THE GREATEST SEA RAIDER
Korvetten-Kapitan Burgraf Graf Nikolaus zu Dohna-Schlodien, commanding officer of the *Moewe*, coming ashore on March 22, 1917, after his second raiding cruise.

THE SEA-RAIDERS

by
E. KEBLE CHATTERTON

AUTHOR OF
"GALLANT GENTLEMEN", "THE BIG BLOCKADE"
"THE KÖNIGSBERG ADVENTURE", ETC.

The Naval & Military Press Ltd

WITH 34 ILLUSTRATIONS

Published by

The Naval & Military Press Ltd
Unit 5 Riverside, Brambleside
Bellbrook Industrial Estate
Uckfield, East Sussex
TN22 1QQ England

Tel: +44 (0)1825 749494

www.naval-military-press.com
www.nmarchive.com

In reprinting in facsimile from the original, any imperfections are inevitably reproduced and the quality may fall short of modern type and cartographic standards.

PREFACE

THIS is the story of Germany's marvellous raids, not by submarines but by surfaceships, during the period 1914–18. The exploits of *Emden*, being so well known, are purposely omitted, but the general public may find more than ordinary interest in the marvellous world-wide organization and the thrilling events which marked the German endeavour to destroy liners, tramp steamers, colliers, food ships, sailing craft, and others. In its vastness, its carefully thought out detail, daring and originality, its bluff and deception, its amazing situations and fierce duels, we have one of the most gripping narratives in the whole story of the sea.

The author has been privileged by the British Admiralty to examine the requisite documents in the Admiralty archives, and to obtain information from participants in the case of certain happenings. This is not the story of how sea-borne trade was carried on during the war, nor is it a record of the work done by the crews of brave merchantmen. My object has been to present a picture of German-American liners and other units being sent out as armed raiders to make the seas dangerous for traffic; and to show to what extent they were assisted by regular, naval, cruisers. The problem of finding food and fuel on voyage, the ramifications of secret agents in North and South America, West Indies, and along the Pacific coast are now capable of being appreciated as a whole.

No more risky enterprise day after day, week after week, can be conceived than that of hovering about on the sea-lanes, usually within wireless range of British cruisers; and the narrow escapes, the coincidences, the exciting moments rival breathless fiction. But it is not merely a campaign of iron men, steel ships, wireless, secret cyphers, strong passions, delicate diplomacy, but a cinematograph-like panorama of wide oceans, tropical seas, romantic islands, snow-capped mountains, lonely hiding-places, and terrible gales of wind. And we can study these adventures with the knowledge that this was honest warfare. For none of the submarine brutalities and the mean tricks, the murdering of women and children comes into these chapters. On the contrary, these raider captains fought with clean hands and had scrupulous regard for civilians. The days of privateering being long since passed, and piracy being now confined to Chinese waters, there is something about this modern steamship raiding which affords in its reading a secret vicarious pleasure. Most of us in the younger days had a sneaking regard for rovers of the sailing ship era who sallied forth to "refresh" themselves from peaceful merchantmen and then go off to find fortune in another locality. We had the feeling that this must be glorious fun to live exciting life at its fullest.

So, in the ensuing pages, we shall cruise as far north as the Arctic, as far south as Cape Horn, eastward across the Pacific, westward across the Atlantic, in and out of secret bays, through mist and fog, sunshine and moonlight. It all reads like a piece of exaggerated fiction—one of those novels that make one forget the monotony of safety—yet every word is historically true and supported by facts. These were living men in real ships, and the crises were more wonderful than any human imagination could invent. For those who take a serious interest with regard to naval problems there emerges from this narrative a valuable set of data touching the necessity of cruisers. We see, as in a concentrated plan, the world's marine highways spread out before us, and the highwaymen pouncing upon the rich cargoes. The drama which arises is the means of illustrating by actuality all that was mere theory. But, because it is a story so human and filled with the glamour of the unexpected, and the contest of brains is so keen, we find ourselves led on and on without stopping to worry about principles.

PREFACE

I desire to return thanks to the Admiral of the Fleet, Sir Charles Madden, late First Sea Lord, and to Rear-Admiral B. E. Domvile, C.B., C.M.G., late Director of Naval Intelligence, for the facilities so courteously granted in making researches at the Admiralty; to Vice-Admiral J. D. Allen, C.B., and Captain Selwyn M. Day, C.B., D.S.O., R.N.R.; to the Imperial War Museum; to the Cunard Steamship Company, and the Isle of Man Steam Packet Company, for valuable assistance in supplying information and for permission to reproduce illustrations. The photographs of *Kent* and *Dresden*, taken on such unique occasions, form an historical record of particular interest.

E. KEBLE CHATTERTON.

CONTENTS

	PREFACE	-	-	-	-	-	-	5
	LIST OF ILLUSTRATIONS	-	-	-	-	11
CHAPTER								PAGE
I.	THE ART OF RAIDING	-	-	-	-	13
II.	THE FIRST RAIDERS	-	-	-	-	24
III.	MINELAYING RAIDERS	-	-	-	-	34
IV.	ON THE TRADE ROUTES	-	-	-	-	50
V.	THE ELUSIVE "DRESDEN"	-	-	-	60
VI.	THE GREAT GAME OF HIDE-AND-SEEK	-	69
VII.	THE RAIDERS' RENDEZVOUS	-	-	-	98
VIII.	THE CAREER OF "KARLSRUHE"	-	-	111
IX.	"KRONPRINZ WILHELM'S" CRUISE	-	-	128
X.	RAIDERS AND WIRELESS	-	-	-	143
XI.	AN HISTORIC DUEL	-	-	-	-	152
XII.	"PRINZ EITEL FRIEDRICH'S" VOYAGE	-	165
XIII.	"RAMSEY" AND "METEOR"	-	-	-	183
XIV.	"MOEWE'S" FIRST VOYAGE	-	-	-	193
XV.	LOOKING OUT FOR RAIDERS	-	-	-	214
XVI.	THE RAIDERS RESUME	-	-	-	-	230
XVII.	SINKING THE RAIDER	-	-	-	-	248
XVIII.	A MODERN SEA ROVER	-	-	-	-	265
	BIBLIOGRAPHY	-	-	-	-	-	281
	INDEX	-	-	-	-	-	-	283

LIST OF ILLUSTRATIONS

THE GREATEST SEA RAIDER	*Frontispiece*
	FACING PAGE
THE FIRST GERMAN RAIDER	16
H.M.S. "HIGHFLYER"	16
GERMAN MINELAYER "KONIGIN LUISE"	17
H.M.S. "AUDACIOUS" SINKING	40
THE SWEDISH CRUISER "FLYGIA"	41
H.M.S. "KENT"	56
OFFICERS OF H.M.S. "KENT"	57
WATCHING "DRESDEN"	57
DANCING ON THE QUARTERDECK	80
SAWING UP WOOD	80
EVERYBODY AFT	81
"DRESDEN" AT JUAN FERNANDEZ	96
"DRESDEN" AT JUAN FERNANDEZ	97
"DRESDEN" AT JUAN FERNANDEZ	120
THE LAST OF THE RAIDER	121
SAILORS ABOARD H.M.S. "KENT"	128
ARTICLES PICKED UP	129
CAPTAIN NOEL GRANT, R.N.	160
COMMANDER J. C. BARR, R.N.R.	161
"CARMANIA" READY FOR ACTION	176
"CARMANIA'S" RANGEFINDER	177
"CARMANIA" SINKING THE RAIDER "CAP TRAFALGAR"	192

LIST OF ILLUSTRATIONS

	FACING PAGE
AFTER THE FIGHT	193
ARMED BOARDING STEAMER "RAMSEY"	208
GERMAN MINELAYER "METEOR"	209
ABOARD THE RAIDER "MOEWE"	224
AT SEA IN THE RAIDER "MOEWE"	225
THE RAIDER REWARDED	240
ARMED MERCHANT CRUISER "ANDES"	241
CAPTAIN SELWYN M. DAY, R.N.R., C.B., D.S.O.	256
H.M.S. "ACHILLES"	257
CAPTAIN K. A. NERGER	272
CAPTAIN K. A. NERGER WELCOMED BACK TO KIEL	273

THE SEA-RAIDERS

CHAPTER I

THE ART OF RAIDING

THE story of the German surface sea-raiding campaign is one of extraordinary interest, alike for its meticulous plans as for the determination and daring in its operation. In comparison with the submarine efforts, we shall find in these surface attacks not the same persistent policy: yet there is a series of brilliant achievements and of enterprising successes that composes one of the most thrilling sections of naval warfare. And to-day, now that at last we are able to have the facts before us, we can view the whole fascinating drama in its right perspective.

If, however, this phase of hostilities was more intermittent than that of the U-boat periods, yet the sphere was far wider. It demanded an organization that had to be in perfect working order long before the European War broke out; and there had to be trustworthy, reliable officials overseas who would maintain this secret system throughout the months when communication with Berlin would be difficult and even impossible. The German pre-war plan in regard to merchant ships was twofold : the preservation of her own property and the destruction of her enemies' vessels.

How was this to be brought about ? What were the problems which presented themselves ? In actual practice we shall observe that the carrying out of well-considered schemes was adequately rewarded : the vast machinery for assaulting ocean commerce was set going with remarkable celerity, and it worked extraordinarily well. That same enterprise, far-sightedness, and astute cunning which had built up the German Mercantile Marine in seventy years, contrived likewise that its rivals should suffer when peaceful competition ended. Germany in 1914 was second only to the British Empire as owner of steamships, but there was a greater solidarity and cohesion.

For, about 60 per cent of German shipping was in the hands of ten lines which amounted to one powerful union ready for the Government's instant service. These ten comprised the Hamburg-Amerika, the North German Lloyd, the Hamburg South American, the Hansa, the German-Australian, the Kosmos, the Roland, the German East Africa, the Woermann, and the Hamburg-Bremen-Africa lines. This huge association represented 3,194,000 gross tons, and there was also the German Levant Line of 155,000 tons. Subsidised to the extent of £107,950 annually, the whole of this mercantile navy was in effect a powerful national combine. Down to the early nineteenth century the Honourable East India Company had been the largest shipowners in the world's history: but in August 1914 the Hamburg-Amerika Line with its fleet of about 500 vessels, its seventy-five distinct services calling at four hundred of the principal ports and carrying over 400,000 passengers yearly, was the biggest shipping corporation that had ever existed. Founded in May 1847 with a capital of 465,000 marks, it began with three sailing ships of 717 tons, and so prospered that on the eve of war it possessed 1,093,000 steam tonnage.

Similarly the North German Lloyd Company rose to rapid affluence. Their first Atlantic steamer was the *Bremen*, built by Caird of Grennock in 1858, but such was the wealth of their passenger trade that in 1897 they were able to launch the twin-screw *Kaiser Wilhelm der Grosse*. It was this vessel which with a speed of 22·81 knots was able to outstrip the *Campania* and *Lucania*, and thus for the first time the "blue riband" of the Atlantic passed from Britain to Germany. The historic part which this four-funnelled liner was to play

THE ART OF RAIDING

in commerce-raiding will presently emerge. Another of the North German Lloyd modern liners was the *Berlin*, built in 1908, and she likewise was destined to play an important part in our story. Altogether this company owned 716,000 of all Germany's tonnage when finally the Great War broke over the sea.

It is, however, to be noted that the policy of the German Mercantile Marine was to rely chiefly on liner trades; and she was able to build her costly mammoth passenger steamers, often capable of breaking Atlantic records, because she had cleverly attracted a considerable amount of emigrant traffic from the continent of Europe. Just as seventeenth-century Holland built up a magnificent commercial navy on the herring fisheries, so two hundred years later Germany created hers largely through poor emigrants from Russia. At one period there was an average annual emigration of 113,000 Germans to the United States, but in the decade ending in 1914 this figure had dropped to only 34,000. On the other hand, the stream of Russians wishing to change their homes for habitation in North America gradually increased from an average of 2000 in the decade ending in 1874 to 199,000 just prior to the Great War. Now in the year 1894 the German Government erected what were known as control stations at various parts of the Russian frontier. The original aim was to prevent the spread of cholera by Russian emigrants passing through Germany. But the erection and management of these controls was placed in the hands of the Hamburg-Amerika and North German Lloyd companies, who continued to use them in such a profitable manner that it was most difficult for any intending emigrant to get through unless he were about to travel by one of these two lines. The Government legislation made it still more awkward and costly for these passengers to reach the United States except in German ships. The facilities of through-rates over the continental railways, and the geographical position of Germany's ports contrived to guide hordes of travellers into German-American vessels and thus maintain a steady revenue.

The British Isles depended for its supplies and overseas trade largely on what is known as the tramp steamer, a name that scarcely does justice to the many excellently built and well-conditioned steamers of moderate tonnage. It was these vessels which were keeping the country's factories, institutions, finance, and actual human bodies from perishing. Thus, whilst Germany concentrated rather on ocean-going passenger ships (and especially in the Atlantic), 60 per cent of British tonnage was made up of tramp steamers, and only 40 per cent were liners. All this "loose", mobile superiority arose because British shipping had become the chief carriers of the world, just as at one period of history the Netherlandish craft were the great "waggoners of the sea".

Very valuable, as it turned out, was this tramp fleet when the Royal Navy demanded so many auxiliaries after July 1914, and such heavy pressure was put on cargo-carrying steamers for maintaining supplies at home. The fast Atlantic passenger ships could never have had enough space available. But the pre-war cause of all this tramp tonnage is traceable to the seasons of nature. Whilst there was a steady trade to be done outward-bound in taking coal from Cardiff or the north-east coast of England, the homeward-bound voyage was modified by the reason that the earth's crops become ripe in different countries at different times. In order, therefore, to return with such commodities as corn, wheat, rice, sugar, wool, cotton, jute, the collier must needs wander from one part of the globe to another and not according to strict schedule. She went where she was wanted and when required. In the month of January the Burmah rice crop was waiting to be shipped before the monsoons occurred; the Calcutta jute season opened in August; the Australian wheat trade began in December; the United States grain trade in July; and so on.

On the other hand, there was a steady flow of cargo borne in British steamers which also carried passengers, though these were not the fastest ships. Some liners were confined, however, to the transport not of human

THE FIRST GERMAN RAIDER
The North German Lloyd *Kaiser Wilhelm der Grosse*.

H.M.S. *HIGHFLYER*
The British cruiser which sank *Kaiser Wilhelm der Grosse*.

GERMAN MINELAYER *KONIGIN LUISE*

This photograph was taken on August 3, 1914, the day before she left the Ems to lay her mines in the North Sea.

THE ART OF RAIDING

beings but of commodities which were needed with regularity and despatch. The collier could amble along at slow speed, but foreign meat and bananas and certain other produce must not be delayed. So it came to this : if war should ever arrive, it would be sound strategy for Germany to hide her own liners in the most convenient harbours, and send out cruisers to harass all vessels bringing cargoes to the British Isles. For reasons which will presently become apparent, it was not the best wisdom to attack purely passenger liners, nor even those which carried half cargo and half people. The finest effect would be when a big steamer was caught fetching meat from South America, or grain from North America ; or, in fact, any supplies that were relied upon for the continuance of life and war.

It followed naturally, then, that the raiding cruisers must first reach those trade-routes along which this traffic should pass. For the few sailing ships which still survived there were recognized routes across the world based on the direction of the trade winds. The steamer tracks were as definitely laid down, subject to navigational dangers, as a road stretches across any country. Just as a highwayman used to find the crossways a most excellent locality for ensuring opportunity, so the meeting of two sea routes suggested a lucrative station to any raider. For example, the vicinity of the Canary Islands is the converging area through which passes an enormous amount of shipping. Hither steamed vessels from New Zealand, via the Horn ; others from the Pacific, via the Magellan Straits ; others from Buenos Aires, Monte Video, Rio Janeiro, Pernambuco ; and all to mingle with that other trade coming up from the West Coast of Africa, the Cape of Good Hope, and even the East African ports. Thus we shall not be surprised when we see this part of the ocean off Africa's north-west shoulder much frequented by German raiders.

Another obvious spot was the north-east shoulder of Brazil near Cape San Roque, for here the traffic divides into that which proceeds north-west to the West Indies and the Atlantic seaboard of the United States, and that which flows north-east across the Atlantic to the Canaries. It was thus logical enough that German raiders should be found operating off Cape San Roque and its contiguous Rocas Reef. The North American route from the United States and Canada to Europe was the most valuable of all. Nevertheless, it presented difficulties for a raider. Civilized warfare demands that some respect must be had for non-combatants. However much German submarine commanding officers on certain occasions displayed callousness and brutality, this accusation can never be laid against the captains of their ships which raided on the surface. There is no parallel, among this more strict brotherhood, to the *Lusitania* episode.

The aim of the surface raider was to destroy but to conceal both his whereabouts and his existence. If he cruised much over the North Atlantic routes, he would sooner or later be seen by some fast passenger steamer who would by superior speed have every chance of escaping, and meanwhile of reporting the raider's position by wireless to one of the British cruisers. On the other hand, if the raider were fortunate in stopping and capturing this Atlantic flier, what could be done with two or three thousand passengers? Certainly there would be no room aboard the German vessel, and it would be consequently useless to sink the prize. Altogether the latter would be an embarrassment. Unless she were well laden with munitions of war, or carrying an impossible cargo of food supplies, the raider's efforts would be wasted, and the risks have been enormous. For this reason, then, there was little North Atlantic raiding, except later by submarines, and on those lucky occasions when some surface raider happened to cross the traffic track whilst proceeding to or from her assigned operational area.

During the last four hundred years whatever sea route was used to India became an attractive path for the enemies of merchant vessels. In different ages the rich commerce being carried to European ports from the Orient has been waylaid as close to its source as the Indian Ocean, and as near to its destination as the Bay

THE ART OF RAIDING 19

of Biscay and English Channel. But, seeing that under modern conditions the Eastern route passes through the Suez Canal and Mediterranean, the obvious areas for a raider must be either outside the Gibraltar Straits or east of the Red Sea. The *Emden* chose the latter, and during a meteoric period of activity caused considerable havoc along the Indian Ocean. Here was an area additionally suitable because there were so many lonely islands where she could arrange to meet her colliers without the likelihood of being disturbed for a while. She found such localities as Minikoi, Felidu Atoll (in the Maldives), and Diego Garcia (in the Chagos Archipelago) invaluable to this end.

Raiding has become more difficult in the age of steam. So long as a sailing ship had fresh water, meat, and biscuits—supplies which were not so difficult to obtain—she could roam the seas for many months till the hull become so foul that the ship must be careened. But the modern raider is limited by the amount of her fuel, which means that at the best she can operate only for a few weeks. Moreover, there comes a time when boilers need to be cleaned and engines to be overhauled. But besides these factors there must be reckoned the element of speed. If the raider is slow, but economical in coal consumption, she is obviously no match for fast modern cargo ships, and she cannot hope to overtake any vessel which has got a fair start before nightfall. Nor must the raider be capable of high speeds, for that would mean extravagant use of fuel and frequent recourse to a collier. Further complications are bound to occur when, through some special emergency, the engines are driven beyond their normal speed and become inevitably ruined.

Our inquiry does not concern *Emden* more than to remark that her principles of commerce raiding were in accordance with those manifested by German onslaughts in other waters. Her career is too well known, and it was confined to one area. At the same time her compact and picturesque adventures exemplify both the strength and weakness of modern steamship raiding. In greater detail we shall notice from the following chapters the four facts which are basic. Firstly, that when once the raider has reached a regular trade route, nothing but very bad luck can prevent her from doing an immense amount of damage to shipping. Secondly, this series of captures and sinkings can go on for months at a time. Thirdly, the raider must rely either on (a) her own colliers always arriving at the secret rendezvous to time, or (b) the colliers which must first be captured along the traffic tracks. Of these two the first is risky, and advisable only as a temporary makeshift till the enemy's vessels have begun to be made prizes. Fourthly, with very few exceptions, the raider (however fortunate and destructive) will not be able to evade being herself destroyed eventually, so long as there is an efficient cruiser force hunting her. The chase may be weeks or months, but sooner or later she will become a victim as surely as the average crook finds that crime cannot ultimately succeed.

Let us elaborate this for a moment and consider the problem from the German's point of view. It is obvious that if she is to do any good she must be on the move most of the time ; continuously steaming along or across the steamship lanes, ever keeping a keen look out for the first signs of smoke coming over the horizon, and always nervous lest the upper works of the stranger may turn out to be the bridge of a cruiser. The suspense, the strain on human endurance, the intercepted wireless messages indicating that the net is gradually closing round her have a cumulative effect on the crew. At the end of a year—if not earlier—these men will decline in moral, a disgruntled mutinous spirit will manifest itself and the captain's hand may be forced to intern his vessel in some neutral port. It is either that or fighting to a finish some rival cruiser or concentrated superior naval strength.

Or, again, picture the successful raider, who has sunk several big cargo ships, now reaching the limit when bunkers must be replenished at all costs, else she must give up the game. She is making for her rendezvous at the back of some island and recognizes the familiar markings on the funnel of her anchored collier. But

THE ART OF RAIDING

that collier has already been captured by a British cruiser, there is a prize crew on board, and the raider steams straight into the trap: H.M.S. *Nonesuch* is watching and waiting round the corner to pounce on the raider and shell her with 4·7-inch salvoes. And even if the *Nonesuch* be mortally wounded, other cruisers will now be on their way in answer to wireless summons: the result is predestined.

But, supposing the raider has terrorized one or two colliers of slow speed into surrender and sent them in charge of an armed party to wait the other side of a reef till more important and bigger vessels have been sunk; what then? As soon as the holds have been emptied of their coal supply, all the accumulated prisoner crews must be transferred from raider to collier and within a few weeks at the most sent into port. Will those angered crews keep their mouths shut when landed? Will not the indignant master mariners inform the Press reporters, the British consul, their owners, and the available authorities that in a certain latitude and longitude the raider was last seen on a particular date? From that moment cables will be busy, messages will pour into the Admiralty, and from Whitehall will be sent orders immediately across the seas. For a little longer the game of hide-and-seek will be played, but then one day the raider has no more luck: she must be sunk or she must surrender. Her machinery has been too long denied its overhaul, the breakdowns have become more serious and more frequent. Moreover, the old trade routes are no longer crowded but empty: shipping has been warned to keep fifty or a hundred miles away along new lanes. Nor is this all. The raider has noticed that most of the merchant ships now carry a gun aft for defensive armament; and, whilst this is of distinct inferiority to the German's, yet it is capable of holing the latter on the water-line, of penetrating through into the engine-room, or flooding the stokehold, or turning the bridge into a roaring furnace. In either case the raider is not efficient for many more of these duels. She must either limp home—if near enough, seeing that her colonies no longer exist—or she must steal through the nocturnal darkness into some convenient neutral harbour.

Whether she will be allowed to effect her repairs and hurry forth again will depend on the local authorities and the force at their disposal for imposing obedience. It is one thing to defy international law when using the facilities of an isolated Chilean harbour that cannot even boast of a telegraph cable : it is something quite different if this resting-place is Newport News or New York, with Customs officers, pilots, harbour-masters, and warships at hand.

There remains to be considered the Pacific as a sphere for raiders. In general this was not given the attention which belonged to the Atlantic, and the reason was sound enough. The Panama Canal had not been opened for traffic when war began. Still, there was a certain attraction in the 5000-mile track from the Far East to Vancouver and San Francisco ; in the routes between Western America and Australia ; in the local shipping between Sydney and New Zealand. After the United States had entered the war, there was an even greater possibility of a raider's cruise in the Pacific being worth while. In due course we shall note how German cruisers, both regular and improvised, utilised lonely Pacific islands and unfrequented channels with utter disregard for international law but with considerable benefit to themselves. Romantic Crusoe-like bays and adventures, scenes and narrow escapes, introduce additional colour and drama into the story, as if to prove that the drab North Sea with its highly mechanized grey battle-fleets was not the only theatre of war.

In the main, however, it was not the Pacific with all its vastness and limited shipping that formed the most tempting region for commerce attacks, but that part of the South Atlantic where the ocean is at its narrowest and there steamed the greatest concentration of valuable cargo-cruisers. No Navy could hope to dispose her protecting cruisers so as to ensure that merchantmen proceeding on their lawful occasions should escape molestation all the time. The most that could be attempted was to be at hand in selected areas, such as

THE ART OF RAIDING 23

those of the Canaries, the Cape Verdes, with visits to islands and reefs suspected of being rendezvous for coaling ; and the patrolling of vicinities where captures had definitely taken place.

All this was far more complicated than may be immediately realized. The commanding officers entrusted with the job of upsetting overseas trade were all handpicked and used every possible circumstance at their disposal. They were able by clever management to create a sense of mysterious uncertainty, simply by ensuring that between their actions and the tidings of their operations a sufficient period should have elapsed which allowed the raider to shift herself north, south, east, or west. For the British cruisers matters were further complicated by the spreading of unsubstantiated and often worthless rumours. And in the meantime an elusive game was being played which, even if confined to that portion of the ocean where the South American coast comes nearest to Africa, was apt to become tantalizing when the hunters never came in sight of the pursued.

Such, then, were the possibilities and particular problems in the campaign for striking violent blows against the most sensitive part of Britain's national organization. Privateering being no longer permissible, the raiders' efforts on the part of armed merchant cruisers against defensively lightly-armed non-combatants were the nearest approach to the olden days when letters of marque were granted. Let us now pass on to watch how the Germans devised their plans and how these plans were transformed into action.

CHAPTER II

THE FIRST RAIDERS

INASMUCH as Germany was inferior to Britain in nominal naval strength, but owned so many ocean liners, she foresaw that in the event of hostilities there was a large potential fleet of fine steamers which in a few hours and by careful organization could be transformed into cruisers. They would require no external alteration, except what could be done with black paint; and, in fact, the more they looked like liners so much the less would they create suspicion when met at sea. Having coaled and provisioned, they would be armed with guns and sent out to waylay those merchantmen whose existence was vital for a nation of islanders. In certain localities there must be arrangements for a supply of coal; and at least part of this supply must be mobile. That is to say, a number of well-filled colliers must be stationed at suitable centres and ready to steam to given rendezvous. But, on the other hand, a very important factor could be relied upon: of all Britain's exports, not less than seventy-five per cent consisted of coal. In other words, these armed liners could always be sure of helping themselves to as much sea-borne fuel as they required.

As far back as six years before the Great War, Germany had issued her instructions to the captains of her liners. If hostilities seemed imminent, and the ship chanced to be lying in a neutral port, then she was to remain there. If she were on passage, she must make for the nearest neutral harbour and wait till the receipt of further instructions. As recently as February 1914 these orders were supplemented. Every master of a North German Lloyd vessel equipped with wireless received a document marked "Strictly Con-

THE FIRST RAIDERS 25

fidential", which told him that, in order to announce the outbreak of war, news would be transmitted by the Norddeich wireless station. All German ships were accordingly to listen-in at 7 a.m., 1 p.m., and 11.10 p.m. In April of that year directions were given for wireless practice to take place daily between German trading vessels and men-of-war.

The German Admiralty also compiled a "Cruiser Handbook", and in this was given a list of secret rendezvous, where liners so ordered could make for immediately and be fitted with their guns. One of these places was near the Bahamas : another was off that lonely South Atlantic island of Trinidada, a most inhospitable spot several hundred miles east of Brazil, notorious alike for its terrible land-crabs, its heavy seas, and for the futile visits of treasure searchers finding nothing but desolation. It was off the Bahamas that the *Kronprinz Wilhelm* was to be changed into a raider, as we shall soon see : Trinidada was the rendezvous where *Dresden* and *Cap Trafalgar* both bunkered from German colliers during the first few weeks of the war, but it was also here that the Hamburg-Amerika steamship *Navarra* with supplies for German cruisers was found on November 11 (1914) by the British armed merchant cruiser *Orama*. After a chase, *Orama* was able to sink *Navarra* and rescue the crew.

It was typical of Germany's pre-war thoroughness to have taken the greatest pains with regard to supplies in the Atlantic. This, being the richest of all the seven seas, must inevitably be the principal sphere for raiding operations, so it was dotted with a number of Supply Centres, each supervised by a Supply Officer. These centres were at New York, Las Palmas, Havana, Rio Janeiro, and Buenos Aires ; that is to say, at the north, east, west, and south of the Atlantic trading area. There were also smaller centres at the Danish island of St. Thomas in the West Indies ; at Para in Brazil ; at Pernambuco and Bahia in Brazil ; at Santos further down the same coast ; at Monte Video in Uruguay ; and even as far south as Punta Arenas in the Magellan Straits. A reference to the map will show that there was thus a chain of stations all the way up the east American coast from Cape Horn to New York. On the opposite side of the Atlantic there were small centres at Lome in Togoland ; at Tenerife in the Canaries ; whilst at Horta in the Azores there was a mid-Atlantic rendezvous.

Each Supply Officer was responsible for seeing that the requisite colliers were in his appointed area. The raider had only to consult her "Cruiser Handbook" and select one of the rendezvous, go alongside, and begin bunkering. There was no necessity to send out wireless messages saying she required so many hundred tons by a certain date : the coal was already there waiting. The Supply Officer-in-Chief, or Controller-General of all these centres was that German naval officer, Fregatten-Kapitän Boy-Ed, of the German Embassy at Washington. Extremely able, astute, cunning, dangerous, this organizer did his share of the work till late on into the war, when he left the United States and came back to Europe.

After the first few days of war Korvetten-Kapitän Leonhardi was the Supply Officer in charge at Las Palmas, and his activities caused no little trouble to the British Navy. A number of German steamers were here interned, and not all of them were content to remain thus immobilized. Whilst British cruisers had to be employed keeping watch to prevent these vessels all emerging and assisting the attack on commerce, there was the unpleasant fact that during this first critical ten days of war it was still possible for the internees, and for Leonhardi, to communicate with the German Admiralty in Berlin. This was effected by the following chain. In accordance with the orders previously enunciated, a number of German steamers had availed themselves of neutral ports in Spain, Portugal, and elsewhere. Among those in Spanish waters was the cable ship *Stephan* at Vigo, and the *Frankenwald* at Bilbao. These picked up the wireless messages sent out from Nauen, and then sent them on to the German Embassy at Madrid, whence in turn the telegrams were transmitted to Cadiz. From there the

THE FIRST RAIDERS

cable connected with Tenerife and Las Palmas, but also across the Atlantic to Pernambuco, Rio Janeiro, and Buenos Aires, so that the Supply Officers could be advised quite effectively.

During the first week of war German colliers with coal from Cardiff and Barry were able to reach Las Palmas and, as we shall witness, come out to supply the raider *Kronprinz Wilhelm*. The Hamburg-Amerika Line chartered a number of neutral steamers to carry coal and provisions from Atlantic ports for other raiders, Newport News being a favourite supply base. Indeed, later events will show that the raiders were generally more than attracted by this Virginian port. The wide entrance to the Chesapeake was much to be preferred, when British cruisers were hovering about somewhere in the darkness, to some narrow and tricky channel. But there were the ship-repairing yards, dry docks, and the facilities for coaling which encouraged drooping spirits after months of strenuous roving. One of the neutral supply ships thus chartered by the Hamburg-Amerika Company was the Norwegian S.S. *Thor*, but between September 7 and 13 the British cruisers of the West India Squadron captured *Thor* as well as four other supply vessels.

The close co-operation between the German steamship owners and their Government was such that in time of emergency the former became practically a department of the latter, employing a huge Atlantic organization as a kind of extended Admiralty. The Hamburg-Amerika Line had contracted, in the event of war, to provide 75,000 tons of coal each month to German cruisers working in the Atlantic, and the intention was to maintain these supplies from North American ports. This grandiose scheme, however, collapsed owing to the very fact of the war itself. There were not enough colliers available, credit could not be granted, and the United States Government showed a firm hand. None the less, Boy-Ed succeeded in sending as many as fifteen ships out from his area, and still had four more ready.

The instruction for German liners to make for the

nearest neutral port was not always the wisest precept to practice. Better for them would it have been if the order had been thus : "Make for the nearest port of a neutral country that is most likely to remain neutral." On August 3, 1914, two of the Hamburg-Amerika liners were off the western entrance of the English Channel, when their wireless informed them that war had broken out between Germany and France. These two steamers therefore selected the first neutral port, which happened to be Falmouth, and I saw them anchored up the Fal. Not many hours elapsed before Britain became a belligerent, and Falmouth ceased to possess neutrality. Off the entrance one saw the arrival of British cruisers, a small steamboat was lowered, and hurried up the Fal alongside the first liner. Three naval officers stepped out on to the gangway and were met by a German mercantile officer ; both liners were detained, and later condemned. German crews and passengers were taken ashore, and before the month was out these two Atlantic ships steamed to the open sea, but with the White Ensign flying at the stern over German colours and a prize crew on board. The first was the *Kronprinzessin Cecilie*, of 8689 tons, and the other was the slightly smaller *Prinz Adalbert*, of 6030 tons.

In like manner those German ships which had interned themselves in Portugal and the United States were at later dates to suffer irreparable misfortune.

Now the first of the German merchant cruisers to get through the Narrow Seas into the Atlantic was the *Kaiser Wilhelm der Grosse*. This four-funnelled passenger ship, which had once been the fastest liner afloat, still belonged to the North German Lloyd. Seventeen years previously she had been built by the Vulcan Company on the agreement that she was first to run a trial trip to New York, and if during this voyage she failed to reach the requirements of the contract, then the North German Lloyd need not accept her. In October 1907, whilst homeward bound, she encountered bad weather and lost her rudder when about seven hundred miles from Halifax ; but that did not prevent her from steaming safely another 2300 miles

THE FIRST RAIDERS

to Bremerhaven, calling at Plymouth on the way. *Kaiser Wilhelm der Grosse* was of 14,349 tons and at her prime could attain a mean speed of over 22 knots. Internally, she was regarded at one period as the most decorative ship afloat and is certainly still remembered as one of those vessels which have made steamship history so notable.

At the beginning of August she was lying at Bremerhaven, but on the third of that month her familiar yellow funnels and white upperworks were all painted black, she received her guns, a naval crew came aboard, and Captain Reymann took over command. On August 4 she came out of the Weser, stood up the North Sea, and then adopted a course that was to be followed by other raiders which were subsequently to leave Germany for the Atlantic. The great nervousness created in the raiding captains by the British blockading cruisers, and the desire to reach the ocean without being seen by one of the patrols, brought about a route which long before the end of war was pretty well stereotyped, receiving modifications only because of weather, atmosphere, or the amount of daylight at the particular season. Thus, it would be a raider's aim to utilise fog, heavy gales, dark moonless long wintry nights, for passing through that portion of the British waters where likelihood of encountering warships was most possible. Daylight hours must therefore be as few as practicable, and spent in some high latitude away from close patrols. Eventually it became a matter of choosing a ship with the right speed to bring her to the patrol area at the proper time. It also meant, and became the practice, that outward-bound raiders had better leave Germany in either late November or December, returning home not later than about March.

Kaiser Wilhelm der Grosse was the first of the pioneers, and she had far greater speed as well as tonnage than most of them. She was also—like the rest of these crack fliers—most extravagant with coal, and consumed over 250 tons a day at half-speed. The seriousness of this is at once appreciated, since her cautiousness took her by such a roundabout way that she had used up most of her fuel by the time she had reached her area. For she could never have dared to rush the Dover Straits and down the short English Channel, but instead had to hug the coast of Norway, then go right up north to Iceland waters, next well to the westward of the British Isles and so down to that previously mentioned busy trade south of Tenerife. By August 7 this black liner was no further than 50 miles WNW of Stalberg, Iceland, where she wasted effort by sinking the British 227-ton trawler *Tubal Cain* and took the crew prisoners.

She had to steam another eight days before she met her second ship, and this was the Union Castle liner *Galician*, passing through the Canaries area on voyage from Capetown for London. Had the raider only known that the Cruiser Squadron, which was to act as the Northern Patrol, was still in the English Channel when *Kaiser Wilhelm der Grosse* came up the North Sea, much time might have been saved. By the time the latter reached the Canaries district there were only two British cruisers—*Vindictive* and *Highflyer*—in the assigned area. Captain Reymann had certainly arrived on the right spot, and his wireless soon intercepted *en clair* signals from steamers ordering coal for them at Tenerife. As they gave their names, it was quite easy for Reymann to open Lloyd's Register, turn over the pages of that volume till his finger stopped at the column where full particulars of her tonnage, ownership, and so on could be at once noted.

The occasion was not without humour. "Is the track clear?" *Galician* was heard to inquire on the air, and Reymann flashed back to Captain E. M. Day an encouraging message, so that at 2.45 p.m. the two liners met. "If you communicate by wireless I will sink you," was the German's greeting. But at five the following morning came another signal releasing her. Why was that done? The answer is the *Galician* could be nothing but an embarrassment to the raider. Here were 250 passengers from South Africa, of whom some were women and children, who would soon eat up the *Kaiser Wilhelm der Grosse's* provisions. But two hours

THE FIRST RAIDERS

after dismissing *Galician* there arrived the S.S. *Kaipara*, 7392 tons, on a voyage from New Zealand and Monte Video, with 4000 tons of meat and no passengers. This was ideal. She was promptly sunk and her crew were taken prisoners; but on the same day the Royal Mail liner *Arlanza*, bound from Buenos Aires, was stopped and then released because she was a 15,000-ton passenger ship with women and children. Still on the same August 16 came next the S.S. *Nyanga*, a 3000-ton cargo vessel with a cargo of African produce, so her crew were removed and the ship sent to the bottom.

Thus twelve days and considerable steaming had brought about the destruction of only one trawler and two cargo steamers. The raider herself had now run out of coal and proceeded eastward, but on the same night reached that lonely and unfrequented anchorage of Rio de Oro, which is in Spanish territory on the northwest shoulder of Africa. Administered by the Governor of the Canary Islands, it has on the settlement a sub-Governor; but a German raider paid scarcely any more respect for rulers of white men's settlements than would have been shown to a cannibal chief. Might was right, and opportunity was always legitimate. She now waited for supply ships to reach this rendezvous and bring her coal as well as provisions. Thither after five days came therefore the German S.S. *Duala* and the *Arucas*. The former had defied the Spanish authorities at Las Palmas by staying forty-eight hours and then proceeding on a pretence of being bound for New York. The latter had escaped from Tenerife. A few days later two more supply ships came to the raider's succour. One was the Austrian *Magdeburg*, with 1400 tons of coal and provisions, and the other was the *Bethania*, which had brought from Las Palmas Supply Centre some 6000 tons of coal.

On the few occasions when these raiders were boarded at anchor, the excuse was always the same: they had come in to effect engine repairs. A Spanish official having come to inquire as to the presence of *Kaiser Wilhelm der Grosse* spending several days in these territorial waters was given the usual lie, but he was completely fooled into believing she was nothing more than a liner: for the crew were wearing on their caps the ribbon of the North German Lloyd. She was still completing her coaling when on August 26 there suddenly appeared a three-funnelled British cruiser. This was the 5600-ton *Highflyer*, well known as a training ship, armed with eleven 6-inch guns as opposed to the raider's six 4-inch. The latter, having refused to surrender, was engaged and eventually sunk. Captain Reymann, nine other officers, and seventy-two of the crew reached the shore and walked to the Spanish fort, where the sub-Governor took charge of them. They were later interned aboard three German ships in Las Palmas. Four hundred others escaped in the *Bethania*, which steamed across to the North Atlantic coast of America, where she was sighted by H.M.S. *Essex*, who chased her, captured her, and brought her into Kingston, Jamaica. The other supply ships had made off before *Highflyer* opened fire, and aboard *Arucas* went the transferred crews of *Kaipara* and *Nyanga*.

So the first raider from Germany had not achieved much success. Whilst she destroyed about £400,000 worth of shipping, she had lost her own more valuable life. But she was not quite suitable for the job, her appearance (with that characteristic German gap between the second and third funnel) being not materially altered by paint, and her coal consumption being both a danger to herself and a terrible strain on the supply organisation. It was indeed just because she had to spend so much time waiting and coaling in Rio de Oro that news reached *Highflyer* in sufficient time. Except for special "rush" incursions of short duration British record-breaking Atlantic liners likewise were not the useful war auxiliaries which it had been hoped they would become. To use them in the best manner was to turn them into either (*a*) minelayers, or (*b*) hospital ships. And the same remark very much applied to steamers of the cross-Channel type, such as the Dover-Calais class.

In the first month of war Britain made the same mistake and learned the same lesson as Germany. The

THE FIRST RAIDERS

fast Cunard liners *Lusitania, Mauretania*, and *Aquitania* were found too extravagant with fuel and altogether of too great a tonnage for cruiser work, which demands moderate consumption of oil or coal, a reasonable amount of mobility (seeing that she will have to be stopped and manœuvred when arresting or fighting another steamer), and a speed somewhere between 14 and 18 knots. It was for this reason that both *Lusitania* and *Mauretania* were handed back to their owners, as indeed was *Aquitania* after she had been in collision. The first-mentioned did excellent work in maintaining rapid communication between America and England until torpedoed, and *Mauretania* was invaluable as a hospital ship when hundreds of sick and wounded had to be rushed home from the Dardanelles, whilst *Aquitania* was to render notable service as a transport. Similarly the rapid, handy, but short-radius class of cross-Channel packets evolved by such vessels as *Riviera, Empress, Engadine* could be usefully employed either to carry seaplanes during some particular brief occasion, or to lay hurriedly a minefield and then scurry home.

CHAPTER III

MINELAYING RAIDERS

THE story of how Germany sent out one of the biggest North German Lloyd passenger liners to lay a minefield off the British coast is to be considered not so much as a separate incident but rather as part of a raiding policy. Under different circumstances this warfare against traffic was carried on by demolition charges, by opening the sea-cocks of arrested steamers, by shelling them from guns, but there was also the adoption of minelaying tactics.

At 7.30 p.m. on August 4, when the *Kaiser Wilhelm der Grosse* was leaving the Weser astern, a smaller two-funnelled steamer owned by the Hamburg-Amerika Line received by wireless in the Ems an order to proceed at utmost speed towards the Thames and lay a cargo of mines. Her name was the *Konigin Luise,* and she was a popular excursion screw vessel which sometimes came as far west as within the Isle of Wight. Her instructions now were to lay a minefield as near as possible to the east coast of England, but not to the north of Lat. 53 : in other words, the area was to be in the North Sea's southern portion. This vessel had been chosen because she was most appropriate for those waters. As soon as her yellow funnels and white hull were painted a hurried coat of black, she very much resembled any of those Great Eastern Railway steamers which plied regularly between Harwich and the Hook of Holland. Consequently no suspicion would be aroused if she were espied along the imaginary line which joins the Maas Lightship to Orfordness. Another convenient feature was that her after-deck was very suitable for the space and little railroad track required in the operation of dropping mines overboard.

MINELAYING RAIDERS 35

Armed with her explosive cargo and two guns, she put to sea under cover of darkness at 10 p.m., steamed westward past the Dutch coast, picked up the Terschelling and Haaks Lightships, and was off the Maas Lightship about 8 a.m. (both of these being German time). She then altered course to get hold of the East Anglian shore and had made up her mind to foul the East Swin Channel, which is one of the busiest thoroughfares for merchantmen trading between London and the North Sea or Baltic ports. But *Konigin Luise* was destined never to get anything like so far. At 10.40 a.m. (G.M.T.) on August 5 she was steaming at 16 knots and was now some thirty miles east of Orfordness, when she was sighted by H.M.S. *Amphion* with her flotilla of destroyers. In command of *Konigin Luise* was Commander Biermann, and he became alarmed: the last thing in the world to be desired was an engagement whilst all these explosives were still on board. He therefore threw his deadly cargo into the sea, altered course first to the south and then south-east in the effort to run back homeward. This, however, was not possible.

At 11.15 a.m. (G.M.T.) the flotilla began shelling her, though not before she had sparked off a wireless message informing the High Sea Fleet that the mines had been laid. Within three-quarters of an hour she had been sunk, and her survivors taken prisoners aboard *Amphion*. The tactical error consisted in the hour selected for her setting forth. Had she so worked her schedule as to enable the mines being laid during the dark hours, then she would probably never have been caught, but the minefield would have dramatically revealed itself later as an undefined danger area causing heavy losses. And this is exactly the result that was obtained when three weeks later during the night of August 25–26 extensive minefields were laid off the Tyne and Humber. The minelayers were undetected and got away safely back to Germany.

Konigin Luise really owed her finale to a British trawler which happened to be in the neighbourhood and noticed her "throwing things" overboard as soon as the destroyer flotilla had been sighted. The trawler informed *Amphion*, and the action followed. But on the next morning *Amphion* herself hit one of those mines and foundered. That, however, was a mere incident. What mattered was that the initial German minefield had been discovered as soon as it was laid, the area could be in future avoided, the North Sea charts off Orfordness given a pink patch to indicate danger, and the minesweepers told exactly where they could work. To the end of hostilities this Southwold Area, as it was always known, was not more dangerous to British shipping than it remained for German submarines which eventually would hunt those very waters.

Now the next phase centres round a much larger minelayer, and the sequence of events shows the intimate relationship between psychology and operations. It will be recollected that on August 28, 1914, was fought the Battle of Heligoland Bight. The result of this was so alarming that the Kaiser insisted on a future naval policy that was characterised by extreme caution. History always shows that enforced inactivity is most disastrous through its effect on the moral of fighting men, and by September this defensive attitude towards her greatest naval enemy was already injuring the moral of Germany's crews. Some sort of raid beyond the Heligoland Bight, without risking the High Sea Fleet was, however, likely to improve the marine tone. The tremendous potentialities of the mine having been proved off Orfordness, the Tyne and Humber, suggested that a more ambitious attempt might do wonders. The question still remained: should the mines be laid to entrap merchantmen, or should the British Grand Fleet be the target?

We know to-day that in September 1914 the German naval intelligence had not yet been able to discover where the Grand Fleet was based, but believed that Moray Firth was the locality. This was a natural enough inference, for the British Navy had been using Cromarty Firth in the years immediately preceding the war. Also it was true that the last-mentioned anchorage was being used by the First Light-Cruiser Squadron and Second Cruiser Squadron. The Battle-Fleet and

MINELAYING RAIDERS

Battle-Cruisers were, however, based on Scapa Flow, whence periodical sweeps were occasionally made down the North Sea towards the Heligoland Bight.

It is at this stage that we introduce the North German liner *Berlin*, another noble twin-screw, twin-funnel vessel. She had been completed for her owners in 1909 at Bremen for the Mediterranean–New York service and to carry 3630 persons inclusive of crew. She was of 17,324 gross tons and 590 ft. in length, with typically lofty upper works so characteristically Teutonic. She was taken over by the German Navy, repainted, fitted out as a minelayer, and assigned the duty of fouling areas not in the North Sea, but at the north-west approaches to the British Isles.

The intention was twofold. Many ships were steaming in and out of the Clyde, and a blow was thus to be struck outside Glasgow. There was also an indirect but extremely sound reason for laying a trap athwart the Clyde channels ; for a huge convoy of 33 steamships was about to leave Canada and cross to the British Isles with troops eventually destined to reach France. Germany got to know not merely this fact, but that the sailing date was to be September 23. That which she did not definitely ascertain was the port for which these ships were bound. It was, however, fair to assume that they would make neither for Liverpool nor some harbour on the English Channel, but for the nearest and most direct terminus via the north of Ireland to Glasgow. Thus the laying of a minefield at the Clyde entrance would be a menace to the Canadian convoy and all other shipping alike.

Next came the choice of a suitable moment. Arguing from the general to the particular, the matter worked out thus. The mines should be deposited under cover of night, on a date not too far from new moon when darkness could be ensured, but the time must not be too much ahead of the convoy's probable period for arrival in the Clyde. Now it happened that new moon was on September 19, so preparations were made for *Berlin* to leave Germany on September 21. She was placed under the command of Captain Pfundheller, carried 200 mines, had a speed of 17 knots, and, being armed with six 4·1-inch guns, was also a powerful cruiser capable of playing havoc with any merchantman. As the German Admiralty possessed the names of the convoy units, *Berlin* was disguised to resemble several of these ships; the hope being that if she were found anywhere between Ireland and Scotland she would be taken for a British liner.

The sailing instructions to *Berlin* were dated September 11, and thus showed how unhurriedly the raid had been schemed. She was to lay her mines athwart the Glasgow approach between Garroch Head and Fairland Head; or, failing that, the principal channel on or south of the line Garroch Head–Cumbrae Lighthouse; or else between Pladda and Turnberry Head. The mines were to be set so that they floated at two metres below the surface of the sea at low-water spring tides. Having thus got rid of her dangerous cargo, *Berlin* was to begin her return voyage, passing through Iceland waters far north of the British patrols, and to make raids on British trawlers fishing off that island. Thence she was to carry on north-eastward to raid the mercantile traffic between England and Archangel. This being done, she was at liberty to find her way down the North Sea to Germany if the autumn conditions of weather, with the usual rain, fog, and heavy seas should thus come to her assistance. But, otherwise, she might take refuge in some Norwegian, Swedish, or Danish harbour, and preferably one where a railway connected.

If *Berlin* should find herself hemmed in at the north so that she could not evade the patrols in high latitudes, and were compelled to escape south down the Atlantic after her minelaying, she was ordered to carry on cruiser warfare after the manner of the *Kaiser Wilhelm der Grosse*. Captain Pfundheller was reminded of the great advantage which a liner such as *Berlin* possessed over genuine regular naval cruisers. A passenger steamer of more than 17,000 tons, designed to be comfortable in any Atlantic gale, was bound to show her superior seaworthiness over warships of consider-

MINELAYING RAIDERS

ably smaller tonnage. "Bad weather," read one of the instructions, "and, above all things, high seas, is the most favourable condition; for the steamer will be able to hold on whilst the enemy light forces and the old cruisers on the Northern Patrol will have their speed seriously reduced."

As to the navigation, Pfundheller was given precise orders how to steer when outward bound. "If possible, you should pass the line South Norway–Scotland under cover of darkness, unless very thick weather rules." Then, "after passing this line, it may be appropriate, under certain circumstances, to hug the Norwegian coast, in order to enable you, if you are chased, and cannot escape, to enter territorial waters." He was advised that a good time to pass the South Norway–Scotland line would be at about 9 p.m., so that he would cross the Bergen–Shetlands line at 7 a.m., when there was usually early-morning fog in September and the enemy might not be extraordinarily alert. "Moreover," ran the wording, "the state of readiness for action of the personnel is likely, at this hour, to be less than usual."

After passing the Northern Patrol line, *Berlin* was to lay a course between the Faroes and Iceland, and thus have a channel of about 180 miles in width. Thence he was to turn south, keep well clear of the Hebrides, and make for his area by crossing the line joining the islands of Inishtrahull (North Ireland) and Islay. From there he would steer betwixt Rathlin Island and the Mull of Cantyre, whence he would begin to be in the proximity of his appointed area. "If possible, do not lay your mines on one bearing, but in an irregular line, to render the sweeping of the field more difficult, and to increase the uncertainty as to its extent."

It was at 11 p.m. that *Berlin* steamed out of the Weser on September 21 with the utmost possible secrecy. Indeed her departure had been kept so quiet that the patrols in Heligoland Bight knew nothing of her and reported her as being an enemy. But it so chanced that the next morning broke with a clearness that was most unusual for a September day. The 22nd was in

THE SEA-RAIDERS

fact one when Admiral Jellicoe in the *Iron Duke* found visibility of the North Sea "very good". Berlin became nervous : the conditions of atmosphere would not be favourable for her passage. She would be much too conspicuous an object at a long distance before nightfall could again cover her up. Thus at 8 a.m., when only about 80 miles NW of Heligoland, she put her helm hard over and steamed back home. The first effort had failed.

On this same September 22 another German merchantship, transformed into a minelayer, named *Kaiser*, came out of the Jade and made towards the Moray Firth, the object being to entrap the Grand Fleet within their suspected base. *Kaiser* showed a keen determination, held on across the North Sea and at noon next day was favoured with misty weather. At 1.25 p.m. she was about 150 miles east of Aberdeen when she was startled by hearing loud British wireless signals, and out of the Scotch mist there burst a British warship of sorts steering NW towards the Moray Firth. She was one of those railway-owned vessels of about 2000 tons which had been commissioned as Armed Boarding Steamers. Their duty was to patrol off such areas as the Pentland Firth, Moray Firth, and the Hebrides on the look out for suspicious craft, but especially potential minelayers.

This Armed Boarding Steamer promptly made for *Kaiser*, who altered course four points to starboard and began running away at a speed of 13 knots, which was her limit. After heading for some time in the direction of the Skager Rack, the German managed to get well clear of the patrol, but the meeting had entirely capsized *Kaiser's* plans. The raider's presence would have been already wirelessed to other vessels, and at the end of an hour *Kaiser* was now about 170 miles from the Moray Firth. What to do ? If she adhered to her orders, she might reach the mine area by 3.30 a.m., but that would mean cutting it very fine, for the darkness would end one hour later. If she were sighted, with or without her explosive cargo, in clear daylight off that coast, she would encounter the gravest risks. So at 3.30 p.m. her captain abandoned

H.M.S. *AUDACIOUS* SINKING.

After striking one of the mines laid by *Berlin*. This unique photograph, which was taken from the White Star liner *Olympic*, shows a destroyer standing by the big battleship.

THE SWEDISH CRUISER *FLYGIA*

This was the cruiser which *Dresden* pretended to the lighthouse-keeper at Rocas Reef that she really was. See illustration of *Dresden* later.

MINELAYING RAIDERS

the whole operations and made for home. His nerves were thoroughly shaken up, and on the morning of September 24, when he had reached a spot 40 miles NW of Heligoland, he had another shock. A British submarine appeared—one of those which were maintaining a watch on the Bight. This happened to be E 4, and *Kaiser* lost no time in scurrying along eastward so as to gain the shallow water off Schleswig-Holstein. He certainly got back safely, but fright had somewhat energised his imagination, and off the River Eider he was convinced that E 4 had fired a couple of torpedoes. This was not the case, she did not attack : still, one torpedo would have detonated all those terrible mines and made an appalling disaster. She was an unlucky ship, for she made another attempt on September 28 to carry out her instructions and got caught in such heavy weather that at 2 p.m. she again turned back, and afterwards went into dockyard hands for a refit.

Both *Berlin* and *Kaiser* had thus failed in their minelaying expeditions, but they had been even nearer to danger than was realised. Admiral Jellicoe was at sea with the Grand Fleet and at dawn of September 22 his forces were covering a line that extended west for over a hundred miles from the Norwegian coast off Stavanger. It is true that at 10 a.m. the Fleet went off to the northwest, but two battle squadrons were detached to support cruisers searching North Sea areas for expected German cruisers, destroyers, and submarines reported to be coming north. Thus the receipt of a wireless message from the Admiralty, or some patrol vessel, would have soon brought about such dispositions as would make escape almost impossible. Furthermore, it will be remembered the morning of September 22 was so clear that Lieutenant-Commander Weddigen in U 9 between the hours of 7.30 and 8.35 a.m. had been able to make that extraordinary achievement of sinking off the Dutch coast the three British cruisers *Aboukir, Cressy,* and *Hogue.*

As a result of that incident, one light cruiser and seventeen destroyers were sent out from Harwich towards Heligoland Bight in the hope of waylaying any submarine going home. Thus, it needed a very slight extension of this search to bring minelayers and the eighteen hunters into the same picture. *Berlin* and *Kaiser* would have been overwhelmed. There was still another unsuspected risk awaiting *Berlin* as she would have gone north past the Norwegian coast and thence through the Faroes–Iceland area. The two armed merchant cruisers *Mantua* and *Alsatian*, which were part of the Cruiser Squadron engaged in the work of intercepting all vessels bound through the northern entrance of the North Sea, had been despatched at 10.30 p.m. on September 22 to make for a position off the Norwegian harbour of Trondhjem and remained thus patrolling till the 28th. (The German liner *Brandenburg*, lying therein, had been heard using her wireless and was likely to emerge. She was, however, definitely known presently to have been interned.) Much more unlikely things might have happened than the meeting of *Berlin* with *Mantua* and *Alsatian*. But what chance would the former have had when the first shell burst among the two hundred mines?

Those particular few days are additionally interesting now that we can see what a small margin existed to separate either side from disaster. The more one looks into the detached episodes, and pieces them together till they make a composite whole, the more surprising does it seem that cause and effect were barely disjoined. Thus on September 23 and 24 the Second British Cruiser Squadron was engaged sweeping up the Norwegian coast and would have been very unlucky had they not met with *Berlin*. But on the evening of September 25 this squadron, which had its base at Cromarty, arrived back there through the Moray Firth in order to coal. Except for the fact that *Kaiser* had accidentally stumbled into sight of the Armed Boarding Steamer 150 miles from land, the Moray Firth minefield would have been laid, and a few hours later the Cruiser Squadron would have steamed into it. Such are the chances and coincidences of history. But others were to follow very shortly.

MINELAYING RAIDERS

At first it seemed as if *Berlin* had forfeited all opportunity for waylaying the Canadian convoy; yet the latter was delayed in leaving, so that the date was changed from September 23 to October 3. But there was a new moon on October 19 and the dark autumn nights would be favourable for a more ambitious mining operation. This was to include the *Berlin's* original plan, and there was also one for mining the Grand Fleet off its Scottish bases. The second portion was to be carried out by the regular, specially designed, pre-war minelayer *Nautilus*, a two-funnelled craft with clipper bow and bowsprit that made her look like a steam yacht. It was this vessel which had so successfully laid the Humber minefield on the night of August 25–26.

We find October 16 selected as the date for this renewed effort, and in order to make certain that the North Sea was temporarily safe, the German battle-cruisers now made a short sweep as far across as the Dogger Bank. Next followed *Nautilus*, escorted by the small three-funnelled cruiser *Kolberg*, and away they steamed towards the NNW. All went well till 4.40 p.m. on October 17, when they were about 100 miles short of May Island, Firth of Forth. They heard some wireless signalling and sighted such clouds of smoke that they became alarmed. Surely here was the Grand Fleet! They accordingly turned right back and made for Heligoland. This was yet another case of nerves; for, apart from coastal patrols of weak fighting ability, there was not a warship nearer than 200 miles. The fact is that at this very hour part of the Grand Fleet was carrying out target practice to the westward of the Orkneys, and part was inside Scapa Flow. On the evening of the 16th no small uneasiness had been created by the report that a submarine was close in to the Swikha entrance of Scapa. It was therefore decided that, until more real security against submarine attack could be provided, Scapa Flow was to be vacated by the Battle Fleet. A temporary base must be sought elsewhere.

From this decision was to follow in a few days a strange sequel. After being at sea for a while, Admiral

Jellicoe took some of his force into Lough Swilly at the north of Ireland, arriving there on October 22. Eight days previously the Canadian convoy had safely reached England—not Scotland—and arrived in Plymouth Sound. Germany did not yet know that the Grand Fleet had withdrawn from the North Sea, nor was she aware that the convoy was already in port. On October 16, a few hours after *Nautilus* and *Kolberg* had gone out, the *Berlin* started from the Jade and went determinedly up the North Sea. Just after dark she crossed the Stavanger–Kinnaird Head line, and not merely did she sight no patrols but there was none working this area between Norway and Scotland. For the cruiser blockade and look-out line had just been withdrawn, owing to the submarine danger; cruiser squadrons and armed merchant cruisers were now north of the Shetlands as well as north-west of the Hebrides.

Berlin was therefore very fortunate this time, and was (had she only known it) incurring no great risk. After proceeding further north, she passed between the Faroes and Iceland on October 19, then stood several hundred miles out into the Atlantic till she was in Long. 20 W, and on October 21, having thus given the British Isles a very wide berth, altered course to steam east along the 56th parallel so as to arrive off the north Irish coast at dark, after a further 300-mile run. We can feel something of the subdued excitement, the suspense and nervousness, as she at length got nearer to the land and began to intercept wireless signals. From these she ascertained that British naval units of the Second Cruiser Squadron were patrolling off the Hebrides, though she could not identify them.

Closer and closer she drew towards that bottle-neck which separates south-west Scotland from northern Ireland. To the north of her on her port flank were the battleships *Albemarle* and *Exmouth*, whilst away on her starboard side to the south-west were other warships. Between the Irish mainland and Scotland the Armed Boarding Steamer *Tara* (one of the London & North Western Railways steamers) was on watch for any stranger. Nor shall we fail to appreciate the

MINELAYING RAIDERS

tensity of the situation when we remember that only a very few hours before *Berlin* steamed into this area, Admiral Jellicoe with part of the Grand Fleet had just come into Lough Swilly. Neither German nor Briton suspected each other's presence, yet they were separated from one another by only a few miles. It was a most singular coincidence.

The short daylight of an autumn afternoon disappeared; the wind tore through the liner's rigging; the heavy swell of the leaden Atlantic thudded against *Berlin's* black hull; the engines steadily hummed to maintain her 17 knots. Anxious eyes were scanning the limited view of inky wilderness ahead as the officer of the watch kept her on a south-east course. Anything at any moment might now happen. Captain Pfundheller was surprised that the neighbourhood was so strongly patrolled: the next few minutes, perhaps the next half-hour, might find him in sudden action with a cruiser. Two hundred mines still on board! Anxious time this. Would she ever get through the North Channel to the Clyde? Could she expect to get back, when all these enemies were hovering around? And now onwards the navigation was becoming a more tricky matter. No longer the spacious Atlantic, but rocks, islands, confined tracks, the possibility of collision with unlit shipping. And, mingling with the pure ozone of the ocean, came now that soft smell off the land which makes the deep-water sailor uneasy for his heavy-draught vessel.

Mines and guns were now being got ready for immediate employment. At 10 p.m. this twenty-second of October soundings had been taken, and indicated that Ireland's dangerous coast was not far off. Then away on the starboard something loomed up. Aran Island! So *Berlin* altered course further to port, and edged away from the shore a little. At 11 p.m., according to his reckoning, Pfundheller believed himself to be off Tory Island, but the flashing lights of neither Tory Island nor Fanad Head were functioning during this war period, and it was impossible for *Berlin* to fix her position by cross-bearings. By this time, at the end of a six-day voyage and continuous uncertainty, and with the immediate prospect of no lights burning on Rathlin Island, Mull of Cantyre, or up the Clyde, the raider's captain considered the risk of attempting the North Channel too great.

So he gave up the original intention of mining the Firth of Clyde, and decided instead to deposit his cargo north of Tory Island. This operation began at 11.33 p.m. and was carried through without interruption, enabling her to steam off again to the north-west without being seen, although at 1 a.m. (October 23) she must have passed within about 16 miles of H.M.S. *Albemarle*. With no small sense of relief did she clear out into the wide Atlantic, and further good fortune came at morning: for the weather turned misty, accompanied by rain squalls—ideal conditions for concealment. Day after day sped by, the firemen down below sweated at their job to hurry her to the remotest north-west regions where no man-of-war could possibly be cruising, and at the end of a week she was right off the European map with the chilly shores of Greenland to port and Iceland to starboard. On October 27 her wireless had intercepted the British warning to all ships that the Tory Island minefield was existent.

These days had enabled her to get rid of any characteristics which might suggest she was a minelayer, but now all this steaming at high speed had begun to manifest itself seriously. She had been built not to perform "stunt" raids lasting over a fortnight and during part of which she was driven at forced pressure through heavy seas: her engines had been constructed to jog along at a steady scheduled rate. So now she developed boiler defects, and in those high latitudes it was scarcely wonderful she struck such gales and atrocious seas that all the fishing fleets must be safely tucked up in harbour. It was no good hoping to sink any of these. The first of November accordingly saw *Berlin* steering eastward towards the Arctic limits of Norway in the expectation of raiding the route to Archangel, for between Russia and England food ships and colliers were still voyaging.

MINELAYING RAIDERS

On the night of November 7-8 she closed the bleak, rugged, lofty Murman coast, but the nervousness of her commanding officer had not been lessened : he sighted a couple of ships (erroneously), surmised that one was a British man-of-war, so took advantage of a sudden snowstorm in which to escape into the open sea. The raider then went out again into the Atlantic and stood to the south of Lofoden Islands : here, at least, she might be well placed to waylay the Anglo-Russian traffic. But the winds and seas were so atrocious that it would have been impossible to lower boats and boarding parties in that weather. She could not have examined one ship but her presence would have been disclosed. Cruiser warfare being out of the question, her boilers being now worse than ever, and her bunkers (after continuous steaming for a whole month) being almost empty, Pfundheller was at the end of his resources. If he went much further south there was a great probability of being caught by the British, so he must give up all thought of reaching German waters.

Availing himself of the discretion permitted in his original orders, he decided to take refuge in a neutral harbour, and on the morning of November 17 during a thick snowstorm brought *Berlin* out of ocean to the land-locked fjord and at 9 a.m. came to anchor off Trondhjem. Twenty-four hours later, with only a little coal-dust in her bunkers, she was finally interned, and would never do any more raiding.

What had she accomplished ? She had neither endangered the Canadian convoy, nor laid an ambush in the Clyde. As an armed cruiser she had not captured one prize. She had thrown her cargo overboard in none of the alternative channels assigned to her. Nevertheless she had been favoured with the luck of a lifetime, and had accomplished more than she could ever have imagined. The mines had been laid in two legs, and a mean position gives this area as about 19 miles $N\frac{1}{4}E$ of Tory Island, where they were not so much as suspected until at 2.15 p.m. on October 26—just three and a half days later— the outward-bound S.S. *Manchester Commerce*, on voyage from Manchester to Quebec, struck one of these metal eggs and sank with the loss of master as well as thirteen of her crew. Thus, after all, the basic intention of spoiling the Canadian track was achieved.

But a far more serious tragedy was to follow. Unfortunately there was an inevitable delay in transmitting the news concerning *Manchester Commerce*, so that it did not reach Admiral Jellicoe in Lough Swilly till 2 p.m. on October 27. This delay brought about a tragedy. For from Lough Swilly came out the Second Battle Squadron on firing practice under Admiral Warrender, who in H.M.S. *Centurion* led the battleships *Ajax, Audacious,* and *King George V* straight over this minefield. When one thinks of several thousand lives and several millions sterling heading for perdition through delayed information, it is difficult to restrain emotion. Even the seagulls as they soared and wheeled over this squadron must have associated those bobbing black pear-shapes with impending horror. The amazing fact is that only one ship hit any of those mines.

The time was 8.45 a.m. *Audacious* was a mile south of where *Manchester Commerce* had gone down on the previous afternoon, and now on the port side aft, a considerable distance below her waterline, the battleship was fatally struck. Those of us who were engaged in minesweeping during the war noted how rarely it was that a vessel hit one of these obstacles bow-on. In most cases, though there were exceptions, the ship's bow wave had the effect of throwing the mine aside, whence it was immediately sucked in aft towards the propellors. *Audacious* heeled to port, with engine-room flooded, and the port engines stopped. A heavy, ugly Atlantic sea was running, she was steering badly, but with her starboard engines giving her about nine knots she was making for Lough Swilly. The situation rapidly became desperate, the water was rising, and about 11 a.m., when still ten miles from the shore, she ceased steaming altogether. The cruiser *Liverpool* was standing by, but now in response to distress signals there arrived on the scene the White Star Liner *Olympic*. The boats from these two ships rescued all the crew of *Audacious* excepting 250 men.

MINELAYING RAIDERS

Olympic (Commodore H. J. Haddock), in spite of the heavy swell, next took *Audacious* in tow, the line being passed by the destroyer *Fury*, and some very pretty seamanship took place. Possibly no one will ever witness in our lifetime the unusual sight again of a mammoth liner acting as tug to salve a crack battleship. But these efforts were unavailing. *Audacious* became as tractable as a mad bull. Other ships tried towing and failed, and by 6 p.m. she had to be abandoned for fear of her capsizing : three hours later she did capsize. The only casualty now occurred when, in sinking, she blew up and dropped debris over *Liverpool's* deck, killing a petty officer.

At the date when *Audacious* went down, the war was waging none too favourably for the Allies, the Battle of Ypres was at a critical stage, and Britain could not afford to advertise the loss of such a valuable capital ship. Strenuous efforts were accordingly made to hush up the incident, and the Press was kept from mentioning it. But it is always difficult for so important a matter to remain a secret indefinitely. Very few persons in the British Isles unconnected with the Navy were informed till after the war. The *Olympic*, however, was on her way from the United States to Liverpool and carried a good many American citizens who had taken photographs of the sinking battleship. The *Olympic* came into Lough Swilly and was detained there three days, all communication with the shore being forbidden. I myself was confidentially shown one of these photographs reproduced in an American magazine the next month. Not till November did Germany learn that *Audacious* was gone, but it was never admitted by the Admiralty till after the war that the loss had occurred.

Minesweepers were set to sweep up *Berlin's* cargo ; the Grand Fleet units left Lough Swilly on November 3 and returned to Scapa Flow. But as late as the following April a Norwegian grain ship foundered on the Tory Island minefield, which was not entirely clear even in the year 1917.

CHAPTER IV

ON THE TRADE ROUTES

BEFORE the war, Germany had devoted considerable study to the damaging blows which could be made against Britain through attacking the vital trade routes. It was, however, fully appreciated that the task of getting through to the Atlantic, and so to the other highways, would always be difficult when once hostilities had begun.

There were but two methods practicable. If one of her regular naval cruisers attempted to burst through the blockade by force, she would be handicapped from the first: she would be too blatant, too obvious. For, whilst a merchantman can become a disguised warship, it is not always possible to change the appearance of a man-of-war in order to make her resemble a passenger or cargo vessel. (It is true that during the war two or three of the British naval sloops were altered to suggest traders, but they were not a great success and did not always deceive the enemy.) When a cruiser has four, or even three funnels, war-like bow, low freeboard, and conspicuous guns, but a forebridge without any of the high decks of a liner, no amount of paint can fool a seafarer into believing her innocence. Therefore the chances of genuine cruisers running the blockade were rightly considered remote. We have seen that *Kaiser Wilhelm der Grosse* and *Berlin* succeeded because the blockade patrols were not yet of sufficient strength, and these two raiders went hundreds of miles out of their way. But they were also dressed to conceal their true character, prepared to pretend and bluff; and this second method quite definitely was accepted by the German Admiralty as the only means of sending surface

ON THE TRADE ROUTES

cruisers forth when the other genuine cruisers had ceased to exist.

It remains an interesting fact that not one of the latter throughout the whole four years made the slightest effort, either independently or in company, to rush the Dover Straits or get westward of Scotland. At the time when the Canadian convoy was coming over the Atlantic there certainly were both anxiety and a half-expectation at the British Admiralty that German battle-cruisers might break through and do their direst. It would have been a gamble, but certainly a justifiable risk. Transports full of soldiers are always most attractive targets in their helplessness; and it would have been of direct assistance to the German Army if some thousands of British troops could have been shelled or drowned. Whether all the battle-cruisers would have got back to Germany again is quite another consideration.

It may be stated at once that after *Berlin's* meteoric career concluded at Trondhjem, not even a merchant cruiser got out from Germany to the ocean routes again until January 1916. No blockade line between Scotland and Iceland, or Scotland and Norway, can ever be absolutely impenetrable having regard to long dark nights and days of fog. The very few raiders which did pierce this steel ring certainly deserved some reward. Only when these attempts were made by exceptionally brave and determined commanding officers, who had the patience and endurance to go near the Arctic Circle, the care to make the best of nocturnal and meteorological conditions, and the luck of not being discovered lower down the North Sea, was attainment possible.

During the first months of hostilities, then, Germany's units for waging war along the commercial sea-routes consisted of (*a*) those of her regular cruisers which happened to be on the China or West Indies stations, and (*b*) any of her ocean liners which happened to be in foreign waters. It will now be our interesting inquiry to follow one of the most amazing voyages in all records of the sea. Let us open the map at the West Indies, which are so richly endowed with colourful background and memories of maritime rovers. It will help us to vitalise the story if we try to visualise the small German cruiser *Dresden*, which was a sister-ship of that famous raider *Emden*. At the beginning of the war *Dresden* was six years old, and still capable of about 24 knots. Armed with ten 4·1-inch guns, she had three tall thin funnels, two tall masts (with searchlight platforms), and displaced 3544 tons. Her maximum coal capacity was 850 tons, a factor which was to have an important influence on her adventures; and her engines were turbines. Captain E. Köhler was her commanding officer.

Steaming across from Germany to the Caribbean came the cruiser *Karlsruhe*, a bigger vessel, of 4820 tons, with a speed of over 27 knots. She was armed with twelve 4·1-inch guns, had been built only that same year, and was under the command of Captain Lüdecke. A lean, four-funnelled, low-lying ship with a modern bow, and every line of her suggesting speed, this two-master was coming out to relieve *Dresden*, but the two captains were to change over. *Dresden* was then to return home and have a much-needed refit. This is a second factor which will presently gain greater significance. It was at Port-au-Prince, Haiti, that the two cruisers met and on July 25 the respective captains took over from each other. Our immediate concern being Captain Lüdecke's cruise in *Dresden*, we must postpone the career of *Karlsruhe* till a later chapter.

It was on July 28 that *Dresden* left Port-au-Prince and went on to the Danish Island of St. Thomas in order to coal her bunkers before starting for Germany. This little hilly islet of only 33 square miles, with poor soil, occupies considerable strategical importance which has become even more marked since the Panama Canal was opened. Nature has made it one of those key-positions of the sea where four important routes converge. It is the centre whence radiate the tracks to New York and Boston, the Mexican Gulf, the eastern ports of South America, and Colon for the Panama Canal. When aerial travel becomes more firmly established it will doubtless increase the value of St. Thomas still further.

ON THE TRADE ROUTES 53

But in 1914 it was, as we have noticed, one of the German supply centres, and here indeed the Hamburg-Amerika Line had its offices. If it was little more than a port of call, yet its harbour is one of the finest of all the West Indies, excellently placed for raiders to come in, coal quickly, and then on putting out to sea find themselves already on the highway of commerce.

By July 30 European political affairs were advancing towards a crisis, but on the next day *Dresden* steamed out of St. Thomas north-eastwards for the Azores and English Channel. She had not been gone more than three hours when she picked up a wireless message from Porto Rico ordering her not to return home but carry on cruiser warfare in the Atlantic : that is to say, she was to destroy enemy commerce. She was ideally placed with the choice of routes, and no raider could wish for a better beginning. Here she was, already at sea, beyond territorial waters, bunkers full, too far from land to be spied on, but supposed to be making for mid-North Atlantic.

As a matter of fact she turned south and wisely began cruising down the track of shipping bound up from South American ports. Not many days had she to wait. It was erroneously reported that she was off New York, though in truth on August 6 she had passed the mouth of the Amazon and off Para stopped her first ship. This was the British S.S. *Drumcliffe*, 4072 tons, from Buenos Aires in ballast on her way to Trinidad for fuel. A boarding-party was sent to her, but *Drumcliffe's* master had with him both wife and child, who would be an inconvenience aboard the cruiser if the merchantman were now destroyed ; and it would be useless to take the steamer along, seeing that she was in need of coal. After the steamer's wireless had been destroyed, and a declaration signed pledging officers and crew not to take part in hostilities against Germany, *Drumcliffe* was dismissed.

Just over an hour later appeared the British S.S. *Lynton Grange*, 4252 tons, bound for Barbados, and the same experience happened to her. But in the meantime arrived the British S.S. *Hostilius*, 3325 tons,

THE SEA-RAIDERS

bound for Barbados also, and then the extraordinary situation occurred of captain, officers, and crew all refusing to sign the German declaration, yet Captain Lüdecke at 7.40 p.m. released her because he did not think her destruction worth while. *Dresden* then proceeded still on her south-east course towards Rocas Reef, which lies singularly isolated, about 130 miles off Cape San Roque, and just off the position where the north-west track for Barbados and St. Thomas separates itself from that to the Cape Verdes and Canaries. It is worth while calling attention to it at this stage, as Rocas was one of the secret rendezvous for German raiders and likely to become of the greatest convenience.

After cruising about the crossways for a few days, she must needs coal, and such was the good organisation of the Supply Officer that she was now able to enter the little-known, rarely frequented harbour of Jericoacoara, a Brazilian inlet which lies just west of the 40th meridian, between Cape San Roque and Para. There she led the S.S. *Corrientes*, from which she took 570 tons of coal. This supply ship had been waiting in Maranham, a port which is a little further westward, but had been summoned by *Dresden's* wireless and got under way at 6 a.m., August 8, meeting *Dresden* the same afternoon. The operation of coaling occupied August 9–10, after which the two ships in company went to the north of Rocas Reef and Fernando Noronha, having thus intentionally crossed both the north-west and north-east trade routes, but so far with no reward.

Fernando Noronha is another Atlantic island which gives picturesque background to the raiders' story. Lying about 80 miles east of the Rocas Reef, it is only 7 miles long by 1½ wide. We can picture this volcanic settlement as a collection of gaunt rugged rocks, over which the hot tropical rains and against which the smashing thunderous seas beat. Ashore there is nothing lovely in the stunted trees, the 700 convicts of assassins and others who long to escape. But the island boasts of cable and wireless station, and in recent years since the war aeroplane flights between Europe and

ON THE TRADE ROUTES 55

South America have halted here. Liners do not call, but give a wide berth to these bare rocks and shark-infested blue waters.

Now, on the day before she met *Corrientes, Dresden* was still further being provided for. The Hamburg-Amerika collier *Baden* on August 7 with 12,000 tons of coal had reached Pernambuco, which, of course, is only a few hours' steaming from Cape San Roque and therefore excellently situated in regard to the two sea-tracks. So, having spent some more unprofitable days hovering about, *Dresden* sent *Baden* an order to rendezvous near Rocas Reef. This signal was wirelessed through Olinda, the telegraph station which is close to Pernambuco, and out came the supply ship. The perpetual anxiety of every raider's captain was the frequent necessity of having to meet, without fail, some undefended slow-steaming ship at a rendezvous that might become compromised suddenly. There was the further inconvenience, and even danger, of having to take in supplies without adequate protection from heavy swell.

During August 13 *Dresden* and *Baden* were lashed alongside each other under the lee of Rocas Reef: but the Atlantic movement is no respecter of ships or nationalities. The two steel ships rose and fell, rolled inwards and outwards, crashing and banging severely in spite of all the fenders. Hawsers were snapped, and some actual ship damage inevitably occurred. Nor can we ignore these as negligible items. The psychological effect on officers and crew of having overwrought nerves still further strained by this monstrous jarring every few days was bound to be cumulative. Coaling ship is at all times an unpleasant evolution, and when it has to be done hurriedly under a tropical sky, with look-outs posted to report any possible enemy cruiser, and the ocean surge every moment endangering the men at work amid black dust and the din of donkey-engines, the operation each time intensifies the men's annoyance with life.

Dresden did manage, however, to take in 254 tons, but the lighthouse-keeper at the island wanted to know who she was. The German fobbed him off with the lie that this was the Swedish ship *Fylgia* doing some repairs to defective engines. She sent *Corrientes* into Pernambuco, and presently there came two more supply ships, *Prussia* and *Persia*. We thus see that so efficiently planned was the German organisation that, notwithstanding the sudden incidence of war, there were at hand and with full cargoes, colliers perfectly placed to render necessary service. At the opening of hostilities there were 54 German and Austrian vessels in American Atlantic ports, New York alone containing nine large German liners such as the *Vaterland, George Washington, Friedrich der Grosse, Grosse Kurfurst,* and *Kaiser Wilhelm II*. On August 21 the North German Lloyd liner *Brandenburg*, with 9000 tons of coal and having taken in a large quantity of provisions two days previously, was permitted by the United States authorities to leave Philadelphia, under the declaration that she was bound for Bergen. Actually this *Brandenburg*, whose speed was only 12½ knots, was despatched by the New York German Supply Centre to a rendezvous near Newfoundland, and her presence would have been appreciated by any unit raiding the New York to England route. But *Brandenburg* never met a ship, held on across the Atlantic, reached Trondhjem on the last day of August and was interned by the Norwegian authorities, as we have already seen.

From Rocas Reef *Dresden* went south, and resumed her search for victims, being accompanied by *Baden* and *Prussia*. She got well across the north-east trade route and on August 15 captured the British S.S. *Hyades*, 3352 tons, Pernambuco for Las Palmas. The latter carried a cargo of grain, and was consequently sunk after the officers and crew had been taken aboard *Prussia*, the position of this first prize being some 180 miles to the north-east of Pernambuco. On the next day *Dresden* molested but released the British S.S. *Siamese Prince*, 4847 tons, and presently parted company with *Prussia* who steamed into port and landed her prisoners, but not at Pernambuco, Bahia, or any other adjacent harbour. That would never have done; not enough days would have elapsed. *Prussia*

H.M.S. *KENT*

With the battle-cruiser *Invincible* and armed merchant cruiser *Orama* at Port William, Falkland Islands, December 1914, before going to look for *Dresden*.

OFFICERS OF H.M.S. KENT

WATCHING DRESDEN
Photograph taken aboard Kent whilst chasing Dresden on March 8, 1915.

ON THE TRADE ROUTES 57

therefore entered Rio Janeiro, and in the meantime *Dresden*, after steering a false course so as to prevent the *Hyades* officers from providing accurate intelligence, went off towards the land-crab Island of Trinidada.

Here once more we note the Teutonic organisation and arrangements for concentration working out with extraordinary success. The only German warship in South African waters, just immediately before the war, was the little gunboat *Eber*. She was eleven years old, carried only two 4·1-inch guns, her displacement being 977 tons, and her speed $13\frac{1}{2}$ knots. She was of negligible fighting value and likely to be sunk by any of the British cruisers of the Cape station. *Eber* wisely left Capetown on July 30, whilst the going was good, and went across the South Atlantic. Thither likewise proceeded the German S.S. *Steiermark* from Luderitz Bay (German South-West Africa). Now, during the night of August 18-19 *Dresden* was in wireless touch with *Steiermark*, and on arrival at Trinidada with *Baden* there was the assemblage of several supply ships which provided coal, stores and food. For, additional to *Dresden*, *Eber*, *Baden* and *Steiermark*, there had come the *Santa Isabel* which sailed from Buenos Aires on August 9, pretending she was bound for Togoland. Actually she brought out forty bullocks, oil, besides shovels and coal-bags, and a week later was met by another German steamer *Sevilla* which transferred to her both a wireless set and operator. It may be said at once that the useless *Eber* was about to hand over her guns to a crack German liner and enable the latter to go raiding. But this must be read in another chapter, since it led up to a most interesting series of events.

Dresden was now replenished with food and fuel, so that after two days she was able to go south-west and reach the trade route coming up from the River Plate. Thus she met the British S.S. *Holmwood*, 4223 tons on the 26th, when about 170 miles S$\frac{1}{4}$W of Cape Santa Marta Grande. The steamer was bound from Newport with Welsh coal for Bahia Blanca, and, after her crew had been placed aboard *Baden*, she was sunk by bombs.

Already, then, the *Dresden* had reached as far south as the southern boundary of Brazil. But at this hour steamed up the British S.S. *Katharine Park*, 4854 tons, bound from Buenos Aires for New York with cargo for United States owners. She was therefore not sunk, but to her were transferred *Holmwood's* crew, and she was dismissed on the understanding that officers as well as crew were not to engage in hostilities against Germany. On August 30 the *Katharine Park* reached Rio Janeiro, though by this time *Dresden* had carried on still further south till on the last day of August she reached Gill Bay (Gulf of St. George), which is some 800 miles from the River Plate.

She was under way again on September 2 and ready to resume her attacks, though the number of likely victims must necessarily be restricted to only those ships using the Magellan Straits or doubling the Horn. Captain Lüdecke was getting into cold latitudes, so sent on *Santa Isabel* in order to procure warm clothing, as well as materials for repairing his engines that had not been allowed their intended refit. This supply ship entered Magellan Straits and reached Punta Arenas on September 4, whence she was able to telegraph the Supply Centres of Buenos Aires and Valparaiso. She also sent a cable through to the German Admiralty at Berlin, and three days later came a reply ordering *Dresden* to operate with the cruiser *Leipzig* which was then at Guaymas (Gulf of California).

From now begins the second phase of *Dresden's* voyage in which she was to pass from the Atlantic to the Pacific. The former was becoming not too healthy now that British cruisers were steaming up and down sweeping the Brazilian coast ; though in truth a raider with adequate fuel could play hide-and-seek in the wide Atlantic for months, unless she were remarkably unlucky. After Gill Bay, *Dresden* chose not to enter Magellan Straits : she had kept her whereabouts shrouded in mystery and used her supply ship as a link between self and civilisation, thus giving a further instance of the reliance which the German Navy had placed on their auxiliary mercantile craft.

ON THE TRADE ROUTES 59

The beginning of September saw this cruiser butting into the wild seas off Cape Horn and encountering the chilly, depressing weather, grey skies, biting blasts, of a most inhospitable area. Making a wide sweep, she put into Orange Bay, Hoste Island, whence the turbulent ocean stretches direct to the frozen Antarctic. So rarely do vessels of any sort whatsoever use this forlorn anchorage, that it has long been a custom amongst mariners to "leave their card" by writing on a board the name of their ship with date. So when liberty men from *Dresden* were at last allowed ashore to stretch their legs after being at sea for several weeks, they discovered ship names and wrote on a board the word *Dresden* with the date, September 11, 1914. It was a natural, unthinking, but imprudent action; and the record was partially yet not entirely obliterated. There remained sufficient evidence, however, for her visit to be proved later on beyond all doubt.

CHAPTER V

THE ELUSIVE *DRESDEN*

DRESDEN'S war against commerce in the Atlantic had been neither particularly brilliant nor as ruthless as were the assaults by some other raiders. She had steamed from the West Indies to Cape Horn, burnt many hundred tons of coal, cruised thousands of miles, and the net gains were two not large cargo ships. These were the last she was ever to sink in that ocean.

But the few days in Orange Bay, where she could be fairly sure of seclusion away from the world, were welcomed as an opportunity for such overhaul as was possible without dockyard assistance. And now she must so regulate her programme as to join hands with Admiral von Spee who was coming east across the Pacific, and to this end she left her anchorage on September 16. Two days later, taking *Baden* with her, she sighted the Pacific Steam Navigation Company's 8075-ton steamer *Ortega* in the Pacific bound to England from Valparaiso. The cruiser gave chase, but Captain D. R. Kinneir escaped by entering the uncharted Nelson's Strait, and through the splendid efforts of his engine-room staff who got 18 knots out of a 14-knot ship. The sequel was that *Dresden* gave up the pursuit, while *Ortega* felt her way cautiously but riskily into Smyth's Channel and out into the Atlantic. It is worth noting that the cruiser kept shelling this passenger liner, but that no hits were made, and there is other evidence that *Dresden's* gunnery was not very good.

Still proceeding up the Pacific, the latter went into St. Quentin Bay (Gulf of Peñas) where she coaled from *Baden*, coasted further yet but found no more shipping, and then made a tack out away from the land to that

THE ELUSIVE DRESDEN

lonely island of Mas-a-fuera. No one can say that the German Navy failed to use every geographical convenience to the extreme limit. Having entered the war without the advantage of a chain of coaling stations, she regarded all isolated rocks, islands, lonely bays, as her privilege for supplies, refits, or rendezvous. The question of infringing the rights of neutral nations was ignored : necessity was the dominating factor, and absence of that force which imposes obedience to law prevented interference.

The principle was unprincipled, the policy impolitic ; for the cumulative effect of using other nations' property without permission was to arouse indignation, which in turn was to create a hostile reaction. But for the present all was well, and the Chilean Government were five hundred miles away—too far for any immediate protest ; and it was whilst at Mas-a-fuera that *Dresden's* wireless gained touch with the approaching Admiral von Spee on October 3. Spee's immediate object was to obtain a concentration of cruisers and for this purpose he selected another remote spot still further away from the American continent. Easter Island was discovered by the Dutch Admiral Roggeveen on Easter Day, 1722, but now belongs to Chile from which it is distant fifteen hundred miles. It has neither timber nor brushwood, and hither in 1774 came Captain Cook.

In 1897 Mr. Merlet of Valparaiso leased part of the island, and subsequently formed a company to exploit it. Scientifically Easter Island demands interest because of hundreds of strange colossal stone idols, some of which are 30 feet high. There is no regular connection with South America, except for a small sailing vessel which is owned by the company using the island as a ranch. Sometimes this vessel comes once a year ; sometimes not so frequently, and then tarries only long enough to take aboard the wool crop. Of triangular shape, measuring only 13 miles along its base, one can think of this volcanic miniature kingdom rising suddenly out of the ocean with high cliffs and jagged rocks, against which the unfettered Pacific perpetually dashes itself into white spray. Quiet, beyond all the traffic routes, quite untouched by the world's progress, it would have seemed the last bit of territory that could be associated with modern war.

In October 1914 its total population consisted of Mr. Edmunds (the English manager of the ranch) and a German tobacco planter in addition to 250 natives, who are Polynesians. But it so happened that in 1913 there had sailed from England the schooner yacht *Mana* (91 gross tons), which had brought to the island in March 1914 Mr. and Mrs. Scoresby Routledge on a scientific expedition to investigate the mysterious idols. It chanced that in October the yacht had fortunately already been sent away temporarily to South America, leaving Mrs. Routledge and one of the crew on the island. The last visit of strangers had been in June 1913, when a crew of shipwrecked mariners from the schooner *El Dorado*, trading between Oregon and Chile with a deck-load of timber, had sprung a leak and compelled her crew to take to the ship's boat.

In the normal course of Easter Island chronology it might have taken about a year before news of the World War reached its inhabitants. Neither Mrs. Routledge nor Mr. Edmunds had the faintest idea that Germany was at enmity ; that Britain, France, and Russia were plunged in a great struggle ; but on Monday morning, October 12, 1914, the islanders were surprised to find a squadron of German vessels had anchored off the shore. They consisted of the cruisers *Scharnhorst, Gneisenau, Nurnberg*, and *Dresden*. The latter had been towed here by *Baden*, in order to economise coal, and with the arrival of *Leipzig* the concentration of von Spee's force was now complete. Besides these fighting units the islanders were able to gaze down upon colliers and storeships.

What was the meaning of this sudden irruption ? The Germans said nothing about a war : they mentioned that they were cruising from the China station to Valparaiso. So unsuspecting were the handful of Easter Island white people that Mrs. Routledge entrusted the Germans with letters to post, of which

THE ELUSIVE DRESDEN 63

incidentally all but one at length reached its destination. As for Mr. Edmunds, he innocently sold the Germans £1000 worth of meat. The visitors offered to make payment in gold, but the manager (perhaps remembering than an exploiter had once been murdered here) considered it wiser to ask and accept an order instead!

But there was an indefinable mysteriousness about this squadron, and it seemed curious that no one came ashore except very rarely. The natives became annoyed that so few presents were made. Had these Europeans no information to impart? Why were they so secretive? The Germans insisted that they had no newspapers, but at night they steamed out with no lights showing. Strange rumours began to develop, and one day an officer was foolish enough to make the remark that "in two months Germany will be at the top of the tree". The crew had been told to keep their tongues quiet, but when the German tobacco-planter went aboard they gave him the momentous news that the Great War had begun. And that was how the tidings came to Easter Island.

Leading his squadron to sea after dusk on Sunday, October 18, with his flag in *Scharnhorst*, von Spee finally quitted Easter Island.* During a whole week he had knowingly and deliberately delayed, where he had been entitled to rest only a few hours. He had flouted Chilean neutrality by using in the most leisured manner this island as his base : yet who was there of Chile to say him nay? To a belligerent who likes to defy international law, the seas afford many a free station whereon authority sits lightly if it exists at all. Will the spread of wireless stations and the extension of aviation make such proceedings nowadays impossible?

The squadron never came back, though the raider *Prinz Eitel Friedrich* descended on the anchorage just before Christmas. Of her cruise we shall investigate the stages in a later chapter. Whilst the sheep-shearing at Easter Island went on, the German squadron with

---

* I am indebted for some of the above details to Mrs. Scoresby Routledge's interesting volume, *The Mystery of Easter Island.*

their auxiliaries steamed south-east for Mas-a-fuera where they anchored on October 26, coaled, left the next day, and approached the vicinity of Valparaiso two days later. Now during this same month Admiral Cradock had been into Orange Bay and found the inscription proving that *Dresden* had called. On November 1 his inferior squadron met and was defeated by Admiral von Spee at the Battle of Coronel.

On November 6 the concentration again began to be made at Mas-a-fuera, yet once more defying neutrality, and now supplies fairly poured in. For two sailing vessels had been captured, one French with 3500 tons of coal, the other Norwegian with 2634 tons; whilst the German supply ship *Sacramento* had arrived from San Francisco with coal and food. Not till November 15 did von Spee sail, though *Dresden* and *Leipzig* left four days earlier and on November 13 called at Valparaiso, embarked stores, but left the next day. It was on the 16th that the British S.S. *North Wales* with coal was captured by *Dresden* and sunk, and next day the crew were transferred to the latter's supply ship *Rhakotis*, who a month later landed them at Callao.

At St.Quentin Bay von Spee once more concentrated his squadron; this time the rendezvous was to see a veritable squadron also of supply ships. It was now November 21 and five days later von Spee set out for the fate that awaited him, the force consisting of his five cruisers, but also he took with him only the three supply ships *Baden, Santa Isabel,* and *Seydlitz.* Dipping their bows into the heavy seas, avoiding the Magellan Straits, and going outside the Horn the wanderers halted : for, coming towards them on December 2 was the British-owned *Drummuir,* 1844 tons, one of the few survivors of the sailing ships. Through four hundred years "Cape Stiff" had been the sailing ship's deadliest enemy, the graveyard of many a sailor, the nightmare of every sailing-ship master. Drake, Anson, and a host of others had spent anxious times battering round this tempestuous corner of the globe, and now the age of sail was completing its last few voyages. As if to hurry its departure by the dominance of steam, *Leipzig* played

THE ELUSIVE DRESDEN 65

her rôle by capturing *Drummuir*, which was taken to the back of Picton Island; next, after the sailing vessel's cargo of coal had been transferred to the supply ships, followed the sad passing. *Drummuir*, representative of a fine race which revealed the Old World to the New, was towed into deep water and sent to the bottom.

That was on December 6, and in the evening von Spee's squadron got under way for the Falklands; but then on December 8 followed the historic battle with his overwhelming defeat. Had it been a victory, the Falklands would have been transformed into a German base, the Atlantic would have been terrorised for a long time by cruiser raids, and the trade routes would have been death-traps. Finally, the squadron would have been able to essay a return to the North Sea and a conjunction with the outcoming High Sea Fleet might have led to a full-dress engagement with the Grand Fleet. But, as it was, von Spee lost to Admiral Sturdee four out of five cruisers, and two out of three remaining supply ships, so that there remained at the end of December 8 only the *Dresden* cruiser, and the *Seydlitz*. The latter had come all the way from Australia, and was one of the North German liners: she escaped, landed the *Drummuir* crew twelve days later, but finally was interned in February at Bahia Blanca.

We are now at liberty to devote ourselves exclusively once more to the adventures of *Dresden* and to observe the incredible situations, the narrow escapes, and terrible moments of suspense which were to last for weeks and weeks. She was destined to play a lonely game in the loneliest and most cheerless portion of the globe. The desperate condition in which she found herself was not merely that her admiral and sister-ships had perished, but that the whole of the German supply system had recieved a series of disintegrating shocks. Inasmuch as the very life of a raider depended on coal and stores, she could not do much if neither reached her. And owners were preferring to keep their ships in port just now rather than expose them to disaster, so the chances of helping herself to fuel and food in the Patagonian area were not promising. Hitherto life for

E

these cruisers had been rather that of a speculative criminal. They had trespassed flagrantly, their supply ships had by lies and deceit used harbours of South American Republics as the sources for coal, provisions, stores of all sorts, and communication with Berlin. Such insults to the self-pride of neutral nations could not be endured for ever.

Brazil and Argentina were now beginning to tighten up regulations : in future colliers would not be allowed to leave port if there was the slightest suspicion that they were about to serve German cruisers. The Governments of Uruguay and Chile were likewise becoming less patient than before, with the result that German Supply Officers in South America were finding their task impossible. Only across the Atlantic at Canary Islands, Las Palmas, Tenerife were there always several thousand tons of German-owned coal always ready. Captain Lüdecke was compelled to do some serious thinking for the future, and the great lesson to be learned from his subsequent movements is one of moral courage. He refused to bow his head to discouragement and, on the countrary, utilised every conceivable means for outwitting fate.

Dresden was able to survive the Battle of the Falklands because she got away in the thick weather of the afternoon. At first Captain Lüdecke intended making for Picton Island, where von Spee was to have rendezvoused. But Lüdecke's wireless calls could get no reply from a supply ship. *Dresden* needed coal, and must have it : yet how ? Whence ? Punta Arenas—inside the Magellan Straits—that was the only possible place. But surely British cruisers would be hovering off the eastern entrance to the Straits ? Most likely they would. Then what to do ? The answer was found in choosing the tricky Cockburn Channel which he entered on December 10 and came to anchor at 4 p.m. in Sholl Bay, some sixty miles south of Punta Arenas. So desperate had become the fuel problem that Captain Lüdecke had to send his men ashore to cut down trees, and they also brought off water. Forests abound in the Magellan neighbourhood, and when Darwin was there-

THE ELUSIVE *DRESDEN* 67

abouts in the *Beagle* during 1834 he recorded: "So thick was the wood, that it was necessary to have constant recourse to the compass; for every landmark, though in a mountainous country, was completely shut out."

Only 160 tons of the cruiser's maximum 850 tons of coal remained, so *Dresden* could not have carried on much longer. That night the Chilean torpedo-gunboat *Almirante Condell* visited *Dresden*. She was a quarter of a century old and lightly armed, but she represented the law and informed Lüdecke he must not prolong his stay beyond twenty-four hours. At 10 a.m. on December 12 *Dresden* weighed anchor and reached that quite unpretentious little town of Punta Arenas so famous for its driving storms. He knew that the United States collier *Minnesotan*, specially chartered by the German Government, was there lying; but this vessel's master now refused to let him have a shovelful. He was not going to supply a man-of-war.

This was awkward, time was precious, and the British cruisers could not be far away. But the German Roland Line *Turpin* had been lying there since war began, so from her *Dresden* managed to obtain 750 tons of briquettes aboard by the evening of December 13, and at 10 p.m. steamed away south down the Straits. Five hours later the British cruiser H.M.S. *Bristol* arrived! It had been a narrow shave.

From now onwards *Dresden* was to live a hand-to-mouth existence in a grand game of hide-and-seek, with the most impressive scenery for background. She was hunted and searched for incessantly; false clues, all sorts of rumours, were followed up and still the German could not be located. She was like some culprit wanted by the police, and unable to show herself in public. In order to picture the strange environment we have to remember that these Magellan Straits are a bewildering labyrinth of channels and islands that even in this twentieth century still remain inadequately surveyed, and such charts as exist date back chiefly from Darwin and the *Beagle* epoch.

Imagine a kind of Norway with valleys, gorges, snow-clad mountains, precipices, and peaks, and all nature in a savage primitive isolation. Here are channels, sometimes 4000 feet deep, running between mountains rising to 5000 feet. Anchorages are few and even thirty miles apart. To navigate except by daylight is impossible, and dangerous at that if the more unfrequented passages are attempted; for rocks are waiting to hole the ship's bottom. Certainly there is smooth water, but the tides are strong, the light is not generally good, the atmosphere never warm, and out of the twenty-four hours it rains for eleven. Its cold and wet, its damp fogs, are comparable only with an English winter.

The deep ravines, the incessant gales of wind, and what Darwin once called "the death-like scene of desolation"; the gloomy woods inhabited by only few birds; the dark ragged clouds that drive furiously over the cones of snow and blue glaciers, overawe the mind of man. Not even the abundant firewood and many waterfalls make up for the misty sunless weather, the grey seas outside, the heartlessness of the fjords themselves. These are cliffs covered with fern and brilliant moss, and there is something majestic in the crags as well as the ravines. But down come the squally "williwaws" lashing the smooth water into foaming crests and liable to lay any sailing craft flat down. Altogether this stern, forbidding, barren region of South America's extremity was an ideal, if strange, asylum for a turbine cruiser hiding after the most complete naval victory of modern times.

CHAPTER VI

THE GREAT GAME OF HIDE-AND-SEEK

THOSE various colliers which had been used by one or more of von Spee's cruisers and had striven so hard to be at hand always when required, had now become like lost children deprived of protective parentage. In addition to those mentioned we may in passing see how some others fared. *Memphis* was interned at Coronel, *Luxor* was confined to the Peruvian port of Callao, *Patagonia* was arrested by an Argentine warship for breach of neutrality, *Mera* was interned at Monte Video, and *Josephina* was caught. She was trying to reach the west coast of South America in the hope of joining *Dresden* somewhere; but just as she was entering the Magellan Straits on January 6, 1915, Admiral Stoddart in H.M.S. *Carnarvon* stopped her, found her papers unsatisfactory, so sent her in to Port Stanley, Falkland Islands.

The battle-cruiser *Australia*, which had been too big to use the Panama Canal during her voyage from the Pacific to Atlantic, passed through Magellan Straits on the last day of 1914, coaled at the Falklands, and left there at daylight on January 5. Now on the afternoon of the 6th she sighted a steamer which, being outside any normal steam track, aroused suspicions. The battle-cruiser gave chase, the steamer ran away, but the former was limping and could not go fast: she had damaged one of her propellers. The pursuit was therefore prolonged, and by sunset the strange steamer was still ten miles ahead, though when first sighted the latter had been on the horizon.

Finally, by loosing off one round of 12-inch shell from her foremost turret, *Australia* caused the other vessel to stop, which turned out to be the *Eleonare*

Woermann, another German supply ship. She had been waiting at her rendezvous near Puerto Santa Elena on the east coast of Argentina, and was now on her way to find *Dresden*, having been despatched by the Buenos Aires Supply Centre (as also had been *Mera* and *Patagonia*) for von Spee's Squadron. Admiral Patey found she had no papers but 1800 tons of coal, and she had to be sunk, after her crew were taken prisoners ; for no prize crew could be spared. Another of the German supply colliers, *Amasis*, had been detached by Admiral von Spee to Fox Bay (about forty-five miles SSE of Punta Arenas), and thence by boat Lieutenant zur Helle communicated with Punta Arenas. He had been specially sent by his Commander-in-Chief to arrange for the squadron obtaining coal, and an endeavour was made to have *Minnesotan's* cargo transhipped to *Amasis*. On the previous day there had come out of Monte Video the supply ship *Sierra Cordoba*, bound south to reach *Dresden*.

Punta Arenas is the most southerly town in the world ; but at this time it was also an outpost for communication between Germany and the hidden *Dresden*. Amongst its population of several thousands connected with the shipping, wool and frozen meat trades, there were plenty of active sympathisers with Germany, who could be relied upon to do their best for *Dresden* in regard to supplying food and valuable information concerning the movements of the British cruisers which were restless in their searches. Indeed, her friends kept the secret of her location so well that she became a veritable mystery ship to most people. All sorts of naval units were hunting for her ; battle-cruisers, cruisers, and armed merchant-cruisers were combing a wide area. Admirals were studying charts and laying careful plans : but all to no purpose. Hundreds of miles with bays, inlets, channels, open sea, were inspected ; yet, most tantalisingly, there was not a trace of the fugitive. Captain Lüdecke had covered his tracks well. But what had become of him ?

To-day we know, and this is the answer. The region of Barbara Channel between the two largest islands west

THE GREAT GAME OF HIDE-AND-SEEK 71

of Tierra del Fuego, and the archipelago of small islands extending from Cape Horn to the western exit of the Strait, had not been searched : it was dangerous to navigation, and therefore about as familiar to ships as the Sahara is to automobiles. But *Dresden* on leaving Punta Arenas went boldly south through Magellan Straits, through Magdalena Sound and Cockburn Channel with safety, next through rock-strewn passages and so to Hewett Bay at the south-west end of Barbara Channel. There she found that *Amasis* was already anchored, after having shifted down from Fox Bay.

This, then, was to be the first of *Dresden's* hiding-places and she remained here till after Christmas. Such was her excellent connection with the outside world that on December 19 she learned that *Sierra Cordoba* was on the way towards her with 1600 tons of coal. It was on December 20 that Captain Lüdecke sent *Amasis* to Punta Arenas, hoping to get the *Minnesotan's* cargo transferred and thus by a circuitous method to overcome the previous objections. The Chilean authorities, however, forbade the transfer, and *Amasis* was detained as was hardly surprising. Furthermore, the activities of the British cruisers were so intense that *Sierra Cordoba* could not move on at present, but remained hiding in Magdalena Sound. This made it extremely inconvenient for *Dresden*, whose crew now had to be sent ashore once more felling timber and fetching water to conserve existing supplies.

In all such unusual, yet literally true, narratives such as this there crops up some important coincidence that in fiction would never be allowed. On the day after Christmas there came a motor sailing-boat named *Galileo*, owned by a French hunter who spoke to some of *Dresden's* seamen in one of the cruiser's boats, and accused them of being Germans. To this was given a speedy denial. The Frenchman pointed to their tatooed arms. There was German indelibly written on their very skin ! Although evasive answers had been given, it was quite obvious that the Frenchman was not convinced that the men spoke truth. Evidently Captain Lüdecke realised that *Dresden's* concealment would soon be divulged, so it was time to quit. Just as in the olden days of the sixteenth, seventeenth, and eighteenth-century sailing ships, explorers used to feel their way into uncharted waters by sending the ship's pinnace ahead to keep sounding for the big ship; so this Christmastide, on December 27, Captain Lüdecke felt his way into Christmas Bay (at the top of Stokes Bay) by sending his steam pinnace some distance ahead carefully sounding. For the charts were most inaccurate, and the British Admiralty issues had marked this convenient arm of the sea as solid land. Who could ever have thought that a war would make the surveying of these scarcely accessible inlets worth while?

On the occasion when *Dresden* had called at Punta Arenas, she had been urged by the German Consul to intern herself, but Captain Lüdecke was not inclined. And now from that port were sent casks of sausages as well as other provisions aboard the specially chartered small Chilean steamer *Esplorador*. Indeed, by the exercise of caution it became possible to keep up a fairly regular communication, through tugs or motor-boats, between this port and the hidden *Dresden*. Admiral Stoddart in charge of the British cruisers had been informed by a Punta Arenas pilot that there were no good bays in the district where the French hunter had reported Captain Lüdecke to be. It was rather an unfortunate sequence of events that though the Frenchman truthfully reported what he had seen to the British Consul, Mr. Milward, and the latter had in turn informed Admiral Stoddart, and had even telegraphed the news to the British Admiralty; yet amid the suspicious atmosphere of Punta Arenas and its mixed nationalities, its opposing cliques and mutual distrust, it was difficult to know what to believe and whom. In any case there was no little secret work being done, and the telegraph was busy. The Admiral most unluckily would not credit Mr. Milward, and somehow the Consul's telegram never reached Whitehall. Further, to complicate matters, the pilots were suspected of being German sympathisers, and the Admiral felt that any inducement for attracting British men-of-war into

THE GREAT GAME OF HIDE-AND-SEEK 73

a difficult and incompletely surveyed district was a subtle trap.

Such was the mental fog which hung over the problem. With H.M.S. *Carnarvon* and *Bristol* the Admiral made a search of Cockburn Channel, but—most regrettably as it now appears—he could not see his way to continuing his search westward. *Sierra Cordoba* watching her opportunity eluded all vigilance, felt her way through channels and passages, so that on January 19 she joined *Dresden* with her welcome supply of coal. This obviously placed Captain Lüdecke in a far stronger position of independence: he had gained by delaying, and his moral courage in refusing to intern his ship had been justified. There next followed the question of his future movements. What was he to do? Where was he to go? For over a month he had evaded his enemies. True. But that could not continue indefinitely. His Admiral von Spee had won the Coronal victory, only to be annihilated at Falklands.

Through Punta Arenas Captain Lüdecke telegraphed to Berlin, and his Admiralty advised him to come home. He was to use not the ordinary steamship tracks, but the sailing-ship route which comes up north in the middle of the Atlantic. As to colliers, Germany would ensure that they should be found waiting at Lavandeira Reef, which is situated off the north Brazilian coast in Lat. 5 S, Long. 36 W : another of those isolated bits of rock which were carefully selected as rendezvous. This recommendation was for Lüdecke impracticable, for it would mean steaming about 5000 miles, and *Dresden* could not carry anything like enough fuel for all that distance. And this, incidentally, again proved that the ordinary fast but uneconomical cruiser is not the ideal type of vessel for raiding. Much better suited was the kind of merchantman accustomed to long passages at moderate speed with economy. The South Atlantic, both north and south of the equator, was just now not healthy for the solitary survivor of the Falklands battle. She could scarcely hope to avoid being pursued before reaching Lavandeira Reef, and this would mean that the rate of coal consumption must mount up by an unreasonable ratio. But, quite apart from all these considerations, we must remember that *Dresden's* proper dockyard refit had been already postponed six months, during which she had steamed thousands of miles including one burst of excessive speed to escape from sharing von Spee's battle fate.

So Lüdecke decided to let the Atlantic severely alone but to clear out of the dismal Magellan area, and after the manner of Drake and Anson carry on westward across the Pacific, picking up what prey he could. This decision to go commerce raiding in an ocean, whence a general clearance of British naval forces had been made, was sound enough. There were lots of unprotected islands for getting shelter, food, recreation, and by zigzagging across the trade routes he could play the same game that he had once tried off Brazil. The further west he steamed, the nearer would he approach the rich Indian area which his sister-ship *Emden*, now destroyed, had found so convenient for raiding. Nor can we afford to omit the psychological factor in this decision.

He who has had command of ships and crews well knows how bored the sailor becomes by inactivity. After all those exciting weeks of tension, hard steaming, no opportunity to spend their pay ashore, no chance of getting away from the sight and smell of their ship, *Dresden's* crew must have reached that stage of mentality which is known in the Royal Navy by the blunt expression of "bloodymindedness". Every sailor, however faithful to his shipmates, has had the experience of so hating his companions after monotonous days at sea that quarrels spark up with the slightest friction, officers find a mutinous spirit and dull lethargy insidiously growing. But if this is so in temperate climates, what must have been the condition in *Dresden's* mess-decks when the men, day after day, week after week, were compelled to gaze out at those dreary scenes of bleak desolation, to watch the dismal skies and hear the gales shrieking down from the snow mountains ? Which of them could sleep soundly in his hammock, when any moment a couple of British

THE GREAT GAME OF HIDE-AND-SEEK 75

cruisers might come round the corner and shell them to perdition ?

Yes : it was time to make plans for moving. Lüdecke determined to go as far west as the East Indies, and on February 3 sent a telegram to Berlin requesting that a collier be sent to the Dutch East Indies by the middle of April. But the command of the seas was in British hands, whose cruisers were incessant ; and the Supply trickery was just about on its final efforts. Therefore the German Admiralty had to cable :

> Further coal supply for Pacific and Indian Oceans is impossible. Voyage home by sailing-ship route recommended. Collier awaits you in 5° S, 36 W.

It had taken six days for Lüdecke's telegram to reach its destination, and this reply was sent to Punta Arenas on February 10. We can picture the harassed skipper pacing his cabin and reading these not encouraging words, that had been written by somebody enjoying the comforts and security of a warm office and perhaps not able fully to realise all the anxiety of a lonely adventurer. But between the despatch of Lüdecke's telegram and the receipt of a reply a further development had taken place.

On January 28 the *Dresden* was discovered by a German otter-hunter, and a few days later *Esplorador* arrived with a German pilot on board. After she had transhipped her Punta Arenas stores on the cruiser's deck, she was ordered to seek out some other safe hiding-place for *Dresden* and *Sierra Cordoba.** Lüdecke was clearly taking no risks, but was also making the best of valuable local knowledge. So, when he had obtained the information required, he dismissed *Esplorador* back to Punta Arenas and shifted *Dresden* to a new harbour of refuge. The latter according to the inaccurate charts did not exist : where the survey showed the area to be land it was, in fact, water. Hence the local personal knowledge of the German pilot turned out to be a godsend : *Dresden* could conceal herself in

---
* It was a Chilean destroyer which compelled *Dresden* to move on within twenty-four hours, yet the cruiser merely changed her anchorage.

an anchorage that cartographically did not exist. (This will be manifest from British Admiralty chart No. 554. Reference to No. 1306 will afford an interesting study of the previously mentioned Barbara Channel with Hewett Bay as an inset.)

The new refuge was very secluded indeed, lay south of Santa Ines Island and north of William Island. Here Lüdecke let go anchor on February 5, and here the Berlin telegram came to him. Its contents made him abandon the East Indian project, but he still adhered to the intention of commerce raiding in the Pacific, and he must get away before many days were spent. This perpetual necessity of having to move about from channel to fjord, like the impulse which comes to a lurking criminal on the run, was hardly improving the moral of the ship's company. His secondary worry was that unrelenting item of coal. Coal! Coal! Coal! It was the bane of a cruiser captain's existence. How lucky had those commanding officers been in the times when privateers, pirates, naval frigates, and corvettes had only to rely on the wind! How servile a thing was this modern era of engines, furnaces, boilers! Such an expression as "freedom of the sea" might mean something to politicians, but to practical naval minds to-day it was a mere contradiction. The cruiser was permitted only so much liberty as the shore would concede in fuel.

His mind was made up : he must go raiding the Pacific and find his coal by capturing other ships. Before leaving he caused a letter to reach Punta Arenas requesting that if possible a collier should be sent to reach by March 5 a rendezvous in Lat. 37 S, Long. 80 W; that is to say well to the westward of Coronel, but about 200 miles south of Mas-a-Fuera. On February 14, having waited for the cover of night, *Dresden* with *Sierra Cordoba* got under way at 5.30 p.m. and steamed out into the heaving Pacific, with the knowledge that for over two months she had completely baffled her hunters.

When once out in open water, a course was made to the westward, so as to give the Chilean coast a berth of 200 miles away from cruisers protecting the steamer

THE GREAT GAME OF HIDE-AND-SEEK 77

routes. It was *Dresden's* hope to work the sailing-ship route, and she posted *Sierra Cordoba* 100 miles ahead as look-out. The latter, being just a single-funnel ship, was not likely to create suspicion, but she could always wireless the approach of British cruisers and merchant vessels alike. It may be at once stated that little came of this raiding intention, and day after day passed most disappointingly. Had all these coal-carrying barques sailed off the seas ? Both she and *Sierra Cordoba* were consuming serious amounts of fuel even though they were trying their best to economise ; for a good pressure of steam must ever be ready for quick action if need be. It was a boring life to be hovering idle in that area of which the rendezvous just mentioned for March 5 was roughly the centre. To the north lay Mas-a-fuera, and to the north-east was Valparaiso which in the pre-war days was accustomed to the visits of European sailing ships. German barques would come up round the Horn with a cargo of pianos, crockery and general merchandise ; these were splendid craft, well run, and used to make wonderfully quick passages. British barques would come out with coal, and then go home with nitrate : but those days are now over as regards the latter vessels. By the time the war was ended, hardly any were afloat.

At last on February 27 was sighted the British barque *Conway Castle*, 1694 tons, some 560 miles SW by W$\frac{1}{2}$W of Valparaiso, being now on her way from this port to Australia with barley ; and she had every right to expect that with von Spee at the bottom of the Atlantic there was not much likelihood of danger in the Pacific. Lüdecke sank her, took the crew aboard, and a week later transferred them to a Peruvian barque which chanced to come along. But he had not done himself the slightest bit of good, and still the coal went on being wasted. Not merely could *Dresden* not refill her bunkers, but he even had to assist *Sierra Cordoba*, since she was in want. Thus occurred the strange spectacle of a cruiser engaged in deep-sea coaling of an ex-merchantman by the inefficient mode of using her own boats. Finally, however, *Sierra Cordoba* had to be sent into Valparaiso, where she arrived on March 3 but sailed again four days later.

It is quite clear, then, that the Chilean authorities had not yet tightened up their neutrality to any rigid strictness. *Sierra Cordoba* was able to leave with 1200 tons of coal, just as if she had never been an auxiliary warship. Legally, the proceeding was quite unjustifiable. The German Supply Officers at Valparaiso and San Francisco at the Pacific side, as well as at Monte Video on the Atlantic, were striving hard to keep *Dresden* in fuel at this critical period though with only partial success. Certainly from Monte Video the supply ship *Gotha* came forth, and an ingenious effort was made to send coal from as far away as Honolulu in mid-Pacific. The scheme was illustrative of Teutonic thoroughness and persistence.

In the early days of the war the single-funnelled little gunboat *Geier*, which was of no great fighting value, had made her way eastwards across the Pacific after clearing out of Singapore and then disappeared. She was a slow old thing, but she ambled along to the Caroline Islands where she took as prize the British S.S. *Southport*, 3588 tons, and left her (as the Germans thought) too injured for further voyaging. The *Southport*, however, managed to steam out whilst *Geier* was away and duly reached Australia. *Geier* stood on to the north-east and on October 15 had to put into Honolulu to carry out repairs. Here the the United States authorities promptly put an end to her career by internment. But there were other German vessels also at Honolulu, and the commanding officer of *Geier*, Korvetten-Kapitän (Commander) Carl Grasshof, was capable of acting as link with North America.

The Supply Officer at San Francisco got in touch with Grasshof with a view to sending one of the German vessels from Honolulu to *Dresden*. By means of a code the two men were able to arrange a bright idea. But there turned out to be practical difficulties. The only German-owned coal at the island was in the *Holsatia* (another Hamburg-Amerika steamer), and the local authorities were not going to permit her departing with

THE GREAT GAME OF HIDE-AND-SEEK

such a cargo. As to the other coal which came hither, that was either Australian or Japanese, and there was no possibility of this being sold either to Germans or their agents. So once more *Dresden* found her sources for replenishment curtailed.

Another item needs to be stressed, because it is in importance second only to that of supplies.

Not all the most detailed organisation for sending forth colliers is of much avail unless these auxiliaries can be certain of reaching their rendezvous. Occasions arise when, owing to a succession of events, these rendezvous have to be changed, or the dates for meeting have to be altered. In this modern period of steamship raiding wireless communication is absolutely essential. This was realised fully as soon as war started, and steps were immediately taken to fit with wireless sets those colliers not so provided. From that time the cruisers could keep in touch with, and control of, the smaller vessel's movements over hundreds of miles, summoning or warning her away as necessity required.

But the war proved that wireless can be a most dangerous gift. One of the reasons for the collapse of the Russian "steam roller" on Germany's eastern military front was the reckless manner in which Russian headquarters divulged almost daily by wireless their operation plans. We know from recently published history that Hindenburg was amazed that such precious information should be broadcast for the German Army to pick up. To this day it still remains inexplicable that any Staff should never have realised their folly of presenting their enemy with to-morrow's intentions. Hindenburg was able to make his counter-preparations and achieve in the end one of the most successful campaigns in the whole four years of hostilities.

On the other hand, the Germans at the Western Front were nearly as careless ; and Army officers have told me that the amount of intelligence picked up from German wireless was surprisingly great. So, too, with the German Navy. It is now common knowledge that never did the High Sea Fleet get under way for a North

Sea raid than the British Admiralty was aware of this sudden activity. For the wireless signals were intercepted from the other side of the North Sea, and the Grand Fleet were able to leave port about the same hour that the High Sea Fleet was quitting theirs.

Let us transfer such possibilities of wireless to the South American neighbourhood, and add the fact that by the chances of war the German code became decipherable. It follows that sooner or later the lonely raider calling up her auxiliary will give herself and the supply ship clean away. When once it has been discovered that the rendezvous is to be at a certain latitude and longitude, it will be very bad luck if the chasing cruisers do not capture either raider or collier. Sometimes, indeed on many occasions, that misfortune did occur : the bird had just flown before the hunter arrived. Furthermore, the bleating of certain South American wireless stations caused messages to reach British as well as German ships. During January 1915, for example, the Cerrito Wireless Station near to Monte Video flashed a signal to the effect that on February 20 a collier would be waiting for *Dresden* at Lavandeira Reef, as the German Admiralty had already promised Lüdecke ; though now we know that he had no intention of using that facility. But an intercepted message also informed the British Navy that the German collier *Gotha*, which had left Monte Video on the night of February 20, was due to rendezvous from March 5–30 at that other position which we have mentioned, viz., about 200 miles south of Mas-a-Fuera in Lat. 37 S, Long. 80 W. So here, then, was invaluable news which might conceivably be the key to the problem : the solution of that mystery of *Dresden's* concealment. Where the crumbs are to be found, there will be discovered the bird : where the collier is ordered to remain, there should steam into the area the raider.

But amid all the messages that were broadcast the rumours that were launched, and the intentionally false information that was sent out, it needed patience and discernment to sort the facts from fiction. In practical terms, that is to say, the difficulty was how to operate

DANCING ON THE QUARTERDECK
Whiling the time aboard *Kent* whilst chasing *Dresden* on March 8, 1915.

SAWING UP WOOD
For the furnaces of *Kent* whilst chasing *Dresden*.

EVERYBODY AFT

To trim *Kent* more by the stern whilst chasing *Dresden*.

THE GREAT GAME OF HIDE-AND-SEEK 81

the hunting cruisers without being on the one hand guilty of uncovering the trade routes, or on the other of affording the hiding raider a period of peace. During this February, for example, there was a rumour that the Germans intended to capture the Royal Mail Line S.S. *Alcantara* in Lat. 7 S, Long. 34 W : that is to say north-east of Pernambuco, on the trade route between Brazil and St. Vincent. The result of this suggestion was that the cruiser H.M.S. *Sydney* had to escort her through the danger zone. At a later date we shall find this merchant vessel making memorable history.

There still survived down in the Magellan area an even more substantiated rumour, and the time had now come when this must be examined with thoroughness. On February 25 Mr. Consul Milward, still convinced that his information of *Dresden's* whereabouts was accurate, chartered that motor sailing-boat *Galileo* and took with him from Punta Arenas a Chilean pilot who knew the channels intimately. The last intelligence had reported *Dresden* in a corner of Stokes Bay, Lat. 54 S, Long. 72.40 W. But before we observe what resulted, let us transfer our attention for a while to the very interesting part which the British cruiser *Kent* was to play in this amazing hunt for a German cruiser. The latter was a newer ship than H.M.S. *Kent* by five years and their respective designed speeds were about the same, though the German was perhaps half a knot faster. At the Battle of the Falklands H.M.S. *Kent* had nobly distinguished herself when she chased *Nurnberg* till the latter burst two of her boilers in trying to get away. On that occasion the eleven-year-old *Kent* happened to be fairly short of coal and this had made her of course lighter in the water. She also had a clean bottom. On the other hand, her boilers were long since past their prime, and it was only by the most determined stoking, together with the unremitting attention of the engineer department, that she worked up to 25 knots—that is to say, two knots better than her designed speed.

Having sunk *Nurnberg*, and having lost four of her

THE SEA-RAIDERS

own men, the British cruiser with seven German survivors steamed back to the Falklands, effected repairs and on December 15 put to sea, thus beginning a long search with other ships for *Dresden* who alone of von Spee's Squadron had to be accounted for. Through the Magellan Straits and into the Pacific, past snow-capped mountains and low green-wooded islands, curtseying to the heavy swell of Cape Pillar, the western sentinel that ruggedly guards the Straits' entrance, *Kent* searched and scanned through telescopes and binoculars every bay and inlet she passed. Meanwhile the armed merchant cruiser *Orama* as well as the two cruisers *Glasgow* and *Bristol* were likewise to spend days of similar activity through the channels of the south and west coast of Chile.

Christmas Day aboard *Kent* was spent in the usual cheery manner customary with the Royal Navy—the decorated mess decks, the impromptu band, the "fun" party and so on. But almost the whole while the cruiser was steaming, steaming, seeking, searching for this mysterious *Dresden*. It was rough on the engineers, and even if *Kent* anchored for a brief space it was no rest for the artificers and their mates who worked night and day to remedy defects which could not be put right when the ship was under way. So the weeks went by in monotonous vigilance, and often it was months before mails from home reached her people. Keeping the requisite three miles distance from neutral territory when coaling from the accompanying colliers, sometimes meant anchoring in water no shallower than 65 fathoms! But all this time *Kent* was a happy ship. There would be sing-songs to keep the men in good spirits, and sports on board such as tug-of-war, 100-yards race, and prizes awarded in the shape of tinned fruit, sausages, chocolates, cigarettes, etc., one of the officers splendidly dressed up as a lady and posing as a Duchess distributing the awards in a most humorous manner.

But on February 4 news came that *Dresden* was hiding somewhere in the vicinity of Magellan Straits. Still, so many yarns had been spread concerning the

THE GREAT GAME OF HIDE-AND-SEEK 83

German that it was hard to know which to believe. Patrolling up and down the Pacific, the cruisers, ten miles apart from each other, would be butting into heavy gales, but somehow *Dresden* was not to be found. Next, on February 22, had come the report that she was hiding in Last Hope Inlet, on the northern side of Magellan Straits: so south from Coronel came *Kent* to join *Glasgow* and *Bristol* in a new search. But no trace of her was found in the inlet: the rumour was once more ill founded.

Still, all news pointed to the probability of *Dresden* being now somewhere in one of the channels at the south side of the Straits, and a determined effort was set going by *Kent, Glasgow, Bristol,* and *Orama*. It was already March 1 and from this date the pace quickens, the suspense becomes keener, and the sphere is narrowed down. In order that the many channels of Magellan Straits might be examined where deep-draught cruisers could not venture for fear of rocks, *Kent's* picket-boat was selected, armed with two 14-inch torpedoes, a Maxim-gun, rifles and ammunition, and fitted with wireless. Commander Wharton of *Kent* was put in charge and she was named H.M.S. *Gillingham* after the well-known Kentish place on the Medway, where in the sixteenth century warships used to anchor as their successors do to this day.

It was decided that *Kent, Glasgow,* and *Gillingham* should work from south to north up the Barbara Channel whilst *Bristol* and *Orama* waited in the Magellan Straits watching the exits from the northern end of the channel. Just before daylight at 4.30 a.m. on March 3 the great search began when *Glasgow* and *Kent* proceeded through Magdalen Sound, through Cockburn Channel and Adelaide Passage, into the southern end of Barbara Channel. Here the picket-boat was hoisted out. The navigation was going to be difficult and big risks undertaken, for the channels had been but slightly surveyed; there were innumerable rocks and islands, many of which were either not marked on the chart or incorrectly shown. Sounding with the lead was not much use as the depths were so irregular, varying from a few yards to 100 fathoms—from no bottom to 17 fathoms.

All guns were kept manned and trained ready to open fire at any moment, for at the other side of an islet or headland the enemy might be lurking. *Gillingham* searched close inshore, with a crew of sixteen officers and men all on the alert. But the long day passed without seeing any clue, night was coming on, the northern end of Barbara Channel had been reached, and an anchorage was found yet no shallower than 75 fathoms, only 200 yards from the shore under a great towering mountain. Thus had an exciting day proved fruitless and disappointing. Every officer and man had been keyed up to expectancy.

But this very night came that above-mentioned valuable intelligence that *Dresden* had ordered a German collier to meet her at a certain rendezvous some 200 miles west of Mas-a-Fuera, so *Kent* was ordered to make for this rendezvous. In command of *Kent* was Captain (now Admiral) J. D. Allen, who has with great courtesy placed at my disposal a detailed diary which he kept from day to day during this memorable cruise. "Now the question was," wrote this officer, "how were we to get out of our present position as quickly as possible?" For the narrows, leading out to the northern entrance of Barbara Channel, consisted of a channel two miles long and only 100 yards wide, with a bend of 45° in the middle, to say nothing of a strong tide—just about as tricky a bit of navigation as any ship could wish.

As soon as it was light enough the picket-boat went off to examine the channel and after a few hours reported that though narrow, it was practicable. *Kent* thus steamed out by a channel that saved her twenty-four hours, though, says Admiral Allen, "it is exceedingly doubtful whether any ship of the size, length, and draught of the *Kent* has ever been through such a place." The operations so suddenly interrupted had been based on the information that *Dresden* was in a corner of Stokes Bay (Lat. 54 S, Long. 72.40 W). But now that the intercepted wireless revealed that *Dresden* had left

THE GREAT GAME OF HIDE-AND-SEEK 85

the Magellanic area, the whole appearance of affairs had taken a dramatic change. It meant that *Kent* had to steam 1100 miles before reaching the *Gotha–Dresden* rendezvous, and it was already March 5, the first day of the period cited in the German message. This is how Captain Allen viewed the prospect :

"We increased speed to 16 knots so as to arrive at the rendezvous just before daylight on March 7. This was quite the best time to arrive, as our approach to the rendezvous would be made under cover of darkness, and we hoped that as day dawned on March 7 we might find the German collier waiting at the rendezvous. We might even find the *Dresden* there, or better still we might find both ships. . . ." So passed that day and the next, as *Kent* went once more up the Pacific.

"An hour before daylight on March 7 orders were sent to the engine-room to reduce the smoke from the funnels as much as possible and our speed was reduced to 12 knots to enable this to be done. As day dawned we were quite ready, everyone on deck searching the horizon for signs of a ship." But to the disappointment of every officer and man aboard, daylight showed there was not a vessel on the horizon anywhere. Whether the collier had come and gone nobody could say, but Captain Allen decided to wait and watch. "We had only 575 tons of coal left, but that was enough for us to remain there a few days and then steam back to the coast. Besides, if we caught this German collier we would coal from her ! We made preparations to try and capture her before she could sink. We had a special boarding party told off and drilled. They included an engineer officer, some artificers and stokers who were to dash down at once to the engine-rooms and boiler-rooms, to take charge of the under-water valves and prevent them being opened or to close them if they found they had already been opened. All the officers and men comprising the boarding party were armed with revolvers and had detailed orders where to go and what they were to do directly they got on board the collier."

The implacable Pacific rose and fell, the hours ticked by, the look-outs scanned the expanse of sea with nothing to report. March 8 found *Kent* with engines stopped and waiting at the rendezvous making as little smoke as possible, yet ready to go full speed at any moment. "The day broke wet and misty, fine rain reducing the visibility to only a few miles—at times to less than one mile. During the forenoon we lowered some boats and cleaned the ship's bottom round the waterline so far down as the men could reach. The bottom was very dirty and was reducing our speed considerably besides causing us to burn a great deal more coal than we ought to have done for the speed attained.

"So the day wore on—sometimes quite clear so that the horizon could be plainly seen, at other times so misty and wet that we couldn't see further than a mile. At 3.50 p.m., just as the weather was clearing, Leading Signalman Hill, who was on watch on the fore bridge, saw a 3-funnelled cruiser about nine miles away. There she was as large as life, broadside on to us, heading north and either stopped or steaming slowly ahead. Immediately the engine-room telegraphs were put 'Full Speed Ahead' and the *Kent* turned towards her. There could be no doubt now that it was the *Dresden*. There was very little smoke coming out of her funnels, and she did not at first alter her course. It looked almost as if she had not seen us.

"We altered course so as to head her off and were working up speed as quickly as possible; we were undoubtedly closing on her and she was still steering across our bow. Then suddenly she turned away till she was stern on to us. It seemed as if she had only just seen us. . . . Now it was simply a chase. We could see she was very light in the water; this of course would enable her to steam faster through the water, but then, on the other hand, it showed she was very short of coal, and perhaps she would not have enough to last out a long chase if only we could keep her in sight. We were now going our best speed and we closed to 16,000 yards of her: this we took with the rangefinder, and was the

THE GREAT GAME OF HIDE-AND-SEEK 87

closest we ever got to her. The extreme range of our guns was 11,000 yards.

"The bottom of the *Kent* was very dirty and foul with seaweed and barnacles; so foul that we knew it reduced our speed by at least one knot." Every conceivable effort was therefore made to increase *Kent's* rate through the water. Spare wood was broken and sawn up for the furnaces—targets, lower booms, spare spars were all passed down to the boiler-rooms.

All canvas screens on the fore bridge were removed, as they caught the wind. Every man not employed in actually steaming the ship was ordered to go aft on the quarter-deck, so as to trim the ship another $3\frac{1}{2}$ inches by the stern. Meanwhile the stokers were doing their work with a marvellous energy and enthusiasm, so that they managed to develop 26,000 horse-power—whereas during *Kent's* trials eleven years previously she had not been able to reach more than 22,300. But now *Kent* was being driven as perhaps no steamer has ever been pressed before: not even she herself at the Falklands battle was so hustled.

"The supports, casings, etc., at the sides and backs of the boilers were red-hot. The funnels", says Admiral Allen, "were nearly red-hot, and from their tops were coming long red flames and showers of red-hot ashes and sparks. What else could be done? And yet *Dresden* was gaining on us. There was no doubt about it now. Black clouds of smoke were coming from her funnels, and she was getting further and further away." Night came on, it was practically certain *Dresden* would alter course and escape: moreover, she would be able to see *Kent's* red-hot funnels and scarlet flames belching forth.

Reluctantly, then, Captain Allen had to reduce speed and back he went to the rendezvous in the hope of at least catching the collier. *Dresden* herself was obviously very short of coal, and still more so after having been chased at full speed for over six hours. She could be heard wirelessing, though *Kent* had jambed that by instantly signalling on the same note. But, adds *Kent's* captain, "once or twice we read the signals she was making and carefully wrote them down. They were in code." *Dresden* as a fact had been that day in wireless touch with both *Gotha* and *Sierra Cordoba*, and had been steaming about awaiting them at easy speed but with steam ready for 14 knots.

Kent was a vessel of 9800 tons, armed with fourteen 6-inch guns, and had a designed speed of 23 knots. It was a coincidence that she had been placed in circumstances similar to those when she was chasing *Nurnberg* and attained a speed of 25 knots, finally to run short of coal. On March 9 *Kent* was back at the *Gotha* rendezvous with only 260 tons of coal, and 320 miles away from Coronel which was the nearest place where she could get any more fuel. By the time darkness again set in there was no form of another ship, so away *Kent* made for Coronel. "After searching for months and steaming thousands of miles we had at last sighted the *Dresden* only to lose sight of her." If only *Kent* had been given the opportunity of a scrub and a coat of antifouling just before this date, she would have sunk *Dresden* as *Nurnberg* was destroyed. *Kent*, in spite of that amazing display of horse-power, could not travel over the ground faster than $21\frac{1}{2}$ knots, whilst *Dresden* was doing another couple of knots. *Kent* cut it pretty fine, for on reaching Coronel only 43 tons of coal remained in her bunkers which were capable of carrying 1600 tons. It is not surprising that at a later date the British Admiralty expressed their appreciation of the fine performance achieved by *Kent's* engineers, and a letter of congratulation was also sent to the Newcastle firm who built the engines.

Now in the meanwhile an interesting discovery had been made in the Magellanic area. After *Kent* had left that locality so suddenly, the motor-boat *Galileo* kept up a search and combed out the southern portion of Santa Ines Island. Thus it was that for the first time this spot, so genuinely reported on as it had been, was at last examined. Irrefutable evidence in a wilderness of stark nature proved that Mr. Milward—himself a retired British master mariner—had been right. His rejected information was found all too correct, and a

THE GREAT GAME OF HIDE-AND-SEEK 89

priceless opportunity had passed. *Dresden* definitely had been hiding here, for yonder were found felled trees that only the hand of man had razed. Over there, too, were water-chutes hollowed out of timber and used for filling the ship's tanks. But—surest demonstration of all—pieces of bread were observed floating. The bird which had flown had also left some crumbs behind her.

When *Dresden* sighted *Kent* on March 8, she who had never seen a British man-of-war for three whole months was thoroughly surprised. That night, having at last shaken *Kent* off, the German still drove her engines at full speed through the darkness. But this machinery was getting worse and worse, and was months overdue for refit at a dockyard. All those weeks of constant wear and tear, then two months in the Magellan Straits with steam always ready at short notice, followed by more cruising in the Pacific and finally this long burst of effort, had just about finished her.

She could now steam at nothing better than 20 knots; she was ripe for *Kent* or any other cruiser that might come along. The idea of crossing the Pacific and reaching the East Indies had to be abandoned: she was at the end of her endurance. But where could she go? She was short of coal, yet had no colliers. She had tried to send them further instructions, but the signals had been jambed. What was to be done? Psychologically the situation is not without interest, if we put ourselves into the situation of *Dresden's* captain. A fugitive from battle, whose existence in the Magellan desolate loneliness must have been one long agony of suspense lest any moment the hunters might pounce; Lüdecke, when once out in the free open ocean, was never so nearly trapped. The meeting of these two rival cruisers is one of the most dramatic incidents in naval history, and for that we have to thank wireless telegraphy.

Lüdecke who had once harried shipping was now being harried himself. He must intern himself: in other words admit failure to carry on. Only a few months ago the Coronel battle had made everything look so rosy for German cruisers. However, now the fortune of war had changed again, and he would enter port not as a victor but as one of the vanquished. He was minded therefore to make for Talcahuano, yet this was to become impossible. Hearing the wireless of British cruisers, he changed his mind and decided on that volcanic Juan Fernandez group of three islands which happened to be the nearest land. These lie less than four hundred miles from Valparaiso, inhabited by only 300 people but owned by Chile. Juan Fernandez was discovered in 1512, and in the next century was destined to become the resort of pirates and sea-rovers who preyed on Spanish sailing-ships that came along the trade routes. Men may die, vessels may discard sail for steam, wood for steel: but geography and strategy remain immutable. This lonely ocean island, 13 miles long and 4 miles broad, was considered by the old raiders to be a capital base and well placed on the flank of the South American trade route. So indeed had thought the German raiders, though they had hitherto used Mas-a-Fuera which is a little further west. The day had now arrived when Juan Fernandez after sleeping for generatons came back into history.

The only anchorage is Cumberland Bay, which is on the north side and so sheltered from the prevailing south-east winds. The island is one mass of mountains, with wooded ravines, and so perpendicular is the scenery that the cattle frequently meet death by falling down the precipices. To every person who can remember his juvenile days Juan Fernandez is still the island of romance. For when Dampier called here on his celebrated privateering expedition in 1704 he landed, at the man's own request, that adventurious Scotsman Alexander Selkirk, where the latter lived such experiences as inspired Defoe to write his *Robinson Crusoe*. To this day Selkirk's cave is still shown to those visitors who arrive in palatial liners on a cruise *de luxe*. But before them have come other venturers armed with spades and pickaxes to dig for treasure said to be left by pirates of the past. To-day its industry is connected with the canning of lobsters, which are

THE GREAT GAME OF HIDE-AND-SEEK 91

carried alive in the tank of a motor schooner that connects with Valparaiso. Juan Fernandez boasts of four gendarmes and an old fellow who is the Chilean Governor.

Cumberland Bay, almost shut in by its overpowering mountains, will always find itself frequented on special occasions because it is such a welcome and unexpected refuge. When Anson was making his celebrated world voyage, the *Centurion* lay here for three months, and it formed a convenient rendezvous till his other units and supply ships could assemble. This was in 1741. And now, on March 9, 1915, *Dresden* came steaming in at 8.30 a.m., with only 80 tons of coal in her bunkers. She could have continued only a few hours longer until at least she could receive her supply ships and overhaul the engines. But that night she received the following message by wireless :

> His Majesty the Kaiser sets you free to lay yourself up.

With that imperial dispensation Captain Lüdecke was entitled then and there to call his chequered cruise definitely off. But it is to his honour that once more he did not immediately throw in his hand. This much may be said. If this officer was not as brilliant and ruthless a raider as some others in these chapters, at least his pluck and patience in playing a long and losing contest can but excite our respect. His spirit refused to accept the logic of defeat, he declined to go out by an easy exit but still possessed that faith in the "old ship" which in all eras of seamanhood has often snatched success from failure. Off came the so-called Governor from the shore, though he combined with his high-sounding office the duties of lighthouse-keeper, and quite rightly informed *Dresden* she must either quit within twenty-four hours, or else be interned. To this Lüdecke protested that he was entitled to make his ship seaworthy without suffering internment ; and this was such a stock argument of raider captains that Germany's staff training must have included the stressing of such a point as worthy to keep in mind. More especially was such indulgence capable of being coaxed when, as in the present case, there was no high authority or any compelling force nearer than several hundred miles across the ocean. In the language of the Army, Captain Lüdecke, so to say, "dug himself in" : he was not going to move till his ship's engines were given such a refit as was in the circumstances practicable. If his good fortune, which had been with him throughout these hectic months, were not suddenly to fail him, then he might still make repairs and be off again. Doubtless it would be found more convenient presently to be interned in a mainland port of South or North America, with railways and civilisation and always the possibility of escaping back to Europe, than to end up at Juan Fernandez.

It needs no excessive imagination to guess the mental strain which this Captain must have been enduring this while. His crew had just passed through a trying surprise, and he knew well enough that British cruisers would not rest till *Dresden* was rounded up. They would hunt *Dresden* as long as the latter had engines to drive propellers. Any hour of the day or night *Kent*, for example, might catch her in an unenviable situation. Lüdecke was too capable an officer not to appreciate all that, so he took precautions against any surprise attack by sending out his steamboat to maintain a watching patrol off the entrance to Cumberland Bay. It is evidence of his increasing nervousness that on March 12 he sent away half a dozen of his officers in a sailing-ship, so that they might avoid any possibility of being interned. But two days later came the grand climax, to which there were preliminaries which belong rather to the nature of a marine detective story. This is how the clues were pieced together till they provided that fitting end which one demands from fiction but rarely finds in real life.

Let us go back to March 8 when *Kent* had startled *Dresden* in the rendezvous area. The further *Dresden* steamed west in her precipitate flight, the further she was going away from her essential colliers. The latter must therefore be given fresh orders. Once again wireless signalling was to became a danger as well as a

THE GREAT GAME OF HIDE-AND-SEEK 93

convenience; for whatever message the colliers might pick up could also be intercepted by *Kent*. Now as the latter bustled along in the chase with smoke belching out of her high funnels and a big bow wave piling up at her forefoot, her aerial took in two distinct signals which the raider was transmitting to some ship or station. These came in quite easily, but *Kent* could make nothing of them as they were in code.

She accordingly called up H.M.S. *Glasgow*, another cruiser off the coast which had also been hunting for weeks, and wirelessed her this incomprehensible message. Perhaps she might be able to decode it. At first this defeated all intellects. But there are certain minds peculiarly gifted for solving ingenious puzzles, and after all the most subtle cypher is not eternally an insoluble riddle. This, none the less, was a teaser, and for days it conveyed nothing but meaningless symbols. Early on the morning of March 13 the cypher surrendered itself to the persistent and clever investigation of an officer in *Glasgow*, who was able to interpret the signals. They were clearly orders for some unknown ship to go to Juan Fernandez.

This discovery was a triumph: it was like finding the switch to flood a chamber with light. If supply ships were being ordered by *Dresden* to rendezvous at Juan Fernandez, obviously she must have intended going there also. That was several days ago. Would she still be at her anchorage? Captain Luce, who had been present at the disastrous Battle of Coronel that was fought in adjacent waters, was the officer in charge of the present operations, and besides his own ship *Glasgow* he could rely on *Kent* together with the armed merchant cruiser *Orama*. He arranged that these should concentrate on Cumberland Bay as nearly as possible simultaneously. Whilst *Glasgow* and *Orama* approached from the west, *Kent* was to arrive from the east.

Early on the morning of March 14 Lüdecke's patrol boat brought the thrilling news that a British cruiser was approaching the island. This was in fact *Glasgow*, with *Orama* coming up from the west, and *Kent* was crossing from the east. Lüdecke prepared to fight, though his ship was not in a fighting condition. Lying about 500 yards from the shore, with not enough steam to make a run for it, he ordered power to be raised in a second boiler for the working of his auxiliary machinery. As the smoke began issuing from her funnels, Captain Luce naturally assumed *Dresden* was getting under way. It was a great moment thus at last to have come upon the "wanted" ship that had caused over three months of fruitless anxiety and had cost thousands of pounds in wasted fuel, but now *Glasgow's* commanding officer was determined there should be no more elusiveness.

Assuming that *Dresden* was about to attempt an escape, Captain Luce was resolved to attack. *Glasgow's* size (4820 tons) and designed speed (25 knots) were superior to the enemy's: but the British cruiser had ten 4-inch to the German's twelve 4.1 inch guns. For the latter there was some genuine respect: Falklands had shown how surprisingly long was their range, and it was said that these were sighted up to 13,120 yards. Whilst Captain Luce's vessels approached, *Dresden* kept her guns trained on them but did not immediately fire. She was flying the German naval ensign and jack.

An engagement was imminent, but Captain Luce, in his anxiety not to cause damage to the few scattered houses which dotted the shore, spent half an hour manœuvring for a suitable position whence no shells would harm the local inhabitants, and then all three of his ships opened fire together. This went on for only five minutes, and then the German hoisted a white flag, having hauled down her colours. The squadron accordingly ceased shelling and closed the enemy, who was now on fire aft and her crew were rowing and swimming towards the shore. Just as the last party were leaving, the Germans arranged for the foremost magazine to blow up, and presently the mountains echoed with a loud explosion as the raider gradually began to sink bows first. Her officers and men had got well clear, and by 12.15 p.m. she disappeared below the water with white flag still flying, but the German ensign rehoisted.

THE GREAT GAME OF HIDE-AND-SEEK 95

As soon as the first party were seen swimming for the land, *Glasgow* had lowered a boat and sent her Commander and Staff-Surgeon to board *Dresden*; but before these could reach her there arrived alongside *Glasgow* a German officer who stated that he had been sent by his Captain to say *Dresden* was interned. (This was a curious declaration, in view of what had actually happened. And, indeed, later on the German Government officially informed the Chilean Government that Captain Lüdecke had refused to accept internment.) To the visiting officer Captain Luce answered that he must have unconditional surrender, and demanded to know the signification of the white flag. The explanation given was that this had been hoisted merely because Captain Lüdecke wished to open negotiations.

These having failed, the German officer returned to his ship, and it was at this stage that her ensign was rehoisted. But the white flag still remained flying and as she sank into the waters, her crew lined up on shore. Led by their Captain, they chanted as her dirge "Deutschland über alles". From the three ships Captain Luce sent every surgeon ashore to tend the wounded, and the serious cases were with Lüdecke's consent put aboard *Orama*, which landed them at Valparaiso where they were received in the German hospital. Seven of *Dresden's* people had been killed, fifteen were wounded severely, fourteen slightly, and one was missing. With the exception of the fifteen, all the survivors (including Lüdecke) were subsequently taken to Valparaiso by a Chilean warship and interned on an island in Valparaiso harbour.

Aboard the British cruisers no casualties or damage of any kind had occurred, but the Governor-lighthouse-keeper had a narrow escape from sudden death. There is something not altogether lacking in humour when we contemplate the old man coming off to board *Glasgow* as she first appeared in the harbour, and not being even observed during these busy minutes. He was flying no flag in his boat, and no one bothered much to wonder who he might be: the main interest was *Dresden*. And then the boat quickly found herself mixed up in a naval engagement, right in the line of fire, with shells dropping so close around that the boat's crew were soaked from splashes and promptly let go their oars. Luckily the lighthouse-keeper managed miraculously to extricate himself from the cruisers' forceful dispute and beat it quickly to the shore.

There he wisely waited till the fighting was over, when he put off again and this time had the wisdom to be flying a flag. He came aboard *Glasgow* to lodge a protest: *Dresden*, he remarked, had been interned. Captain Luce expressed his regrets, but naturally explained that since the German had her flag flying and her guns trained there had been no means of knowing that she was interned. That was one point. Another matter was the damage alleged to have been done by British shells in respect of a small Chilean schooner and the death of 1000 lobsters. This was diplomatically settled on the spot and all claims satisfied by the payment of 10,000 pesos, the lobsters being presently distributed among the British Squadron.

A more serious protest was that of the Chilean Government for the violation of their neutral waters. For this a full apology was made by the British Government and accepted. On the other hand, it was an open secret that the Germans had persistently and continuously been guilty of the same trespass. When the survivors of the sailing-vessel *Conway Castle* were landed at Valparaiso on March 11, the whole waterside soon knew that for two whole months *Dresden* had been utilising Chilean territory before resuming her attacks. But now that *Dresden* had gone for ever there was great Chilean joy: for with her had departed a most embarrassing visitor whose presence had never been welcome.

Such then are the life and adventures during the war of a cruiser that will always be remembered less for her share in battle, engagement, or raids than for the achievement of retaining her halo of mystery for three months. The obvious lesson to be learned is that pluck and determination, allied with local sympathy and favourable geographical conditions, can accomplish

DRESDEN AT JUAN FERNANDEZ.
The white flag at her foremast head can be distinctly seen.

DRESDEN AT JUAN FERNANDEZ
Showing gun cleared away and trained on British cruisers.

THE GREAT GAME OF HIDE-AND-SEEK 97

many things. But there is also emergent the incontrovertible conclusion that without some convenient dockyard and fortified coaling bases the raider can have only a limited life : however brilliant her career, it cannot last. After *Dresden* was no more, the fate of the fast dwindling supply ships was not always the same. Some of them would cease to function, while others would be ready to serve the next raiders. *Sierra Cordoba* and *Gotha* both escaped capture that March. The former got into Callao on the 17th, and the latter reached Valparaiso on the 20th.

There was also a third auxiliary named *Alda*. She left Valparaiso with provisions on March 10 and tried to call up *Dresden* by wireless for instructions. She had pretended that her port of destination was Antofagasta. The Chilean Government declined to believe her, so insisted that one of their officials should take passage in her. That was why she never reached *Dresden*. A fourth ship, the collier *Bangor*, was sighted by H.M.S. *Bristol* coming out of the Magellan Straits, and was arrested.

It remains only to mention again the unfortunate disbelief in the British Consul, Mr. Milward. Had his advice been taken in December, the story of *Dresden* would have been concluded abruptly. But even this incident had a happy conclusion ; for the British Admiralty ultimately made the most courteous amend and symbolised this by presenting him with a gold watch. He has recently died.

CHAPTER VII

THE RAIDERS' RENDEZVOUS

AT 11 p.m. on August 4, 1914, Germany's commercial shipping, in obedience to the handbook of instructions that had been issued to her master mariners, either continued to remain in the ports of neutral countries or hurried onwards to get into some convenient harbour such as might be possible in the United States, South America, Portugal, and Spain in particular. It was because of the immense passenger trade carried on between the United States and Germany that there were soon assembled in New York such giant liners as the *Vaterland* (the newest and biggest afloat), the *Kronprinzessin Cecilie, Kaiser Wilhelm II, George Washington, Friedrich der Grosse, President Grant*, and *Grosser Kurfürst*. Up till August 3 the North German Lloyd liner *Kronprinz Wilhelm*, a vessel of 14,908 tons, which had been built in 1901 and had a speed of 23 knots, was one of this fleet.

For the British Admiralty these powerful merchantmen were a source of no little anxiety during the first days of hostilities, since they could be converted into cruisers within a few hours and be ready for work on the trade routes. Would they one and all break out from New York and harass the Atlantic? That was the possible danger.

To oppose them there were in the Western Atlantic five British cruisers under the command of Rear-Admiral Sir Christopher Cradock. These consisted of the *Suffolk* (flagship), *Berwick, Lancaster*, and *Essex*—all belonging to the old-fashioned "County" class, with a speed of 23 knots, fourteen 6-inch guns, and a displacement of 9800 tons—together with the *Bristol* which carried two 6-inch and ten 4-inch guns, and was of

THE RAIDERS' RENDEZVOUS 99

4800 tons. On August 4 these five were located thus : *Suffolk* was at Kingston, Jamaica, but left at 6 p.m. for a position east of Nantucket, where also from 9.30 p.m. was *Essex* already, as a protection on the New York–England route. *Bristol* was also steaming northwards to that area from the West Indies, though she was recalled two days later. *Berwick* was patrolling the Florida Channel between Florida and Bahamas, but *Lancaster* was in dockyard hands at Bermuda and unable to leave till August 6, when she was sent to patrol the Cabot Strait.

We have seen that in June the modern German cruiser *Karlsruhe* under Captain Lüdecke had come out to relieve Captain E. Köhler's *Dresden*. After meeting at Port-au-Prince, Haiti, and the two captains had changed over, *Karlsruhe* left on the afternoon of July 26 but, steaming through the Windward Passage, went westward along the Cuban coast for the port of Havana, where she stayed from July 28 till 10 a.m. of July 30. It was the news of impending war that made it advisable for Captain Köhler now to remain at sea away from complications of the land ; yet whilst cruising about and evading any possibility of meeting with Admiral Cradock's units or the two French cruisers *Conde* and *Descartes* (which were also in West Indian waters), *Karlsruhe* was able to keep in touch with the political development. By means of his wireless Köhler was soon to learn that his own country was on the brink of war, and he himself acted accordingly. Thus he prepared his ship for action, utilised the waters between Cuba and Florida as convenient for battle practice, and apart from receiving information from other stations he was able twice daily to obtain Press news sent out by Sayville Wireless Station.

Declarations of war against Russia and France came on August 2 and 3, and now the possibility of war with Britain appeared inevitable. Anticipating this, Köhler passed through the Florida Channel and then went east for a certain rendezvous off the Bahamas, where he was to meet a German-American liner from New York. We thus notice how excellently organized was the pre-war arrangement, whereby this newly arrived cruiser and a certain passenger liner were ready to co-operate at a definite position in the Atlantic when hostilities came with no little suddenness. On August 4 Köhler's wireless brought him orders to begin hostilities against Britain, and on opening his instructions he learned that he was to operate as he deemed best in the Middle Atlantic.

One of the outstanding lessons to be learned from these German raiders is that of using every geographical possibility to its fullest extent. Already the reader will have noted how the islands and reefs of the Pacific and South Atlantic, the lonely bays and creeks, had been obviously carefully explored and considered long before war arrived. So, in like manner, *Karlsruhe* was to utilize that maze of islands and tricky passages in the Bahamas for her special purpose. And in these days of mechanical marvels it is deserving of more than passing interest that personal ingenuity availing itself of Nature's opportunities can, with average luck, achieve results of the highest importance. Shells and cordite are not the only deciding factors in the contest. Köhler was in a critical situation, and had three considerations to bear in mind. Firstly, he was in great danger from the British and French cruisers, and must keep himself hidden at all costs. Secondly, this evasiveness must not prevent his meeting with the liner from New York, nor must he imperil that defenceless ship which would fall as a rich prize to the first British cruiser that came along. Thirdly, *Karlsruhe* must act on the defensive for as brief a period as possible : her orders were to wage war against Atlantic shipping. Everything, therefore, in spite of this sudden incidence of war, had to work to schedule. There must be no bungling, and no allowance could be made for the slightest misunderstanding.

Whilst *Berwick* was searching Florida Channel for *Karlsruhe*, the latter was hiding between Crooked Island and Mariguana Island, and at Plana Cays was able to listen-in unsuspected by her foes. She had a little time to spare : she must give the liner the necessary days to

THE RAIDERS' RENDEZVOUS 101

arrive, and in the meanwhile Sayville was an invaluable service for watching the trend of events. Plana Cays is just north of the Windward Passage and on the route from the latter to New York, but the rendezvous which Captain Köhler had chosen for the liner was a little further up this route, so that his destination required him to steam still more to the north. The meeting was to take place on August 6, but on the previous evening whilst *Karlsruhe* was wirelessing instructions to the oncoming New York liner, H.M.S. *Berwick*, having found nothing in the Florida Channel and having proceeded south-east through the North East Providence Channel, was off Cat Island (Lat. 24.20 N, Long, 75.30 W) at 7.45 p.m. and intercepted the German cruiser's signals. Furthermore, *Berwick* realized that the ship being called up was a New York-German liner, though wrongly supposed this to be the *Friedrich der Grosse*.

She was in fact the North German Lloyd *Kronprinz Wilhelm*. This four-funnelled ship was under the command of Captain Grahn, her peace-time master, and was lying in New York at the beginning of August. Captain Boy-Ed, the German Naval Attaché at Washington, sent Captain Grahn his sealed orders through the North German Lloyd Company's offices in New York, and *Kronprinz Wilhelm* hurriedly took on board huge quantities of meat besides other provisions, so that by August 3 she was coaled and ready for an extended voyage. At 8.10 that same evening she received instructions to leave New York and await further orders by wireless. Under cover of darkness, with her engines humming and the stokers sending her along at a fine pace, this great steel ship on the night of August 3-4 sped southward along the New York-Windward Passage track, and on the way her crew were busily repainting the liner's exterior. Captain Grahn in due course was in wireless touch with *Karlsruhe*, from whom he learned that Captain Köhler would meet him on August 6 in Lat. 25.40, N, Long. 72.37 W, that is to say between three and four hundred miles north of the eastern end of Cuba. In the meanwhile *Karlsruhe* was getting ready a couple of 3·4-inch guns, 290 rounds of shells, together with machine-guns. Captain Köhler further had the requisite men ready to be lent as guns' crews, and their kit-bags already packed.

All worked without a hitch, the navigation was perfect, and at 7 a.m. on August 6, when about 150 miles away from the nearest land (Christopher Columbus' historic Watling Island, bearing SW) the two vessels made the rendezvous. No time was wasted, for a British cruiser might be descried on the horizon at any moment, so the towering liner, overshadowing *Karlsruhe* with her high freeboard and lofty upper works, went alongside the slim cruiser. It was an extraordinary sight for these two utterly dissimilar ships to be lying secured to each other in the lonely ocean as the Atlantic swell rolled hull against hull, snapped hawsers and made fenders almost useless. But amid the crashing and grating of steel plates there was the sound of short sharp orders, then came the little puffs of steam as the derricks swung over the two guns, whilst gangs of men were transferring in exchange to the cruiser's deck, below, tons of coal and provisions fresh from New York. The work went on with suppressed excitement and at feverish speed : it was a race against the clock, against serious damage to hulls, against surprise of enemy cruisers.

Captain Grahn went aboard *Karlsruhe* and learnt that *Kronprinz Wilhelm* was to become from now an auxiliary cruiser, to which one of Captain Köhler's officers, Lieut.-Commander Paul Thierfelder, was appointed as captain, Grahn acting henceforth as his assistant. Thierfelder was a navigating specialist. Now he and Grahn were still aboard *Karlsruhe* when at 10.15 a.m. the work of unloading was going on with animation, but suddenly there came a report from the look-out. "Smoke to the southward !" Instantly the excitement broke forth irrepressibly. "British cruiser ! Must be the *Berwick* !" Something not far from a panic ensued, all operations had to be cancelled instantly, boats were still over the side in the water, the two guns were not yet mounted in their positions, and

THE RAIDERS' RENDEZVOUS 103

all too little ammunition had been taken aboard. There was barely time for officers and men to be rushed across, hawsers to be cast off, and the two ships to separate. *Karlsruhe's* launch could not be taken on board : there was no time even for that, so it was abandoned, but eventually it drifted over the sea and brought itself into a United States harbour. *Karlsruhe* scurried away to the north, and *Kronprinz Wilhelm* to the north-north-east.

As we know from one of the latter's officers,* the Germans had been taken completely by surprise. The inconvenient arrival of a strange ship had entirely upset the carefully arranged meeting. But actually this was not *Berwick* : it was her sister *Suffolk*, in which was Admiral Cradock. It might at first seem as if it was not a little curious that a British cruiser should come right on to this scene at such a moment, and that in the wide Atlantic one tiny spot should lose its seclusion at the critical hour. But the facts are quite simple. *Suffolk* was on her way from Jamaica to the Nantucket area, as also was *Bristol*, who was now in Lat. 31.30 N, Long. 73 W, that is to say about half-way between New York and the Windward Passage. Thus *Karlsruhe* had *Suffolk* to the south of her and *Bristol* to the north. Admiral Cradock's intended track was essentially not far off that of the combined *Karlsruhe–Kronprinz Wilhelm* routes, for *Suffolk* had come up through the Windward Passage. Moreover, before the Germans had effected their rendezvous, *Suffolk* could hear *Karlsruhe* that morning making wireless signals. It was therefore not impossible that a good look-out might reveal something interesting.

The incident illustrated again the advantages and evils of wireless. If it had been the means whereby the two German units had been able to meet, it had certainly assisted in their being discovered. On the other hand, Admiral Cradock was able to flash by the same system an order across several hundred miles to *Bristol*, telling the latter to intercept the escaping German cruiser whose position of departure and course

---
* *The Cruise of the "Kronprinz Wilhelm"*, by Lieutenant Count Alfred von Niezychowski. New York, 1929.

were known. It was therefore not impossible for *Bristol*, by laying down her own position on the chart, to steer so as to cut off *Karlsruhe*. Now unfortunately *Suffolk* was inferior to *Karlsruhe* in regard to speed : the more modern ship had soon whacked her engines up to 22 knots and was steaming well. Through hour after hour that day did *Suffolk* chase her, but it was of no avail : Captain Köhler got right away and by sunset was out of sight. Thus ended the first exciting phase of *Karlsruhe's* war period, though the second was to begin immediately.

It was an early moon that night, and *Bristol* had been so well navigated that at 8.15 she sighted *Karlsruhe* on the port bow. There was the latter showing up under the moon some half-dozen miles away, and in this picture of two lean warships about to begin a lonely nocturnal duel we have a glorious subject for any imaginative marine artist, and full of dramatic suspense. *Bristol* altered course to port so as to bring her starboard guns to bear, and at 7000 yards opened fire. *Karlsruhe* turned to the east and replied, but again her superior speed saved her so that she was able to make off to the south-east pursued by *Bristol*. The chase continued till 1 a.m., by which time the German had well extricated herself from an awkward position without having once been hit, and this episode shows how useless it is to rely on mere statistics in regard to a ship's capabilities. On paper *Bristol* was supposedly a 26-knot vessel, whereas her speed actually dropped to 18 knots in spite of all the stokers' strenuous efforts. What was the reason for this great disparity ?

The answer for both *Suffolk's* and *Bristol's* indifferent steaming on that important occasion was found by attributing it to the unsuitable Pocahontas coal which these two cruisers were at the time burning : otherwise there can be little doubt but that within the first three days of war *Karlsruhe* would have been sent to the bottom. On the other hand, the latter had obtained at Havana excellent coal, which served her well. Besides filling her bunkers to utmost capacity, she had also taken a deck cargo of 200 more tons. Still, such is the

THE RAIDERS' RENDEZVOUS 105

rapid consumption by a fast cruiser, when pushed, that not even all this did more than barely suffice; and, whilst neither *Suffolk* nor *Bristol* appreciated the fact fully, they had done excellent work in compelling the German to keep on wasting invaluable fuel. *Karlsruhe* was in a serious predicament, and had to reduce to her economical speed, which was 12 knots. Her captain was now taking her to that notorious base at St. Thomas, the Danish island, and hoped there to replenish before beginning his raids. But as he came south on August 7 the ship heard the wireless signals of a British cruiser so strongly that it was expected to be in action at almost any hour.

The nerves of everyone became in a state of high tension, and the outlook seemed still more desperate when it was found that the coal would not last out as far as St. Thomas : if *Suffolk*, *Bristol*, or *Berwick* were to appear, the fight would have to be fought out without accelerating so much as one knot. And that would mean complete annihilation; for the British cruiser could choose her range and position of attack, cross the German's bows and concentrate a broadside, whilst *Karlsruhe* would have only her minimum of guns bearing in reply.

But once more she was exceptionally lucky; no British cruiser came in sight and she managed to reach San Juan, Puerto Rico, on August 9. This was only as much as she could do, for out of all that fuel which she had taken at Havana there now remained a mere dozen tons. Nor were her troubles ended. Puerto Rico being a United States island, the authorities were going to suffer no nonsense : the German would be allowed that to which she was legally entitled and not more. She could take just so much coal as would be enough for her to reach the nearest non-American neutral harbour, which was St. Thomas, and her stay would be limited to twenty-four hours.

This was a little awkward, and St. Thomas was too obvious when it came to be considered again. But *Karlsruhe* was not destitute of friends, for, lying in San Juan was the Hamburg-Amerika liner *Odenwald* which was able to transfer some reservists to the cruiser and lent assistance also in taking aboard 550 tons of coal. Furthermore, at the other side of the island there happened to be lying another steamer belonging to the same company, a vessel of 3000 tons named *Patagonia*, whose master offered his services to Captain Köhler. The latter instructed *Patagonia* first to enter St. Thomas, coal there from German supplies, and then meet *Karlsruhe* off Barbados. *Karlsruhe* had taken no risks through delaying, for she had reached San Juan at daybreak and left at 7 p.m. At first she steered as if she were making for St. Thomas, but then came night and she altered course to the west of south, went right across the Caribbean till she came to the Lesser Antilles, and at dawn on August 12 reached the Dutch island of Curaçao. Here she managed to obtain 1200 tons of coal with such celerity that at 8 p.m. she steamed off to sea. But during this short sojourn there came in the German S.S. *Stadt Schleswig*, so the latter was given orders to follow with more fuel and meet *Karlsruhe* at a certain rendezvous.

We thus observe the impossible situations into which the modern steamship raider of the fast cruiser type is bound to find herself unless her country has convenient bases where supplies can be relied upon, or a chain of colliers can be maintained without a break. *Karlsruhe* was being driven from port to port, as a beggar is dismissed from house to house with small bribes of food. The only other procedure was to evade the British cruisers, get on to the trade routes as soon as possible and live on prizes, just as an invading army may exist on the captured towns and villages. So for the present let us leave *Karlsruhe* well filled with fuel and steaming eastward along the Venezuelan coast in the hope of falling in with British steamers.

What had happened to the four-funnelled liner *Kronprinz Wilhelm*, now that she was an armed merchant cruiser?

Her days had been less exciting than was *Karlsruhe's* experience. Having escaped from *Suffolk* on August 6, she carried on across the Atlantic and during the voyage

THE RAIDERS' RENDEZVOUS

had full opportunity to settle down to her new capacity. The guns were made ready for service; all woodwork was protected with mattresses, carpets, and bagging; the grand saloon, which had so recently been the dining-hall for first-class passengers, was turned into reserve bunker space for coal; and the comfortable smoke-room was made ready as a hospital. On the way over the ocean between the Bahamas and the Azores *Kronprinz Wilhelm* had not the good fortune of picking up a single prize, but on August 17 safely reached the Azores. She had now been at sea for a whole fortnight, since slipping out of New York just before war with Britain began, and she required coal as well as water. How were these to be obtained?

We here see a condition of affairs exactly opposite to the situation in which *Karlsruhe* had to struggle. Off the Azores there should be waiting somewhere at hand, according to plan, a German supply ship. At first *Kronprinz Wilhelm* could not find her, but on August 18 the meeting took place in Lat. 35 N, Long. 25 W, that is to say, between the Azores and Madeira. Up came the S.S. *Walhalla* which had been hanging about for a fortnight in readiness. On August 2 she had left Las Palmas with a surprising quantity of coal and provisions, so here she was in accordance with German thoroughness all ready to furnish the raider's needs.

In accordance with the practice now familiar to the reader, the two steamers lashed up alongside each other in the open Atlantic, and the weather was such that in this manner they could steam ahead at two knots whilst coal and other commodities were being transferred to the *Kronprinz*. This went on for three days, at the end of which 2500 tons of coal—enough for only one week's steaming at good speed—had been bunkered. The *Walhalla* was then dismissed and reached Las Palmas again on August 26, whilst the *Kronprinz* went south and south-west in order to work the South American trade route with its rich cargoes of meat and cereals. But a week passed and nothing happened till on August 27 she stopped first the Danish schooner *Elizabeth*, which obviously could not be detained, and then the Russian barque *Pittan*. The sinking of the latter would not have been worth the embarrassment of having an extra crew as prisoners, so she was scornfully released.

This had happened in mid-Atlantic and then another week passed by so that it was the third of September when she met the S.S. *Asuncion* a couple of hundred miles east of Cape San Roque, Brazil. This was one of the supply ships, and belonged to the Hamburg-South American Line, being a vessel of 4663 tons. She was to be useful also to *Karlsruhe*, as we shall soon observe, and certainly played her part in the war against commerce. It was not till the next day—September 4—that at last *Kronprinz Wilhelm* made her first capture when at night she fell in with the British S.S. *Indian Prince* about 210 miles E by N of Pernambuco.

When one considers that this prize was of only 2846 tons, that *Kronprinz Wilhelm* had been steaming about for a whole month at enormous expense and risk, during which she had crossed the Atlantic twice, it scarcely seems as if the cost had been commensurate with the reward. Passengers and crew had to be taken off and accommodated, coal was also emptied out of the prize, and finally *Indian Prince* was sunk by means of a bomb, though not immediately. The steamer was two days out from Bahia, and was at first made by the Germans to steer SSE, whilst the raider followed astern. It was at 9 a.m. on September 9, when a couple of hundred miles north-west of Trinidada Island, that *Indian Prince* was finally despatched. Two days later *Kronprinz* was joined by another of those numerous German supply ships which used to come out from some South American port with provisions, coal and information, returning not infrequently with prisoners off captured ships. *Asuncion* on September 3 had brought such quantities of necessary supplies that it took a whole day to unload them aboard Commander Thierfelder's raider, and now it was the Hansa Liner *Ebernburg* which brought further replenishment in addition to South American newspapers that were almost as welcome.

THE RAIDERS' RENDEZVOUS

But there likewise arrived two colliers, *Pontos* and *Prussia*. The former belonged to the Hamburg-Amerika Line and had left Monte Video three days after war broke out between Germany and Great Britain. The latter had left Pernambuco on August 4 and for some time was tender to *Dresden*. *Prussia* was then sent into Rio with the crew of *Hyades* which Captain Lüdecke had sunk on August 15, but sailed out again on September 5 having been able to fill up with more coal. She also was a Hamburg-Amerika liner, and the whole scheme by which these different units worked is abundantly clear. Whilst the raiders dared no longer risk entering any but the loneliest South American port, yet their tenders could bring them all that was needed. As to a rendezvous, whilst Rocas Reef and Fernando Noronha were convenient for raiders operating on the trade route north-east of Cape San Roque, the Island of Trinidada was excellently situated on the flank of the route from such busy ports as Buenos Aires, Monte Video, and Rio Janeiro. Trinidada was just far enough for the usual steamer track to be unobserved, yet near enough to the South American coast when holds had been emptied and further stores had to be fetched. Thus, actually though quite illegally, Trinidada at this time was nothing less than a German Atlantic base, where *Pontos,, Prussia*, and any other tenders could wait till they were summoned by wireless. They were at the disposal of any and all the raiders as convenient, and it was no small satisfaction for the latter's commanding officers to know that off this remote island Brazilian exports could be obtained with such dependence.

But how long could the secret be maintained? Surely, sooner or later some British cruiser would come along? But the truth is that patrols were not immediately available, and indeed on the outbreak of war H.M.S. *Glasgow* was the only unit off the Brazilian coast. Still, it could be after only a very few weeks that some sort of protection for the trade routes would be afforded, and then there would be complications.

The sudden development came on September 14

with devastating effect. For on August 22 the Hamburg-Amerika liner *Cap Trafalgar* had escaped from the River Plate, and then met off Bahia the obsolete German gunboat *Eber*, which had come from Capetown. From her *Cap Trafalgar* picked up both armament and personnel and took on the character of a commerce raider, but in this capacity she was singularly and completely unsuccessful. On September 14 she was coaling at Trinidada from the Woermann liner *Eleonore Woermann* and the American S.S. *Berwind* (chartered by the Hamburg-Amerika Line) when the armed merchant cruiser *Carmania* (of the Cunard Line) suddenly arrived and interrupted proceedings. The details will be discussed in another chapter, but for the present it is sufficient to state that after a hot duel *Carmania* sank *Cap Trafalgar*.

Now this incident occurred whilst *Kronprinz Wilhelm* was being coaled at sea from *Pontos* and *Prussia*, and the distance was less than 150 miles away or about seven hours' steaming. The news reached *Kronprinz* by wireless, but she continued to fill her bunkers slowly, this essential operation occupying a period of about September 11–19. On the 17th Commander Thierfelder transferred the prisoners of *Indian Prince* from *Kronprinz* to *Ebernburg* and *Prussia*, and sent them into port, *Ebernburg* landing her contingent at Santos on the 24th and *Prussia* bringing hers to Rio on the 25th. The raider was now free of human encumbrances and prepared to resume her warfare along the South American sea-lanes.

CHAPTER VIII

THE CAREER OF *KARLSRUHE*

WE last witnessed *Karlsruhe* steaming slowly eastward from Curaçao along the coast of Venezuela, and on the morning of August 18 she picked up that German S.S. *Patagonia* which Captain Köhler had ordered to meet him off Barbados. There was no intention at present to raid West Indian islands : it was British shipping that mattered, and *Patagonia* was taken along to act as tender in accordance with the practice of other raiders.

That same afternoon when about 480 miles E by S of the West Indian island of Trinidad (not to be confused, of course, with the South Atlantic Trinidada) *Karlsruhe* encountered the British S.S. *Bowes Castle*, 4650 tons, coming north from Monte Video to New York, and captured her, transferring her crew to *Patagonia*. This was *Karlsruhe's* first prize, and the steamer was presently scuttled. Captain Köhler then went southeast along the shipping track and three days later coaled from *Patagonia* off Maraca Island at the mouth of the Amazon ; on the 25th crossed the equator, and on the same day reached Sao Joao Island, another isolated bit of Brazil further down the coast towards Maranham. At this island she found the *Stadt Schleswig* awaiting her, who now yielded up her coal and received the *Bowes Castle* prisoners instead. The latter were taken into Maranham, where they landed on September 2.

Still keeping *Patagonia* with her, *Karlsruhe* now settled down to attacking the shipping which must inevitably be found off the north-east shoulder of Brazil. For within a restricted area, which she selected, there was the choice of several routes : (*a*) those coming north-west to New York, Barbados and Trinidad from

Pernambuco, and (*b*) those branching off north-east for St. Vincent, Tenerife, and Las Palmas from the Plate, Rio Janeiro, and Cape Horn. Even allowing for modification of the peace-time tracks, the raider could hardly fail to find this focal region fruitful : for, by criss-crossing east and west, she would eventually cut athwart the seaborne traffic. *Dresden* in this squared section had captured *Hyades* and *Siamese Prince*, *Kronprinz Wilhelm* was presently herein to capture *Indian Prince*, and others at a later date. But before the end of October Captain Köhler's ship was to bring about the loss of sixteen more.

Whatever results might be obtained depended therefore on sound strategy. It was to be not so much a gamble but merely a question as to whether the dividend would be moderate or exceptionally good. Failure was impossible—unless Köhler fell in with superior naval strength. So, after coaling again at another secluded spot on August 30, he steamed eastward and attracted to him by wireless those faithful tenders of the North German Lloyd, *Asuncion* and *Crefeld*. Captain Köhler had therefore under him quite a little squadron and it proceeded in single-line-ahead. Success came immediately, for on the afternoon of the 31st he sighted the British S.S. *Strathroy*, 4336 tons, which was carrying 5600 tons of coal from Norfolk, Virginia, to Rio Janeiro.

Here, indeed, was beginner's luck. Could anything be more suitable than this cargo of fuel coming as a gift ? The position of this occurrence was equally fortunate, for Rocas Reef was only 50 miles to the east-south-east. At first Köhler sent *Asuncion* and *Crefeld* thither, whilst keeping *Patagonia*, but presently after examining the prize led her to the shelter of the Reef likewise, arriving there at eight next morning. Now *Strathroy* had a crew consisting partly of Europeans and partly of Chinamen. Köhler transferred the former to *Asuncion*, but kept the Orientals aboard *Strathroy* which was far too useful to be sunk. He was minded to employ her for his own purpose in a particular way. Under care of *Patagonia* he despatched

THE CAREER OF *KARLSRUHE* 113

her to a secret base in a certain secluded anchorage, whither *Karlsruhe* could always come and replenish her bunkers without incurring the damage and inconvenience of having to coal on the exposed ocean. For a long time after the war was ended this base was still not ascertained, but we now know that it was Lavandeira Reef (Lat. 5 S, Long. 36 W) which has been mentioned in a previous chapter.

Once again is presented an instance of the Teutonic appreciation for utilizing every geographical facility. These thousands of tons of fuel would be available for any other German warship, and Köhler took the opportunity of sending letters to Germany by *Patagonia*, who posted them in Pernambuco which she reached on September 6, after having safely escorted *Strathroy*. *Patagonia* now fades out of this chapter, for during this same month she proceeded from Pernambuco to Bahia Blanca, where she had to go into dry dock to effect repairs. She was leaking badly and bore evident marks of damage received whilst having lain alongside *Karlsruhe* coaling. From Bahia Blanca she reached Monte Video at the end of November, and left there in December with provisions and coal, but was arrested by an Argentine warship and brought into Bahia Blanca the same month. She, too, had certainly played no mean part in succouring her country's navy.

Karlsruhe could now be relieved of all coaling anxiety for some time, provided the Lavandeira base were not compromised, and forthwith proceeded along the north-eastern track, to look for victims. This route passes close to Fernando Noronha, leaving Rocas Reef on the west and St. Paul Rocks on the east but several hundred miles further to the north. The latter islets are only a few yards in area and not more than thirty feet high, yet they form a natural confine to traffic at a point about one-third across the Atlantic to the Cape Verdes. It was on September 3, when still 250 miles SW of St. Paul Rocks, that the raider captured the Liverpool S.S. *Maple Branch*, a vessel of 4338 tons, bound from England to Punta Arenas with a valuable cargo that included prize cattle. The latter were taken from her to provide welcome meat supplies, the crew were put aboard *Crefeld*, and the steamer was sunk.

Two days later the cruiser had to leave her warfare alone, as her bunkers were getting low, and at 14 knots she made for Lavandeira Reef, where she spent a couple of days coaling, but by September 9 was back again on the rich north-eastern trade route. She was still wonderfully fortunate, for *Macedonia* (a British armed merchant-cruiser) had passed within thirty miles of her, and H.M.S. *Bristol* narrowly missed catching her in the act of coaling. During the early hours of September 14 *Karlsruhe* sighted the lights of a steamer coming south-west down the route, and at dawn found her to be the Liverpool S.S. *Highland Hope*, 5150 tons, bound for Buenos Aires to fetch a cargo of Argentine meat. She was captured, but whilst the crew were being taken aboard *Crefeld* there happened to come along the Spanish liner *Reina Victoria* on her way to Monte Video. Seeing this cruiser with two merchantmen, the Spaniard's curiosity was aroused, and she inquired what they were. Köhler replied : "Convoy of British ships."

This incident took place 190 miles SW of St. Paul Rocks, and again *Karlsruhe* had the narrowest of escapes. For it so happened that H.M.S. *Canopus* was on her way down this lane escorting a tanker to Pernambuco, and Köhler became uneasy when he heard the Spaniard talking by wireless to a British warship. She had been passing information as to the suspicious happening. Although *Canopus* obtained the position of the alleged "convoy", the British warship held on her course, whereas only 20 miles away to starboard *Karlsruhe*, *Crefeld*, and *Highland Hope* were lying at her mercy. Doubtless her first duty was towards her tanker, but one can only imagine the certain fate that would have been dealt out to the German raider had *Canopus* got within range for a few moments. This was, of course, the battleship which was to open fire three months later on von Spee's Squadron approaching the Falklands. If only those same guns this September day could have seen *Karlsruhe*, the latter would have been blown out of the water and many thousands of pounds'

THE CAREER OF *KARLSRUHE* 115

worth of shipping saved. As it was, however, Köhler scuttled *Highland Hope* and scurried off to the westward.

Wisely, then, did the German now clear out of a suspected area, and he transferred his attentions from the north-east to the north-west track for a period. He had not long to wait, and three days after sinking *Highland Hope* was 145 miles N by W of Cape San Roque when he sighted the British collier *Indrani*, a 5706-tons steamer with 7000 tons of American coal. It was decided not to sink so valuable a ship, but to retain her as one of *Karlsruhe's* tenders. A prize crew was put aboard, her Chinese ratings were kept to assist, but the European officers were transferred to *Crefeld*.

Next day the cruiser went to Lavandeira Reef to coal once more from *Strathroy* for two days, and on the 20th she met her tenders to try the north-east track again. Quite close to where *Maple Branch* had been sunk she now captured on the 21st the Dutch S.S. *Maria* carrying wheat to Ireland, and sank her. On the same day but slightly more to the west she captured and destroyed by bombs the British S.S. *Cornish City*, of 3816 tons, carrying coal from Barry for Rio Janeiro; and on the 22nd similarly treated the British S.S. *Rio Iguassu*, 3817 tons, carrying 4800 tons of coal from Newcastle-on-Tyne for Rio Janeiro. This prize had been discovered further up the route, 155 miles SW of St. Paul Rocks, only 45 miles beyond the position where *Highland Hope* had been scuttled.

To be able to despise coal cargoes was a great contrast with the days when she could find fuel only with the greatest difficulty. But to-day she was so well filled that she even had a deck cargo of coal. What with the *Strathroy* source, and the certainty of always meeting British tramp steamers coming out from South Wales or Newcastle, to say nothing of the German tenders that managed to get what they wanted in some South American port, *Karlsruhe's* anxieties consisted solely in keeping away from British cruisers. This was more easily done than the chart would suggest, for the Atlantic was too wide and there was always the covering protection of night to follow the day.

But another weak feature of the modern steamship raider, when compared with the old sailing days, now manifested itself. There comes a time when engines must be allowed a rest for overhaul, and boilers be given their periodical clean. Owing to continuous steaming all these weeks, and by reason of the damage done to hull through coaling, *Karlsruhe* now needed urgent repairs which would occupy several days. During this period she would be in no condition for fighting, and she dared not risk being surprised in some port with no means of escaping. Her only alternative was therefore to choose some part of the Atlantic not too far away from her hunting area, yet sufficiently remote from the likely tracks of enemy cruisers.

For this reason she went west till she was in the locality of Lat. 1.10 S, Long. 33.30 W, that is to say, in mid-ocean. Here she could be alone, and from September 25 to 27 she got on with the job of reconditioning. That being accomplished, she must needs go to Lavandeira Reef to refuel from *Strathroy*. By the time she had filled her bunkers and stacked her upper deck with coal a yard deep it was the last day of September. A strange sight she presented, with her waterline submerged and coal everywhere except round the guns. No such phenomenon had been beheld since the days of Rodjestvensky in the Russo-Japanese War, and it would have been impossible for her to have attained her best speed with this increased displacement. Had she been brought to fight an engagement with another man-of-war in this hampered condition, she would have been severely punished. But her captain was thinking rather of her radius of operation as destroyer of unarmed ships : he could never forget that lack of coal had once nearly ended his ship's career.

And now *Strathroy* had at last delivered up the last of her coal, so her prize crew were taken off and she was scuttled. The tenders continued to be used not merely as means of communication with South America : they were employed as innocent-looking scouts and thus between them were able to cover a wide front, wirelessing to *Karlsruhe* as required. On October 2

THE CAREER OF *KARLSRUHE* 117

Asuncion brought her some important telegrams which contained news that *Cap Trafalgar* had been sunk; that von Spee was crossing the Pacific to South America; that H.M.S. *Good Hope, Monmouth,* and *Glasgow* were steaming south; and that all Brazil was short of coal. It was thus that *Karlsruhe's* commanding officer was by no means isolated from the world, and could still keep his finger on the war pulse. If von Spee should desire him to join up with the squadron, the order could reach him overland from Chile to Brazil and thence over the sea. In the meanwhile the duty of remaining in wait along the highways could not fail to be well rewarded.

Lying just so far from each other as to keep in visual touch, the cruiser's scouts were forming an ambush across the north-eastern route, and on the evening of October 5 a little to the eastward of the spot where *Rio Iguassu* was captured, there now fell another victim. This was the British S.S. *Farn,* 4393 tons, and the position was just below the equator in Lat. 0.46 S, Long. 30.50 W, or 140 miles SW¾S of St. Paul Rocks, therefore in much the same area as before. This vessel was bound from Barry for Monte Video with 5810 tons of Welsh coal and coke, so another South American republic would have to go short. Britain's numerous tramp steamers and colliers were essential to the raider's very livelihood.

Farn, under the present circumstances, was not to be sunk but became another tender. In command was placed a German Reserve officer, Lieut.-Commander Lubinus, with a crew that could easily be spared now that *Strathroy* was no more. But, after sending *Farn* away, *Karlsruhe* heard the wireless of a British warship, and this was observed of such strength that the German became alarmed and moved off further to the east so that she was now more directly in line with St. Paul Rocks and actually clear of the normal north-eastern sea-lane. It was H.M.S. *Cornwall* that she heard, and this cruiser was making a sweep first to Fernando Noronha (which she visited on the 6th) and then carried on up the trade route, so that during the forenoon of the 7th she passed quite close to the very spot where *Farn* had been captured at 6 p.m. on the 5th. Indeed, so near did *Cornwall* and *Karlsruhe* approach each other that at 7.30 a.m. on the 7th they were not more than 90 miles apart. If therefore fate had quite reasonably contrived that the two ships should be steaming towards each other at 15 knots, they would have met in three hours and sighted each other long before.

The raider was thus running an enormous risk, and the least accident might settle her destiny: yet she was blessed with that exceptional luck which not infrequently accompanies the adventurous. But she was more fortunate than she could ever have a right to expect. For she was 40 miles to the eastward of the normal shipping tracks, and she could not hope to find traffic so much out of its way. Köhler had yet to learn that, in accordance with the British Admiralty's direction, vessels were not always adhering to the peace-time lane; they were giving it a wide berth. Thus it happened that on the afternoon of October 6, when 100 miles S by W¼W from St. Paul Rocks, he encountered the British S.S. *Niceto de Larrinaga*, 5018 tons, bound for England with cereals from Buenos Aires, and he sank her that night with bombs. Next morning he captured the British S.S. *Lynrowan*, 3384 tons, 90 miles SSW of the same Rocks and destroyed her in like manner. She too was carrying food cargo from South America. On the 8th another homeward-bound British steamer *Cervantes*, 4635 tons, was caught 10 miles further on and similarly dealt with. Soon after midnight the 4408-ton British S.S. *Pruth*, coming north-east, made yet another victim; so that in one tiny area four good ships in three days had steamed straight into an unintended trap. *Cornwall's* wireless had been the accidental means of driving the raider to a ripe harvest.

Nor did this amazing luck suddenly desert *Karlsruhe*. Being in need of fuel, she now proceeded west towards Lavandeira Reef whither *Farn* had been ordered to rendezvous with her coal. But before this meeting-place could be reached, *Karlsruhe* sighted *Farn* having some communication with the 5153-ton British S.S. *Condor*. This was in Lat. 2 S, Long. 34 W, or 215 miles N by E of Cape San Roque. *Condor* was bound from New York for Chile, but for safety's sake had elected to keep over a hundred miles eastward of the usual shipping route.

This, in truth, was to be her undoing. She had a temporary engine breakdown and on sighting *Farn* flying the British ensign requested the latter to stand by. This was easy enough, and the *Farn* under German officers managed to detain *Condor*, well knowing that *Karlsruhe* was coming along. It was thus that on the 11th at 3 p.m. *Condor* was trapped, and during the next two days the cruiser was busy helping herself to the valuable cargo of lubricating oils, provisions, and dynamite cartridges. The oils would come in handy as additional fuel for *Karlsruhe's* furnaces. Finally, having cleaned the prize out of all that could be taken, *Condor* was scuttled. The cruiser then proceeded further west and spent October 14–16 coaling from *Farn* at Lavandeira Reef. Her subsequent adventures will presently be considered.

By this time, however, Captain Köhler was faced with a problem which is an inevitable accompaniment of every successful raider. The more that ships were sunk, the more seriously and inconveniently would the number of prisoners mount up. His tender *Crefeld* was at this date inordinately crowded out with about 400 people. It was impossible to add any more crews, and those whom he had must be landed somewhere. He had kept the accumulation with him as long as possible for obvious reasons : as soon as these prisoners of war were released in some neutral port, full information would be broadcast concerning *Karlsruhe* and her doings ; British cruisers would be sent to patrol that region which he had found so profitable, and it would no longer be healthy for him to continue.

Köhler therefore made two decisions. Firstly, he would send *Crefeld* not into some South American port (since that would be too near and enable the tidings to be known before he had time to get clear), but across to the other side of the Atlantic right away from this scene. By thus resolving, he would be giving himself extra days in which to operate. Secondly, he must change his strategy altogether and relinquish this harassing of the South American trade routes. The British cruisers might patrol and search for him in vain : he would be elsewhere on another mission that would equally well aid Germany in her warfare.

At 4 p.m. on October 13 Köhler finally dismissed *Crefeld* by signal, and she steamed away to the northeast bound for Tenerife, but with orders not to reach there before October 22. With her also went letters from him for Berlin, which would have little difficulty in eventually reaching their destination. On October 22 *Crefeld* reached Tenerife and at last set at liberty the crews of a dozen ships. Notwithstanding that this German vessel had been acting in the clearest possible manner as tender to a warship, the Spanish authorities refused to intern *Crefeld*, and the result was that to cover her as well as three other ships it became a necessity for British naval cruisers to include the blockading of Tenerife as part of their duty.

We can admire the resourceful ingenuity of the way in which the German raiders were so ably backed up by their agents ashore, even if we censure their utter disregard for the rights which pertain to neutrality. The supply of intelligence, for instance, was almost as essential as the supplies of food and fuel. Köhler's movement would have to depend on the bigger events which were happening at sea. It was necessary that he should be given every possible information as to what British cruisers were doing off South America, who they were, and how many ; but in a wider sense he required to know if any momentous naval engagement had taken place to modify the trend of progress in the North Sea, Atlantic, or Pacific. There might, for example, be new circumstances which would demand his return home. Nominally he was playing a lone hand out of touch with any theatre of war other than a restricted section of the trade routes.

But by means of a very simple relay system Köhler

DRESDEN AT JUAN FERNANDEZ

She is seen at extreme left hand, taken from H.M.S. *Glasgow's* boat, with Juan Fernandez Island in the background, March 14, 1915.

THE LAST OF THE RAIDER
Dresden finally sinking at Juan Fernandez.

THE CAREER OF *KARLSRUHE*

was well linked up with the outer world. The German-owned Roland Line, which was to incur a few months later the Brazilian Government's anger for breach of neutrality, was a notorious offender. Ever since the outbreak of war one of its ships, the S.S. *Holger*, had been lying in Pernambuco, which was situated most suitably in regard to the focal point of the trade routes we have just been discussing. This steamer used to signal by weak wireless the movements of both merchantmen and British men-of-war, and the news was picked up by *Asuncion* who kept in communication with the raiders. The value of this method could scarcely be overrated.

But a good deal of intelligence was obtainable from newspapers published in South America and found aboard the captured ships within a few days of the latter having left port. It was, for example, worthwhile news to learn that certain mercantile steamers had reached or were leaving harbour, or that British warships had been reported. From such newspapers did Köhler ascertain that H.M.S. *Good Hope, Monmouth*, and *Glasgow* were about and had called at Monte Video. By collating all these details, listening-in on his wireless, using a little imagination, and plotting positions on his chart, he would be able to get a pretty useful appreciation of the present situation. Being a sensible man, he could see that this raiding adventure would be attended by increasing difficulty now that the number of regular cruisers and armed merchant-cruisers of the *Carmania* type was being so efficiently increased. Lonely, natural, improvised bases such as Lavandeira Reef, Rocas Reef, Fernando Noronha, Trinidada, could not be regarded as secret indefinitely : but when once they had become no longer practicable, there would be considerable difficulty with regard to coaling and rendezvous for the tenders. Nor was it to be expected that the running in and out of South American ports by *Asuncion* and her sisters would be tolerated much longer by any of the republics. In short, then, Köhler was compelled to revise his plans, face the change of outlook, and realize that this cruiser warfare against commerce was not to be regarded as a steady campaign but, at the best, was merely an ephemeral series of exploits.

Karlsruhe now entered upon her last phase, and there was just time to make another venture along the northeast route before the British could react from the data which *Crefeld's* prisoner seafarers would speedily supply. After coaling for the last time at Lavandeira Reef in mid-October, Köhler went east and began drifting about in wait for something to come along. On the 18th he captured the British 3021-tons S.S. *Glanton*, 195 miles SW of St. Paul Rocks, yet it was not till October 23 that he took also the British S.S. *Hurstdale*, 2752 tons, when 205 miles SW of those Rocks. Both vessels were destroyed, the former by bombs and the latter by scuttling.

But already it was about time to quit, so on the 25th, having given instructions to her tenders *Rio Negro, Asuncion,* and *Indrani* for the next few weeks, *Karlsruhe* went off with *Farn* westward, the intention being now to take up the previously abandoned plan of raiding West Indian islands, and to make a beginning with Barbados. The German cruiser was thus well away from her notorious north-east area by the time *Crefeld* could create activities, and *Karlsruhe* was now running up that north-west route which would lead through Trinidad to New York. It was therefore hardly surprising that on October 26, when to the north of Jericoacoara (mentioned in an earlier chapter), in Lat. 1.14 S, Long. 40.42 W, she came across the British S.S. *Vandyck*, 10,328 tons, which was on the regular Cape San Roque–Trinidad track. This was a well-known fast ship of the Booth Line, and carried women and children among her passengers. Such a capture was a rich prize, but it necessitated wirelessing *Asuncion* to come and receive these numerous prisoners. All on board were transferred from the Booth Liner, so that what with the crews of *Glanton* and *Hurstdale,* the *Asuncion* was crowded out with 461 survivors. The unpleasant conditions aboard the old 4663-ton Hamburg-South Amerika steamer under the equatorial sun may readily be imagined. On the 27th *Asuncion* was sent away with instructions to

THE CAREER OF *KARLSRUHE* 123

land all these people at the nearby port of Para, but not to arrive there till the first of November, thus giving time for *Karlsruhe* to disappear. *Asuncion* therefore steamed about dead slow, and it was not till November 2 that the unfortunate people set foot ashore.

Having ransacked *Vandyck*, the Germans sank the latter on October 28, and she was to be the last vessel that *Karlsruhe* captured. For on the 27th she stopped the British S.S. *Royal Sceptre* a little further up this same track, but released her through fear of offending New York owners of her cargo.

And now at the end of a highly successful cruise, just when Köhler was about to attack Barbados, the hand of fate gripped him, seized him tight, and squeezed the life out of him. The story of this fine cruiser with her brilliant flashes of daring, her elusiveness, and her destructive adventures, ends with that inevitability which justice demands of a great drama. Köhler must have often realised that his run of luck could not possibly continue for ever : sooner or later he would receive a nasty blow. But the irony of the whole finale is that the knock-out blow should come *after* the raids against commerce had ended. Still more remarkable is the fact that death should arrive not through the fortune of a fight or by the impact of British shells. *Karlsruhe* was at the critical moment in anything but a fighting mood : her crew were resting, and enjoying a few moments of peacefulness. It was then with an intense, sudden, and devastating effect a mysterious blow came out of the blue tropical sky.

On November 1 she coaled for the last time from *Farn*, then continued towards Barbados in company of *Rio Negro* and *Indrani*. Three days later *Karlsruhe* was only 300 miles short of Barbados, and Köhler was on his forebridge. If he was looking forward to the surprise which he would soon present to the British subjects in Barbados, he could look back with satisfaction to what he had already accomplished for his own fatherland. Seventeen steamers had he captured or sunk in a few weeks, of whom all were British save one Dutchman. Over seventy thousand tons of shipping had been wiped off the register, and much-needed cargoes had been prevented from reaching England. Altogether he had done damage to ships and produce up to a million and a half sterling, and had beaten the achievements of *Emden*.

And now the fierce sun set into the warm Atlantic sea, most of the crew off duty were only too glad to recline forward and get some benefit from the cooling breeze as the lithe cruiser cleft her way through the hot atmosphere. The ship's band was playing, men were humming to the music, and the engines were maintaining a steady vibration; when for no apparent reason there came a flash, a terrible explosion, flames and smoke. *Karlsruhe* had been severed in two, and the forward half with Köhler as well as 260 of his shipmates perished. The after portion floated for twenty minutes, which enabled 146 officers and men to be picked up by *Rio Negro* and *Indrani*. Thus by a miracle Barbados was relieved of the danger that threatened within a few hours.

Köhler was a popular officer with his men, and certainly acted humanely with regard to his prisoners. Resourceful and courageous, able and prudent, he organised his raiding operations in accordance with sound strategy and with efficient tactics. And when once he had got on to the trade routes he was careful never to use his wireless except in the case of absolute necessity. His reliance chiefly on captured colliers certainly relieved the German Supply Officers ashore from anxiety.

It was a clever intention to have selected such a time for attacking West Indian islands; for the effect would have been not inconsiderable. At sea further anxieties would have been placed on British cruisers in the Atlantic, and there would have been awkward demands from citizens for protection. That would have interfered with the Admiralty's more comprehensive and general strategy. But there would have been another unhappy result if Barbados had been bombarded. On November 1 had been fought the disastrous Battle of Coronel, and the British public mind already, depressed with the military situation on the continent of Europe,

THE CAREER OF *KARLSRUHE*

would have been in no mood for receiving tidings such as would soon come along the Atlantic cables. If a German cruiser had been allowed to raid West Indian islands there would immediately have been raised the cry of, "Where is the British Navy? What are our cruisers doing?"

The loss of *Karlsruhe* was for a while a well-kept secret, and in the meantime she was being diligently searched for by various units, an important feature of this effort being the endeavour to locate her bases. Thus on October 25 H.M.S. *Defence*, a cruiser, examined Rocas Reef, and on the previous day the armed merchant cruiser *Edinburgh Castle* examined Lavandeira Reef. Of course nothing was found, but it is not without interest to bear in mind that *Karlsruhe's* visits to Lavandeira were on August 30, September 9, 18, and 30, whilst her final call there was October 15. *Edinburgh Castle* therefore missed her by a few days. It was one of the chances of war that these diligent cruisers never passed sufficiently close to the Reef whenever the German or *Strathroy* was there: for not till long after peace had been signed was the situation of that mysterious base known in London.

It was spontaneous explosion which had brought about *Karlsruhe's* loss, though at the moment her people imagined she was torpedoed. The surviving senior officer was Lieut.-Commander Studt, and he acquitted himself as would be expected. Two duties impressed themselves upon him: the first was to reach Germany, and the second was to prevent the world from knowing that *Karlsruhe* was lost. He accordingly took charge of *Rio Negro* and sank *Indrani*, though *Farn* was never taken into his confidence, so that the latter during two months went steaming about hopelessly ignorant of the new conditions, till at length she put into San Juan, Puerto Rico, on January 12, 1915, where she was interned. When *Karlsruhe* exploded, *Farn* happened to have been not with the squadron.

One cannot but admire the courageous determination of Studt in his resolve to risk getting through the British blockade into the North Sea; and now *Rio Negro* started off on her voyage towards home. Lest the news should reach British cruisers that the search for *Karlsruhe* might be cancelled, he carefully avoided entering a neutral port even for a short time, but made a circuitous course so that he went right to the north of Europe into such icy latitudes that his shipmates in their scanty tropical clothing suffered severely from winter's cold. To try avoiding the cruisers which were watching in areas between the Shetlands, Faroes, and Iceland, as well as to the north-west of the Hebrides, was in practice easier than appeared theoretically. "The whole of the cruisers were beginning to show signs of overwork," Admiral Jellicoe has recorded in his *The Grand Fleet*. During the gale of November 12 the old *Edgar* class of cruisers on this patrol suffered much damage, began to leak, lost boats as well as ventilators, so that it was decided to pay off the whole 10th Cruiser Squadron and employ armed merchant cruisers, which could keep the sea for longer periods. Incidentally, this was exactly the same conclusion which months of warfare against commerce had brought about in the mind of the German Admiralty: cruisers, like destroyers and race-horses, are too lean and delicate except for special demands under short periods of speed.

It may be said, then, that just about the time when *Rio Negro* made her big detour towards Iceland waters and thence south-east in the direction of Norway, her risk was not considerable: the British blockade was in a state of transition and not yet effective. At the same time, even under the best conditions, it would be quite impossible ever to guarantee that no enemy ships should succeed in breaking through an area so vast that it reached as high as the Arctic Circle and even the North Pole. Bad weather and long nights were the conditions always easiest for the blockade-runners, and most difficult for the patrols. It was only when a Germany-bound raider got south of Bergen that he became especially nervous, since the distance across to the Shetlands is too short and too easily patrolled. This was in effect a defile of some 200 odd miles, which either had to be gambled with or not attempted.

THE CAREER OF *KARLSRUHE*

Now it so happened that on November 27 and 28 there was a strong gale at the northern end of the North Sea, making the chances of an elusive single ship during the short daylight most promising. Thus, in short, on November 29 *Rio Negro* came to the end of her venture by entering the Norwegian port of Aalesund, which is well to the north of Bergen. From there it was not impracticable for her crew to reach Germany, which they did a week later. So well had the *Karlsruhe's* loss been kept that not even Berlin was aware on November 27, when Nauen wireless station sent a signal to Captain Köhler giving him the Kaiser's permission to return home, and this message was actually taken in by *Rio Negro* whilst approaching her last anchorage. One can readily imagine the feelings of Studt and his companions!

That imperial permission, however, is significant: for it shows that the *Karlsruhe* was just about at the end of her usefulness as a raider, and that even while von Spee's Squadron was still undefeated the cruiser was not deemed indispensable for Atlantic work. Nine days after *Rio Negro* took herself into a Norwegian harbour was fought the Battle of the Falklands, so that the Atlantic was rid of all German cruisers just four months after the outbreak of war, and the only unit of this type still to be accounted for was *Dresden,* whose end we have witnessed. There still remained, however, the armed merchant cruisers *Kronprinz Wilhelm* and *Prinz Eitel Friedrich,* and we shall now proceed to follow out their careers. It is worth nothing that thus from quite early in the war, in spite of the spectacular exploits by *Emden, Dresden,* and *Karlsruhe,* the main operations by surface ships against the trade routes were carried on not by regular naval cruisers built for war, but by ships designed for commerce and then readapted for destroying commerce. In this respect we come back to the conditions of the sailing-ship age when an East Indiaman—the equivalent of our modern liner—was so similar in appearance to a man-of-war that the one was frequently supposed to be the other.

CHAPTER IX

KRONPRINZ WILHELM'S CRUISE

IT was no small relief to find, as time went on, that there was not a number of liners escaping out of North American harbours and emulating *Kronprinz Wilhelm*. The latter had, it will be recollected, hurriedly left New York on the very eve of war. On August 22 the North German Lloyd *Brandenburg* in escaping from Philadelphia had eluded H.M.S. *Essex* but ended up only at Bergen. The United States authorities disallowed both German and Austrian vessels to arm whilst in neutral waters, kept a careful watch to prevent any of them infringing the law of nations, and thus banished what might have been a very serious crisis had the Atlantic trade routes been harassed by converted liners in great numbers and during the same period.

There was only one other which broke out, and this was the Hamburg-Amerika liner *Graecia*, which skipped away from New York on August 29, 1914, and made for the Azores neighbourhood where (like other German steamers) she hung about for day after day in readiness to supply coal and provisions to the first of her country's ships that should come along. The raiders knew that they could expect to find supplies off those islands, and it is a proof of the excellent German supply organization that storeships managed to reach there. The latter owed their immunity partly to good fortune; partly to the large amount of patrolling and watching which had to be done by British units off Tenerife, Las Palmas, and St. Vincent; partly also because these were so busy seeking *Karlsruhe* and *Kronprinz Wilhelm*; but, further, because it is so easy for a single ship to zigzag about the Atlantic without being seen. Nevertheless, on October

SAILORS ABOARD H.M.S. *KENT*
Watching *Dresden* sinking, March 14, 1915.

ARTICLES PICKED UP
After sinking of *Dresden*.

KRONPRINZ WILHELM'S CRUISE 129

10 H.M.S. *Argonaut* was off the Azores, and in Lat. 38.31 N, Long. 25.22 W sighted what purported to be the Norwegian S.S. *Björgvin*. On being boarded, the latter was found to be *Graecia* and was arrested.

At this time there were anchored at St. Vincent eight German merchant ships, and the large number of these steamers in the various harbours of the Canary Islands was the counterpart of an idle Teutonic fleet in the United States. There was, however, this essential difference : as the weeks sped by, the possibility of these east Atlantic vessels trying to make a dash for the open sea was still considerable. It was believed that some of them were ready to sail with coal, stores, and even ammunition at the first chance. There can be no gainsaying the fact that there was a strong anti-British, pro-German feeling to contend with during the first stages of hostilities. At Las Palmas, for example, the British Consul was not permitted to transmit wireless messages in cypher; yet the German and Austrian Consuls there were reporting the movements of ships by cypher to the German and Austrian embassies in Madrid. This was possible by the following chain of high-powered wireless-stations : Las Palmas to Tenerife, then Tenerife to Cadiz. But any German ship which happened to be within a thousand miles could also pick up such important signals and thus know the movements of British cruisers. Between October 10 and November 11 no fewer than twenty-five messages addressed in Spanish to the German embassy at Madrid and signed by the Austrian Consul, Mittelstrasse, were intercepted by H.M.S. *Victorian*. Admiral de Robeck (who was in command of the British cruisers down here) protested against this favouritism, and Madrid had at length to allow cypher messages to be sent by all nations. Seeing that in Las Palmas were lying the two steamers *Duala* and *Arucas*, which had coaled *Kaiser Wilhelm der Grosse*, there was every reason for suspecting some sudden activity afloat accompanied by the transmission of messages in cypher.

But *Kronprinz Wilhelm* had, as we have noticed in a previous chapter, gone across towards south-east South

I

America. After dismissing the crew of *Indian Prince* on September 19, Thierfelder remained in the neighbourhood of Trinidada till the end of the month. He was not the most able or most successful of the raiders, and the weeks of fruitless steaming about are in striking contrast to the conception that this kind of warfare is one closely packed series of thrilling surprises. The days of boredom, the long periods devoid of any excitement, could not fail to have a cumulative effect on the spirits of officers as well as men, and this depression hardly made for sparkling efficiency. *Karlsruhe's* strategy was more simple, compact, and concentrated : having once found the richest area, she stuck to it. *Kronprinz Wilhelm*, on the other hand, was more varied in her choice of localities, less scientific, so that if she lasted longer there was not the same achievement. The clever commanding officer gets on to the most frequented track quickly, cleans it up by intensive work, clears right off the scene but to another busy route, repeats his campaign and then disappears to a different part of the world, thus completely mystifying the naval forces searching for him. The raider *Wolf*, whose career will be studied in a later chapter, is an excellent instance of mobility on a world-wide area after intense concentration over a secluded section.

During the eight months in which *Kronprinz Wilhelm* operated she captured only fifteen vessels, or fewer than one every fortnight. And out of these fifteen only eleven were steamers, the rest being obsolete sailing-ships. Apart altogether from the expense, the question arises as to whether it is worth while employing a large crew for so long a time in return for such meagre results. It was not till October 7 that she made her next capture, though it was a most useful one in every way, causing the loss to Britain of a good steamer and valuable food, whilst supplying the raider with all sorts of items. This was the Houlder Line S.S. *La Correntina*, 8529 tons, which had come out from La Plata with Argentine meat for the British Army, and she was now 320 miles east of Monte Video.

Thierfelder seems to have been no great ship lover,

KRONPRINZ WILHELM'S CRUISE 131

and the manner in which he handled the great four-funnelled liner appears strangely unseamanlike on more occasions than one. *La Correntina* was captured by the strange medieval tactics of boarding : that is to say, the *Kronprinz* came along the smaller vessel's starboard side smashing boats, davits, bridge-deck, and then sending boarders over the side to take possession. But the sinking of *La Correntina* did not occur for a week. After passengers and crew had been taken off, enough meat was transhipped to last the raider till the middle of March : but coal, water, and two fine 4·7-inch guns were also taken. As to the latter their history is rather a sad instance of muddle and delay. They were perfectly good weapons placed aboard just before the beginning of the war, and with them went the two guns' crews, but alas ! no ammunition. That still remained at Liverpool owing to a misunderstanding.

On October 20 *Kronprinz* was joined by the single-funnel tender *Sierra Cordoba* bringing coal, clothes, vegetables, soap, cigars, and so on. Two days later, the weather being calm, the tender came alongside the big liner, and took off *La Correntina's* people. Thierfelder then went further in towards the coast, crossing the trade routes that led up from the Horn and Magellan Straits, and on October 28 in Lat. 34 S, 52 W captured the French sailing-vessel *Union*, bound for the Plate with 3100 tons of Cardiff coal. It was rather hard lines on the Frenchman thus to have got right across the Atlantic and to the very threshold of her destination only to fall into the enemy's hands : but all this coal, so badly needed in South America for the railways and electric-light works, was very much desired by the raider who now took her in tow.

And then a rather ridiculous situation ensued which indicates that Thierfelder had not the ability of Köhler : he was bent more on profiting from his capture than dealing smashing blows to seaborne commerce. Truly there is deep down some of the piratical urge in every sailor who still remembers his boyhood days, and the temptation to make the best of a prize (especially when she carries fuel) is considerable. But this officer might have been better employed had he sunk *Union* forthwith and then kept along those busy routes which brought such rich cargoes in and out of the Rio de la Plata. His primary duty was not to be the pirate or pilferer, but to sink Allied shipping. Instead, however, we find him now neglecting this essential service, avoiding the trade route, trying ineffectually to coal from his prize but prevented by the heavy ocean weather. It was not till November 20 that, after towing *Union* for three weeks, he was able to take 2000 tons of coal and then to sink her, the crew being transferred to the tender *Sierra Cordoba*, who two days later landed also the people of *La Correntina* at Monte Video.

During these high-seas coaling operations *Kronprinz* suffered severe damage. This was scarcely surprising when we think of the four-masted iron *Union* pounding against the 15,000-ton steel liner : but the skill in coaling might have been more proficient, for, whilst 800 tons were still aboard the French vessel, the latter capsized. Still, it is only fair to admit that taking in fuel under these circumstances is at the best of times a risky business, and we can find a comparison with the experiences of H.M.S. *Kent* illuminating. On November 11 the latter arrived off the Abrolhos Rocks (between Trinidada and the Brazilian coast, and the following extracts are from the diary of her commanding officer, Captain (now Vice-Admiral) J. D. Allen :

> Nov. 11th. Arrived at the Abrolhos Rocks at daylight and found two colliers at anchor there, the *Thistledhue* and the *Priestfield*. To save time the *Kent* went straight alongside the *Thistledhue*. We commenced coaling at 9.0 a.m. and finished at 1.0 p.m. . . . It was no easy job coaling, as the anchorage was very exposed and the ships were rolling a good deal all the time. We carried away several wire hawsers and lost some of our big fenders. We learnt by practical experience that wire hawsers are no use under these circumstances. Large coir springs, manilla or hemp hawsers, especially coir, are best as they have so much "give" in them. Wire hawsers are no use for this sort of work.

The same distinguished officer, who it will be remembered sank *Nurnberg* and was present at the sinking of

KRONPRINZ WILHELM'S CRUISE 133

Dresden, also tried the experiment of coaling in the open Pacific Ocean and has been good enough to give me the following details :

> We were now getting short of coal, so we decided to coal at sea the first day that the sea was smooth enough.
> Jan. 10th and 11th. At sea. Fine weather, but a long swell which kept the ship rolling. . . .
> Jan 12th. By daylight the swell had gone down a good deal, so we decided to coal. We turned the ship head on to the swell, so as to keep her from rolling as much as possible and went slowly ahead so as to be able to steer her. The collier then came alongside and we made her fast with manilla hawsers and grass springs. Then we kept steaming slowly ahead with one screw, towing the collier alongside. We found the two ships much steadier when moving slowly ahead than when stopped. For one thing we could keep them under control and head to the swell, and for another thing it kept a steadier strain on the hawsers and springs between the two ships. It was very successful. We commenced coaling at 9.45 a.m. and finished at 4.0 p.m. . . . Seeing that both ships were rolling slightly all the time, this was a very good performance and it proved the practicability of coaling at sea in fairly fine weather. No damage was done either to the collier or any men, though getting in and out between the *Kent* and the collier was a ticklish job. The men had to wait till the two ships rolled towards one another and then jump across. If any man had slipped and fallen between the two ships, he would have been crushed to death.

Kronprinz Wilhelm was able to keep herself well informed of events by means of the wireless station at Olinda (near Pernambuco), and on November 21, being well away from the land on the sailing-ship route, came across the French barque *Anne de Bretagne*, bound from Europe for Melbourne with timber. Those of us who were serving afloat during the war observed how difficult it was for a ship with a cargo of wood to sink, no matter how badly she had been shelled, torpedoed, or mined ; and I recollect assisting to bring into port a big steamer which had been mercilessly attacked by submarine and sank so low that on boarding her I found the main deck only a few feet above the sea-level and the officers' cabins all awash with gurgling water. Still, we managed to get into port after some hours, and she was finally prevented from foundering. So, too, the

THE SEA-RAIDERS

decoy Q-ships, which deliberately went to sea for the purpose of being torpedoed in trapping submarines, were late in the war packed tightly with cork and wood that they kept afloat a long while and could be towed home.

When *Kronprinz Wilhelm* tried to sink *Anne de Bretagne*, the German found this was no easy matter, and finally had to ram her, explode three bombs in her, and fire twenty-five rounds of ammunition before she disappeared in Lat. 27 S, Long. 32 W. And, incidentally, this rough treatment did not fail to damage the bows of the liner herself. It must have grieved her peace-time master, Captain Grahn, to have seen his fine ship thus used.

And now Thierfelder, having had little success on the sailing-ship route, wisely betook himself to that area between Cape San Roque and the Cape Verde Islands which *Karlsruhe* had found so highly remunerative. Indeed, this part of the ocean highway is, for its comparatively restricted length between the two continents of America and Africa, the most attractive of all the world's trade routes to an ambitious raider. He can be as sure of finding victims along this road as a pickpocket can be certain to find opportunities along Broadway or Piccadilly. Since there are far more steamers nowadays than sailing-ships, one wonders that *Kronprinz* did not from the first stick to the locality between, say, Cape Roque and St. Paul Rocks.

Actually she proceeded to operate somewhat to the east of this north-east track, but it served her well inasmuch as shipping was by Admiralty instructions keeping a little off the usual direct line. Thus on December 4 Thierfelder was able to capture the inevitable British collier. This was the S.S. *Bellevue*, with 5400 tons of coal and general cargo bound for Monte Video from Glasgow, and the position was in Lat. 3 S, Long. 29.9 W, or about 460 miles NE from Pernambuco. But whilst engaged with her, he sighted also the French S.S. *Mont Agel*, and the latter being only in ballast was soon sunk, though again *Kronprinz* did not hesitate to perform such an act by the process of

KRONPRINZ WILHELM'S CRUISE 135

ramming. The wonder is that the liner's fine, razor-like bows could stand all this punishment. Did not the White Star liner *Titanic* go to the bottom through ramming an iceberg ?

Thierfelder now made the same mistake of being put off from his primary duty. The contents of *Bellevue* so attracted him that he took her and himself right away from the pick of the sea-tracks and sought seclusion to the north-west in that "dead" zone where shipping is not normally found. For four days he went steaming on, and next from December 8 to 20 wasted valuable time drifting about the ocean removing every conceivable thing of value—coal, whisky, soap, chocolate, cigars, and so on. Then he opened *Bellevue's* sea-cocks and let her sink. But on the day that Thierfelder had captured this steamer, there came out of Pernambuco the S.S. *Otavi*. She was a Hamburg-Amerika liner of 5173 tons and had been lying in harbour ever since August 17, yet now on December 4 she bluffed her way to freedom since the German Consul declared her mission was commercial and she pretended that she was going to Fernando Po. It is pretty well established that she emerged for the purpose of meeting either (*a*) the German battle-cruiser *Von der Tann*, which never did come into the South Atlantic though there were strange rumours that she intended so to do, or (*b*) von Spee's Squadron. The probability is that *Von der Tann* was to try breaking out of the North Sea, going right away up towards Iceland, sinking any of the patrols (which she could very easily have done) and then effecting a rendezvous with von Spee as the latter came north up the Atlantic. The battle-cruiser would have required to be coaled, and *Otavi* was not the only German tender which came out from the South American coast in readiness at the beginning of December.

But the Battle of the Falklands on December 8 completely changed all that, and four days later *Otavi* with her stores joined the drifting *Kronprinz Wilhelm*, remaining till the day after *Bellevue* was scuttled and then taking from the raider all prisoners. It was thus December 21 when *Otavi* parted company, leaving

Kronprinz in Lat. 4.8 N, Long. 37.50 W (that is to say, the "dead" zone which is bounded on the west by the Pernambuco–New York track, on the north by the Para–Madeira track, on the east by the Pernambuco–St. Vincent track), and went across the Atlantic to Las Palmas where she arrived on January 4, and was interned by the Governor within twenty-four hours.

Thierfelder's ship was by Christmas time thus full of stores: the great liner could be independent of the shore for a long time. Still, the German Admiralty had no longer much faith in raiders just now, and they had been able to get a full clear appreciation of the situation from the recently returned survivors of *Karlsruhe*. Berlin was able to send a message through to Thierfelder suggesting that he should give up, lay his ship in some neutral port, and let her be interned. But it is to this captain's credit as a loyal naval officer that he preferred to carry on commerce raiding instead of choosing the easier way. So towards the end of 1914 we find him back on that station where he had found *Bellevue* and *Mont Agel*: that is, eastward of the line Fernando Noronha–St. Paul Rocks. It was a wise decision to make trial of the fruitful locality which he had deserted since December 4, and his reward came when the British S.S. *Hemisphere*, 3486 tons, fell into his hands at six on the evening of December 28. She was another collier, her cargo being destined from Hull to Buenos Aires for the Central Argentine Railway.

Once more Thierfelder forsook his locality, took his prize to the eastward till December 30 (being in another "dead" zone) and removed from her coal, stores, as well as everything else he wanted. The position of the capture had been Lat. 4.20 S, Long. 29.25 W, or about sixty miles from where he had found *Bellevue*. It was to be a fortnight before *Kronprinz* made another success, for not till January 7 did she destroy *Hemisphere* by scuttling. Such leisurely tactics could not bring about rapid results.

Now at this stage we have still further proof of the persistent disregard which Germany showed for international law, and for the South American republics in

KRONPRINZ WILHELM'S CRUISE 137

particular. All sorts of bluff and lies were deemed permissible, provided the supply tenders could do their work. In a previous chapter mention was made of the S.S. *Holger*, belonging to the German-owned Roland Line which earned such notoriety. This vessel as she lay in Pernambuco was in effect a transmitting station keeping raiders in touch with the movements of Allied shipping. For some time did such activities continue, and then on December 2 she was detected reporting by wireless the departures as well as cargoes of British ships. She had clearly been utilising neutral territory for an hostile act.

On the first of January she followed this up by another bit of sharp practice, when without clearance papers she slipped secretly out from Pernambuco and got to sea. At last this flagrant incident roused the Brazilian Government to get busy, and really do something to stop all this abuse of hospitality. Not before it was due, then, came the decision to remove the necessary portions of wireless instruments in every ship that happened to be in Pernambuco, as well as in any vessel at any Brazilian port found to be communicating. The Captain of the Port and the guardship's commanding officer at Pernambuco were dismissed, the wireless station situated on Fernando Noronha Island was now closed, and a thorough search was made for secret wireless stations ashore. Thus the unlawful means of communication with any raider received quite a blow, the German Supply organization was gradually breaking to pieces and the methods of commerce attack would soon have to give way to new ideas. *Holger* joined *Kronprinz Wilhelm* on January 6 north of the equator in Lat. 1 N, Long. 20 W, that is to say, in mid-Atlantic about 550 miles east of St. Paul Rocks, supplied her with stores, and took off the crew that had been aboard *Hemisphere*.

Thierfelder then moved north-west till he was once more a little to the east of the Las Palmas–Buenos Aires track, and therefore in a likely position to trap those steamers making for South America according to the instructions which required them to keep east of the peace-time lane. *Kronprinz* accordingly captured just after midnight on January 10 the British S.S. *Potaro*, 4419 tons, owned by the Royal Mail Line, the exact locality being Lat. 5.48 N, Long. 25.58 W, or more than 300 miles north-east of St. Paul Rocks. She was bound from Liverpool to Buenos Aires in ballast, so she was rather a disappointment, but might come in handy as a scout. A prize crew was put aboard, she was temporarily sent away, repainted navy-grey, and fitted with extra wireless aerials.

Meanwhile *Kronprinz* steamed south, and on January 14 was 70 miles nearer St. Paul Rocks when she sighted the British S.S. *Highland Brae*, 7634 tons, bound from the London river for Buenos Aires. This vessel fell into Thierfelder's hands like a ripe pear; although, being over 150 miles east of the steamer route, she had every reason to suppose the region was safe. But whilst *Kronprinz* was still on this spot there came up the same day the 251-ton three-masted schooner *Wilfred M.* owned in Canada. She was sailing from Nova Scotia to Bahia with a cargo of dried fish, so the crew were transferred and the little vessel sunk by ramming, *Kronprinz's* bows cutting her in half. Thierfelder once more wasted golden opportunities and sheered off eastward away from the lane he had now fully understood, and took with him *Highland Brae* to join *Holger* at the mid-Atlantic rendezvous.

It is strange to note that just when his prospects were so bright he should also now withdraw altogether from this locality, for gradually he went south down the Atlantic and as he voyaged removed coal, stores, and everything of value from *Highland Brae*. Thus passed the sixteen days till he was about a hundred miles SE of Trinidada when, on January 30, the sea-cocks of *Highland Brae* were opened and she was sunk. *Potaro*, after having likewise been stripped, was not used as a scout but sunk, so that the raider now had with him only *Holger*. Thierfelder seems to have got a fright, for he had left the steamer tracks well alone and was concerning himself with the sailing-ship routes once more. The third of February found him back in that

KRONPRINZ WILHELM'S CRUISE 139

vicinity where he had captured the sailing-vessel *Anne de Bretagne* on November 21 ; for when in Lat. 26.30 S, Long. 27 W, or about 930 miles from Rio Janeiro, he captured the Norwegian barque *Semantha*, which he sank because she was carrying wheat to the English Channel.

This was all the luck he had for deserting the St. Paul Rocks area, and finally he had to part with *Holger* in order to get rid of the accumulated prisoners. This vessel was dismissed on February 12 and sent into Buenos Aires where she arrived on the 17th, and was interned by the Argentine Government after twenty-four hours on the grounds that she was an auxiliary of the German Fleet. Thus at length the notorious craft came to the end of her roving. She was very foul below the waterline and could do no better than 8 knots, but right to the last she was extraordinarily fortunate. That morning at 9.30, as she passed within sight of Monte Video, H.M.S. *Carnarvon* was inside. This was the flagship of Admiral Stoddart, though neither ship was aware of the other's presence. The armed merchant cruiser *Celtic* was sent up from the Falklands to cruise off the River Plate in case the tender came out again, but on March 2 the British Admiralty were officially informed that the internment had taken place.

Carnarvon was again unfortunate on February 22, for she had been coaling at the Abrolhos Rocks (the secret British base off Brazil), but half an hour later struck a rock so badly that two of her stokeholds became flooded. Fortunately H.M.S. *Vindictive* was lying anchored at the Rocks guarding the colliers, so *Carnarvon* was beached close to the lighthouse and Admiral Stoddart shifted his flag to *Vindictive*. Temporary repairs were made to *Carnarvon*, which had a rent 95 feet long, but she managed to leave on March 4 for Rio at $6\frac{1}{4}$ knots, arrived safely and went into dry dock for repairs. It was annoyingly disappointing that, in spite of endless searching, the raider could not be located, and at this date the whereabouts of *Karlsruhe* still remained unknown to the British authorities. There were vague rumours that she had got back to Germany, yet on the other hand Grand Admiral von Koesler, President of the German Navy League, stated on February 5 in a lecture at Kiel that *Karlsruhe* was still operating in American waters. This was a curious remark, when we recollect that several months had elapsed since she blew up and that Studt had been home since November.

Whilst every endeavour was being made to find *Karlsruhe* and *Kronprinz Wilhelm* early in 1915, there had arrived on January 12 at San Juan, Porto Rico, a steamer flying the German ensign with *K.D.*3 on her stern. At first it was a little puzzling to guess what *K.D.*3 might signify, but presently she turned out to be none other than S.S. *Farn* which *Karlsruhe* had been using as tender, and the prize crew on board were unable to shed any light on their cruiser's fate. *Farn's* internment by the United States authorities helped to simplify the British cruiser's work; but at Havana, where *Karlsruhe* had coaled on the eve of war, there lay the Hamburg-Amerika liner *Bavaria* which had remained continuously since the beginning of hostilities.

This steamer caused no little uneasiness, for she had taken in large supplies of provisions and fuel so that 1700 tons of coal were aboard, and at the end of December 1914 a German agent had been trying to buy coal at any price from the Havana Coal Company. The only means by which this coal could have been carried from Havana was by means of *Bavaria*, and she was ready to leave at any moment as supply ship. But this was all negatived by means of two counter-moves. Firstly, the manager of the Coal Company being a Briton declined the agent's offer and reported the matter: secondly, H.M.S. *Berwick* was sent to keep a watch on the port.

Another steamer, with the very English name *Gladstone*, created anxiety. She was actually a Norwegian but had a German skipper and became extremely suspect: there was grave reason for assuming she was part of the German Supply organization.

KRONPRINZ WILHELM'S CRUISE 141

She reached Norfolk, Virginia, after the outbreak of war, in November. We next find her at Newport News, and in this United States port she was fitted with wireless. She endeavoured to change her flag to that of Chile, which would have been thoroughly convenient for a German tender operating off South America : but this ruse did not come off. She remained a month at Newport News and sailed on December 15, but under the name of *Mariana Quesada*, which had a sound more in keeping with one who would like to be thought a southerner. Moreover, she had obtained permission from the Costa Rican representative in the port to fly the Costa Rican flag. Proceeding down the Atlantic coast and across the Caribbean, she reached the port of Limon in her suddenly adopted country. Unhappily for her, however, the Costa Rican authorities refused to recognise her as one of themselves, repudiated her change of flag, and detained her as a German supply ship.

Such was her persistency that this rebuff did not thwart her and early on New Year's Day, 1915, she slipped out of Limon without papers or flag, steamed east along the Venezuelan shore, and thence south into that Brazilian port of Pernambuco which had been rightly so suspected. It was now January 23, and (as we have seen) a firmer control was already being kept on German ships within that harbour. The Brazilian Government regarded her movements as highly suspicious, and disabled her machinery lest she should make any further attempt at escape.

The length of the trade routes and their multiplicity; the vast extent of the Atlantic and the complicated situation created by elusive raiders, aided by deceptive tenders; the uncertainty and vagueness of much information that came in; all combined to make the work of British cruisers difficult and apparently without result. Nor shall we forget that at this period the mysterious *Dresden* was still not located, but able to draw off the services of other units. It was inconvenient that cruisers had to be detached for the duty of ensuring that one or more of the supply ships should not run out during the dark hours for her neutral shelter; and, if we would be wise after the events, perhaps the better course when once von Spee's Squadron had gone, should have been to introduce the convoy system at this stage, and escort by cruisers fleets of merchantmen (just as became an essential practice during the last months of the war when ocean-going submarines had for the most part taken the place of surface raiders). The supply ships would then have become useless, for there would have been no raider powerful enough to attack the cruisers in charge of the convoys; such vessels as *Kronprinz Wilhelm*, with their light armament and conspicuousness, would have been overwhelmed, outranged, turned into a mere target. In previous wars the convoy system proved itself efficient and sound. At the beginning of the Great European War there was a prejudice against its adoption, and only the terrible losses of vessels enabled that prejudice to be overcome. To keep compact a fleet of sailing-ships was far more difficult in the olden days than to regulate a convoy of steamers; and the unqualified success of the convoys during 1917–18 makes one regret that the revival had not been instituted as early as August 1914.

Still, the Atlantic cruisers during early 1915 were so active, and so dangerously near on many occasions, that there was a cumulative effect of breaking the raiders' spirit. Lüdecke, Köhler, Thierfelder, with all their skill and good fortune could not expect their run of luck to continue: the longer they kept at sea the more certainly would they be rounded up. And the German Admiralty had (not without due appreciation of the true facts) sent them permission to end each his campaign. Moreover, sooner or later, the necessity of communicating with a tender by wireless was almost certain to bring about a result fatal to the raiding operations. We have seen that this aerial method of conversation led to the death of *Dresden*, and now we shall witness again the danger of having to co-operate with tenders that must be given their rendezvous.

CHAPTER X

RAIDERS AND WIRELESS

LET us for a moment go back to the middle of January when *Kronprinz Wilhelm* was taking *Highland Brae* towards Lat. 1 N, Long. 20 W, that mid-Atlantic rendezvous where she was to pick up *Holger*, before proceeding southwards to the locality beyond Trinidada.

Now this necessitated the exchange of wireless messages, and the interesting sequel was that on January 18 a British steamer when in Lat. 1 N, Long. 24.27 W, that is to say, very near to the locality just above the equator, heard German telefunken wireless signals being transmitted. For this reason H.M.S. *Canopus* made a sweep which included that part of the Atlantic from January 21, and then a strange thing happened which shows that even in the wide ocean it is possible to meet with exact evidence. Just after sunset one of the look-outs in *Canopus* noticed a fish-like smell and this caused his vigilance to be intensified. Presently he sighted something awash, and lo ! it was a wreck ! Here was what remained of the schooner *Wilfred M.*, and it is a further proof of a wooden ship's refusal to sink that though *Kronprinz Wilhelm* had rammed her no less than four times the victim was still there. The position was Lat. 2.40 N, Long. 25.50 W, so the wreck had shifted but little. *Canopus* was an old-fashioned battleship with a ram, and inasmuch as the schooner was a danger to navigation, the warship tried to despatch *Wilfred M.* by her forefoot. This attempt proved a failure likewise, and long weeks afterwards, having been driven many hundreds of miles north-west to the West Indies, the wreck was brought by currents and trade winds till it drifted ashore at the Island of Grenada in the Windward Isles, on April 28, 1915.

So far, then, nothing practical had been obtained except to prove that a raider must have been hereabouts and that she was not working alone. Neither she nor *Holger* was sighted, for the reason that the pair were steaming south from this region. The converted liner was again lucky: the battleship's guns would have made short work of her. If, however, the cruise of *Canopus* had just failed to achieve something tangible, other sweeps were made by British cruisers belonging to that area which included the vicinity of Las Palmas. By intercepting wireless messages two important items were ascertained: (1) a certain rendezvous chosen for meeting *Kronprinz Wilhelm*, (2) that the German collier *Macedonia* would probably try to meet her. This was extremely likely, seeing that supply ships from South American ports were now finding it difficult to get out. As *Macedonia* was lying in Las Palmas a keen watch was for some time set to catch her if she should come forth. This Hamburg-Amerika liner had escaped from New Orleans on August 30, 1914, crossed the Atlantic and reached Santa Cruz, Las Palmas, on October 17, where she had later been interned by the Spanish authorities. Thus, her intention of serving as supply ship seemed to have been brought to a speedy end.

In order to prevent any nonsense, the same authorities took the precautions of disabling her engines by the removal of a cylinder cover. We now pass to March 15, by which time the difficulties of any raider receiving supplies were acute. But the ingenious Supply Officer at Las Palmas had taken the trouble to have a spare cylinder cover ready. *Macedonia* had been allowed to retain her coal on board, and on March 4 the Supply Officer received orders to have her prepared to rush out and join the *Kronprinz Wilhelm*. On March 15, at 1.30 a.m., she escaped out of harbour under cover of night and disappeared. But how was it that there was no cruiser to prevent her?

The answer is that for some time, in order to respect

RAIDERS AND WIRELESS 145

Spanish susceptibilities, and in the belief that strict neutrality was being enforced, the British watch had been removed from these islands, so that there was not one of His Majesty's warships nearer than sixty miles. The question now was, where had *Macedonia* gone? Besides other means of obtaining information regarding secret rendezvous, it was possible to obtain valuable intelligence by decoding messages wirelessed from the high-power station at Nauen, Germany. The conclusion come to was that the delinquent had made for a rendezvous with *Kronprinz Wilhelm* on the equator in Long. 33 W. (This position is to the south-west of St. Paul Rocks, and well clear to the westward of north-east trade routes from Pernambuco to St. Vincent and Tenerife.)

A sweep was therefore begun to include that area, and so we have a kind of nautical detective hunt played over the South Atlantic by ships and naval officers doing their best to follow up the clues available. Picture, then, that beautiful light cruiser *Gloucester* (Captain W. A. Howard Kelly), which had so distinguished herself in hanging on to the skirts of the German battle-cruiser *Goeben* when the latter was scurrying out of the Mediterranean to the Bosphorus at the opening of the war. Captain Kelly now began combing the ocean from the equatorial position just mentioned towards the north-west. This would bring him into the vicinity of that spot where *Otavi* had parted company from *Kronprinz Wilhelm* on December 21 in the "dead" zone between the north-east and north-west trade routes. (See Chapter IX.)

By noon of March 27 the equatorial position was reached and then, twenty-four hours later, after steaming north-westerly, Captain Kelly came up to a steamer flying Dutch colours bearing the name *Hendrick*. The latter was steering to the south-east, and immediately on sighting the cruiser altered course to the north. But it was hopeless for her to try escaping from this fast *Gloucester*, who overhauled her and sent off a boarding party. She was found to be *Macedonia* herself, and thus we have a ship intended for *Kronprinz Wilhelm*

K

becoming herself a prize. The German crew were removed, and a prize crew from *Gloucester* put aboard: but *Macedonia's* chief engineer, four warrant officers, and eight hands all volunteered to work in her, so they received the same wages as they had been paid by the German owners.

To-day we know that the spot where *Macedonia* was to await *Kronprinz* was Lat. 3 N, Long. 37 W, and she was to remain there from April 9 to 23. Thierfelder knew that he would be in want of coal, and it is interesting to remark that in a direct line SE of this spot, some 600 miles distant, he was this self same day making his final capture. But this scoop by *Gloucester*, based on wireless intelligence, was one of the causes for bringing the hectic career of Thierfelder to an end. The supply system had at last broken down, and the inevitable end faced him. He could scarcely complain that the fates had been unkind to him, and even this month he might quite reasonably have been given a knock-out blow. By a slight alteration of odds *Gloucester* could have run him down, but other cruisers were very hot on the track, visiting every rendezvous and coaling base that had become known through intercepted wireless and other collated data. There were few secrets now which the Atlantic still kept unrevealed. Thus British cruisers had been searching Lavandeira Reef, and that mid-Atlantic rendezvous of Lat. 1 N, Long. 20 W, mentioned at the beginning of this chapter. Admiral Stoddart with H.M.S. *Sydney*, the armed merchant cruiser *Edinburgh Castle*, and two wireless colliers were sweeping northwards from Abrolhos Rocks early in March, but without result.

Such was Thierfelder's desperate need for supplies that a second interned German steamer about this time did her best to come out and succour him. This was the *Odenwald* which had been lying at San Juan, Porto Rico, since the war started. On March 22, taking advantage of night, she tried to escape from harbour, yet she was fired on by the port authorities and compelled to return. But the attempt necessitated H.M.S. *Melbourne* being detached to watch off San Juan from

RAIDERS AND WIRELESS 147

March 24 until *Odenwald* was definitely known to have been again interned on March 29.

All this, then, by way of interlude to show how the drama was proceeding as viewed from another angle. We can continue the story as seen from the bridge of *Kronprinz Wilhelm* after the capture of *Semantha* on February 3. This was her furthest south, and after the unsuccessful sally in which she had sunk nothing between that date and January 14, she returned north to the South American trade route above Pernambuco but south of St. Paul Rocks and well to the east of the north-east track. It was a sensible procedure and bound to yield good results as it had hitherto, this area being as nearly fool-proof as it is possible to make any region.

On February 22 Thierfelder captured the British S.S. *Chasehill*, 4583 tons, here (Lat. 6.15 S, Long. 26.10 W). In view of the gloomy prospects for getting fuel from any more supply ships, this prize was most welcome and again one of those colliers bound for South America extricated the big liner from an awkward situation. For *Chasehill* had a cargo of 2860 tons of coal which she was taking to the River Plate. Times were getting difficult for Thierfelder, and this was only the fifth capture since the new year opened. But next day on this spot he captured the French mail S.S. *Guadeloupe* which was bound from Rio for Bordeaux, and was carrying among her cargo a quantity of grey cloth for the French Army. This fabric came in most conveniently, as the liner had been six months at sea and new clothes were needed. Thus out of French material German uniforms were made. *Guadeloupe* was sunk in Lat. 7 S, Long. 26 W, at 7 p.m. on March 9, but *Chasehill* was kept till all the coal had been taken out of her, and in this process the latter was considerably knocked about.

Thierfelder was now in the awkward predicament of having no tender but 294 prisoners from the British collier and the French liner. Some of these were women and children, and there was nothing for it but to send them in *Chasehill* to a near South American port. They reached Pernambuco on March 12. Once again *Kronprinz Wilhelm* had a narrow escape, for on the morning of March 10 the British armed merchant cruiser *Macedonia* (not to be confused with the German steamer of the same name) passed close to where *Chasehill* and *Guadeloupe* had been seized. There followed another unprofitable lull till March 24 when the raider stopped the British S.S. *Tamar*, 3207 tons, a little further to the north and some 500 miles ENE of Pernambuco. But this vessel's cargo consisted of coffee, so she was not much good to the German, who sank her by gunfire. On March 27 a little to the south-west of this position (that is, 460 miles NE½N of Pernambuco) Thierfelder encountered the 3824-ton British S.S. *Coleby*, which likewise was no use as a prize. He therefore set her on fire by shelling her, and the 5500 tons of South American wheat were destroyed.

It was this very day that to the north-west *Kronprinz's* intended supply ship *Macedonia* was captured by *Gloucester*, and this was the climax of the German-American liner's cruise. Thierfelder had now sunk his last ship, he was alone in the world without one single tender; his own fine vessel that once had been the pride of the Atlantic, the last word in safety and luxury, was now in a badly damaged condition with her hull all misshapen owing to the vessels which had been lashed alongside. Her captain recognized that this raiding exploit was just about played out; the British cruisers and more stringent regulations imposed by neutral countries had altogether changed the nature of this war against commerce. Wisely had Köhler in *Karlsruhe* elected to give up the effort and attack Barbados instead, where the only defence consisted of a few local volunteers armed with rifles.

Unable to obtain coal or provisions, many of his crew being down with either beri-beri or scurvy, all of them stale and tired after being afloat during eight months of only moderate success and imminent peril, Thierfelder now decided that it was time to quit. He therefore had no alternative but to intern his ship at some neutral port, and he chose the United States for his asylum.

RAIDERS AND WIRELESS 149

The nearest convenient harbour was Newport News, Virginia, but all risk was not yet ended. Off the entrance to Chesapeake Bay, where three centuries earlier had arrived that little squadron from England bringing Captain John Smith and the first permanent settlers of North America, was now lying another English ship. This was H.M.S. *Suffolk*, and it was a strange but suitable occurrence that this cruiser should be here. Was this not the flagship in which Admiral Cradock at the beginning of the raider's cruise had caught her alongside *Karlsruhe* and frightened her away? But the Admiral had long since shifted his flag to *Good Hope*, in which he went down to his death at the Battle of Coronel.

On April 11 at 5 a.m., having taken advantage of darkness and successfully eluded *Suffolk*, *Kronprinz Wilhelm* steamed into Newport News. Four days previously another raider, *Prinz Eitel Friedrich*, had been here interned, and this was known to *Kronprinz Wilhelm* by intercepting British wireless messages. It was because there was reason to think *Prinz Eitel Friedrich* was about to steam out again that there assembled off the Chesapeake early in April several British men-of-war till it was definitely known that internment had taken place on April 7. Now *Kronprinz Wilhelm*, having learned that the detention had been enforced; having also noticed that the wireless signalling between the British men-of-war had ceased, came to the conclusion that these had all dispersed save one, and it would be a justifiable risk to enter Chesapeake Bay under cover of night. She certainly succeeded, although *Suffolk* was lying stopped at the entrance to the channel. It was from a passing steamer the cruiser ultimately learned that *Kronprinz Wilhelm* had arrived.

But the old game of German bluff was not yet dead. *Prinz Eitel Friedrich* up till April 6 had been showing considerable signs of activity, and Thierfelder seems to have got a second enthusiasm. He requested permission of the United States to remain three weeks so as to have repairs made to his ship that had been caused by ramming the *Wilfred M.* and by coaling. The American authorities firmly refused to allow any repairs where the injury had not been caused solely by the sea. She was allowed to enter dry dock on April 19 and undocked on April 22, during which her weedy bottom was scraped and anti-fouled. But neither her bows, nor the plates along her side, had been repaired, and on April 26 she was at last interned. That was well, for outside there were British cruisers ready for her and resolved that she should not escape again.

During this same month the United States Government objected that British cruisers off New York were in the line of fire from American shore guns, and in the way of ordnance tests being carried on from Sandy Hook. The presence of these cruisers was caused by the fear that some of the thirty interned German liners in New York might break forth and cause further raiding havoc. But the United States having affirmed their intention not to relax vigilance in the maintenance of neutrality, the British Admiralty ordered the cruisers to keep outside the line of fire, i.e. thirteen miles away.

Thus ended the cruise of the converted four-funnelled liner *Kronprinz Wilhelm,* which proved that a huge ship with such an extravagant coal consumption was a continuous source of anxiety to her commanding officer and was rendered helpless as soon as the German supply system was cut off. A smaller ship, with less speed than the unnecessary 23 knots and an economical need of fuel, would have been far more unrestricted in her movements and therefore likely to spend more days in actual warfare. The aim of a raider should not be to loot but to assist in breaking the enemy's will to fight : this the raider does by destroying as many cargoes and as many cargo-carrying ships as possible. The coaling, the transference of provisions and stores, have no direct military value but are a waste of time, though occasionally inevitable.

Kronprinz Wilhelm, whilst exceedingly lucky, certainly did well with such ridiculously weak armament, which would not have been much use later in the war when so many steamers were defensively armed, and utterly useless against any British cruiser that might have been encountered from day to day. Thierfelder had a difficult task, and we cannot but respect his bravery for having kept the sea all those weary months under tropical heat with never a chance of going ashore, and all the uncertainty of finding essential supplies. It is not surprising that lack of good fresh food brought down to ill-health the crew of even a modern liner fitted with all sorts of convenience, refrigerating machinery and perfect cooking facilities. There are indeed many lessons to be learned from this ambitious cruise how not to carry on the raiding of commerce.

CHAPTER XI

AN HISTORIC DUEL

WE have seen how well organized was the German Mercantile Marine, and that those ships acted in accordance with the handbook of procedure telling them what to do and where to go in the event of war. This manual had been issued in 1912 after the Agadir crisis, when Britain and Germany were much nearer to fighting than many people realise. It was laid down that care should be taken to avoid the usual steamship routes, reach port at night, approach it from the open sea; and it was further ordered that the distinguishing funnel markings were to be painted over.

But long before this date the British Government had gone into the question of dealing with its own merchant shipping under such circumstances, and by the agreement with the Cunard Company alone, made in 1903, every vessel of this line was to be at the Admiralty's disposal. Various well-known units, such as *Aquitania, Mauretania, Campania, Caronia,* and *Carmania* were at one time or another commandeered, but it is with the last-mentioned that we are about to devote our consideration, since her exploit is unique in the whole of the Great War's history. Indeed, we have to go back several generations into the sailing-ship age before we find any parallel. Whilst German-American passenger ships were turned into armed merchant cruisers for the purposes of raiding commerce, a number of British liners were similarly converted but for exactly the opposite intention. Germany's commercial shipping as a whole acted on the defensive, sought immunity in neutral harbours, and therefore could not be harried: Britain's liners and tramps generally carried on much as usual.

AN HISTORIC DUEL

Those few passenger steamers which were armed offensively could not be employed to raid German commerce; for all seaborne Teutonic trade suddenly faded out when the bugles of war sounded. But it was for protecting British trade and seeking out raiders that certain liners of the Cunard and other companies were required. Some liners, dating from the first autumn, were needed as we have seen for enforcing the northern blockade.

Our story begins at 8 a.m. on August 7, 1914, three days after hostilities broke out, and the scene is the Liverpool landing-stage, where *Carmania* had just arrived from across the Atlantic and was landing her passengers as quickly as they could step across the gangways; but then she was taken into dock to discharge her cargo, to coal, and fit out as an armed merchant cruiser. The change over from the character of a luxurious transatlantic floating hotel to a grim warship proceeded with amazing speed. Gangs of workmen were soon painting the red funnels black, shipwrights were cutting away bulwarks on one of her decks to allow guns to train round the necessary arcs; armour plates were placed over vital spots, rope protection to deflect splinters was devised, all woodwork between decks was stripped off, passengers' cabins put ashore for fear of fire, magazines built into the holds, speaking-tubes installed to connect with the steering-room aft, eight 4·7-inch guns mounted; searchlights and a naval range-finder were fitted, white upper works were painted a dull grey. All this was completed within a week from the time of her arrival in the Mersey.

In the meanwhile her personnel had been provided, Captain Noel Grant, R.N., being appointed by the Admiralty in command, with Lieut.-Commander E. Lockyer, R.N., as First Lieutenant. Her peace-time master was Captain J. C. Barr, who was made Commander, R.N.R. "On the arrival of the ship at Liverpool from New York," Captain Grant has related, "I went on board and told Captain Barr that I had orders to commission the *Carmania* as an armed merchant-cruiser, that I wanted him to go with me, and I wanted the whole engine-room complement from the chief engineer to the last-joined trimmer. Captain Barr did not hesitate one moment. He said he would go in any capacity. He then sent for Mr. Drummond, the chief engineer, who selected his officers and men, with the result that the whole department, without one exception, volunteered for the job."

Several Cunard officers and a number of ratings remained, and a number of ranks and ratings from the Royal Fleet Reserve and Royal Naval Reserve arrived from Portsmouth, the able seamen being largely composed of those sturdy Scottish fishermen who did such magnificent work afloat in all manner of warships. A number of Marines also joined the ship's company. So on August 15 with her bunkers full, a couple of naval semaphores showing up prominently, and her general appearance suggestive of an interesting warrior, the transformed *Carmania* went steaming down the Mersey, up the Irish Channel, across ocean to Bermuda where she arrived on August 22, coaled, and was next placed under Admiral Cradock's orders. She had taken every opportunity of dropping a target and doing some gunnery practice at sea, and the excellent firing had showed Captain Grant that his scratch crew would be likely to acquit themselves well if they ever went into action.

On September 11 *Carmania* was ordered to intercept, with the co-operation of H.M.S. *Cornwall*, the German collier *Patagonia*, which was about to leave Pernambuco and had been working with *Karlsruhe*, but reached Bahia Blanca this month from Pernambuco, having evaded capture. *Carmania* was now given instructions to inspect that lonely Trinidada Island, which in a previous chapter we saw being used as a raiders' base for coaling. Soon after dawn on September 14 *Carmania* sighted this lofty desolation sticking up out of the sea, and by 11 a.m. was able to make out the upper works of a large vessel lying in the western side. The day was bright and clear, and it was seen that the vesssel had a couple of funnels. Now that fact was significant.

AN HISTORIC DUEL

Was she a British man-of-war? Certainly not. Not one was in the neighbourhood. A British merchant ship perhaps? Impossible. She would not have any reason for being at Trinidada. Obviously, therefore, this was a German. But who was she?

It may be said at once that neither then nor till several days afterwards was her identity known. She could hardly be *Dresden*, for the latter had three funnels; nor the *Karlsruhe*, nor the *Kronprinz Wilhelm*, each of which had four funnels. As a fact this was the Hamburg-South American liner *Cap Trafalgar*, a brand-new ship which had just been built with three funnels. One of the latter was a dummy and used for ventilation purposes, but had been got rid of. This luxurious ship of 18,710 tons and 17½ knots was not very dissimilar from the *Carmania* of 19,524 tons and 16 knots. *Cap Trafalgar* had reached Buenos Aires just before war began and at once became suspect: she was the very kind of craft that would make an excellent armed merchant cruiser. The Argentine authorities had her searched, but could find nothing warlike on board.

It is true that she had 2100 tons of coal on arrival, but her bunker capacity was 4000 tons. After discharging her cargo at Buenos Aires, she sailed at 5 p.m. on August 17, and it was thought that she had taken 3500 tons of coal as well as large baulks of timber for shoring up her gun positions: yet on reaching Monte Video she was again searched, when only 2100 tons of coal and no warlike stores were discovered. She now bunkered, took in 1600 tons and left on August 23 nominally for Europe via Las Palmas. This, of course, was pure bluff, for after leaving the River Plate she met at sea the German gunboat *Eber* which had (as already mentioned in a previous chapter) come across from South Africa with the collier *Steiermark*, and received *Eber's* armament consisting of two 4-inch and six 1·4-inch machine-guns. *Cap Trafalgar* had then cruised for a fortnight with the aim of attacking British commerce, though she had no success whatsoever, and in the meanwhile *Eber* reached Bahia on September 5 flying the German mercantile ensign. Commander Wirth was in command of *Cap Trafalgar*, but so frequently did he hear the wireless of British cruisers that he was frightened away from the trade routes.

For about a week this German raider had been at Trinidada when *Carmania*, a triple screw, turbine-driven eleven-year-old vessel began to approach the island. The Cunarder had been seen, and the Hamburg-South American began to stoke up, smoke issuing from both funnels. Lying alongside the *Cap Trafalgar* were two smaller steamers, but before *Carmania* could raise their hulls on the horizon these two cast off and made respectively for the north-west and south-east.

Captain Grant had to display caution at first. Who knew but at the other side of Trinidada there might be lurking in ambush some German cruisers? Who could say that there was not a signal party ashore to semaphore which side of the island *Carmania* was about to pass? Captain Grant determined to keep any watcher guessing and steered for the middle of Trinidada, intending when close to go suddenly east. But; having discovered this big German liner, he decided to keep the latter to starboard and steered south-west. At 11.30 all hands that could be spared in *Carmania* were sent to dinner. *Cap Trafalgar* seemed inclined to run away, for when the second collier had left her side, the German liner hove up anchor, backed out from the land, then went ahead and followed the first collier that was already out of sight at the back of the island. (The latter was the S.S. *Berwind*, flying the "Stars and Stripes", having been, as we saw in a previous chapter, chartered from United States owners.)

Carmania began to chase, but *Cap Trafalgar* now swung round to starboard and headed across about four points on the former's bow. The enemy was flying no flag, was painted grey, with red "boot-topping", red funnels with black tops. She therefore had the appearance of a Union-Castle liner and might have been about to attack the South African route shortly, for she could have reached the St. Helena neighbourhood in less than four days, and done immense amount

AN HISTORIC DUEL 157

of harm. *Eber* conceivably may have given some useful information as to this trade.

But in spite of her disguise *Cap Trafalgar* was too stockily built, too like such a steamer as *Berlin* to be anything except German. Smart she certainly was, for she had made only one voyage. Surprised she was likewise, for she must have expected to see a Cunarder anywhere save at Trinidada.

At noon *Carmania's* crew were sent to general quarters, and the largest British White Ensigns were hoisted at both mastheads as well as at the staff at the stern. It was still a small matter of doubt as to whether the German was armed, so at 8500 yards the Cunarder fired a shot across the other's bows, and only at the last minute did *Cap Trafalgar* run up the German White Ensign. From now the duel between two nearly matched liners began, and it was to be a fight to a finish. Flashes were seen fore and aft along the German's decks, and shells came shrieking over *Carmania's* bridge to fall some 50 yards to starboard into the sea.

"Let him have it!" shouted Captain Grant, and three guns on the port side which would bear now blazed away. The first rounds fell short, but the range was soon found, and in order that the fourth gun might come into action Captain Grant ported a little. Some excellent gunnery ensued, practically every round being a hit. But one German shell had burst on *Carmania's* starboard side killing one of the gun's crew and wounding others. Hits were frequent on both sides, and next the German closed to 3500 yards so as to bring her machine-gun into use. There came a shell which carried away *Carmania's* fire-control and made it no longer possible to telephone ranges from the bridge to the guns. The German was shelling concentratedly on *Carmania's* guns and bridge, in order to make the duel no longer possible. The danger was that the machine-gun fire might make the bridge quite untenable and thus throw into confusion the direction of the ship. Therefore Captain Grant ported, and in turning away to starboard increased the range, brought the aftermost 4.7-inch to bear, so that for a few seconds five of the eight guns were engaging *Cap Trafalgar*. But the latter ported also, bringing the guns on her port side to bear.

By this time it was apparent that the German had a distinct list to starboard; she had also been on fire forward but this conflagration had evidently been put out. The aim of Captain Grant was now to sink his enemy by direct attack at the waterline, and of course the shells went through the steel plates with disastrous effect so that the Atlantic poured in rapidly. Now this kind of single-ship fight between combatants that had been created for peace and comfort, for safety and luxury, was inevitably bound to cause grievous damage to both parties : there is something painful in the situation of two such noble examples of shipwrightry being put to such intolerable tests. Still, war is war, and raiders had to be fought wherever and whenever found. Those of us who crossed the ocean in *Carmania* when she first began her voyaging, and remember how with a beam wind she was almost as sensitive as a sailing vessel, could not have imagined that she should ever have endured the terrific hammering of battle.

Ventilators, rigging, derricks, and boats were showing ugly scars; German shells had penetrated into the second class smoke-room, where a few weeks previously nothing more explosive than a soda-water bottle had ever been heard. In the petty officers' mess some rounds had fallen with damage to hammocks, beds, and clothing, though happily not to human lives. In a single-ship contest a hundred years previously the decision would have been fought out at close quarters, but in this modern engagement between two crack steamers of rival companies the range never got less than 2900 yards, or about $1\frac{1}{2}$ miles. As the distance widened, it was very obvious that *Cap Trafalgar* had not gained immunity by having closed for the benefit of her machine-guns : she was listing in a doomed manner.

A conflagration had broken forth in Captain Grant's sleeping cabin through the impact of a shell, though soon put out thanks to the arrangements made for

AN HISTORIC DUEL

flooding. But presently the flames below the bridge again broke forth, and there were no means of putting them out, inasmuch as the water main had been shot through. Thus the bridge became uninhabitable and blazed fiercely.

From now, therefore, *Carmania* had to be conned aft, and she was in considerable danger of becoming that awful phenomenon, a burning wreck. But her peace-time master, Captain Barr, who knew her well down to her smallest rivet, did remarkable work in this crisis. "Captain Barr," remarked Captain Grant, "was of the greatest assistance to me during the action, and it was due to his initiative that the fire below the bridge did not extend to the next deck." She presented a battered picture, with this holocaust forward, the decks around the guns knee-deep in expended cartridge-cylinders, the port side of her main rigging shot away and hanging in meaningless festoons, the wireless aerials all gone, long ago, some of the ventilator cowls ridiculously ribboned, a huge hole gaping on the port side of the upper deck, where a shell in its travel had been turned upwards against the side of the wheelhouse and then had passed through the after-bridge. In so doing, steel rails and stanchions had been twisted like bits of wire, whilst everywhere about the decks were fragments of boats and davits in a medley of destruction.

As to *Cap Trafalgar*, the listing of this tall ship went from bad to worse. She was still shelling rapidly, but with decreasing accuracy, and widening the range till the distance was now about five miles. Captain Grant, whilst realizing that this was about the extreme radius of *Carmania's* guns, kept his ship dead before the wind ; it meant increasing the range still further, but it was necessary to prevent the bridge conflagration from spreading. The German was badly alight, too, enveloped in smoke, and was noticed to be heading back to the island. Her guns became silent, she stopped her engines, began to lower her boats, and this was the time for *Carmania* to cease firing likewise ; every effort aboard the Cunarder being concentrated on stamping out the raging furnace that threatened death to all.

In *Cap Trafalgar* another race against destiny was being made. Half a dozen boats had been lowered from her and got away : no easy evolution from a height of 70 feet, with the great hull listing as if to drop on the men any moment. Two or three miles away still waited one of her colliers, an awed spectator of an historic occasion, so to her these escaping Germans pulled. And then, just one hour and a half after the first shot had been fired, the newly built *Cap Trafalgar* heeled her enormous sides over till she capsized to starboard, her funnels lapping the Atlantic, and she disappeared bows first with colours still flying. Her death-agony was impressive, and no sailor could fail to notice how this mass of 18,710 tons seemed for a period to hesitate, heave herself upright with bows submerged, then suddenly tilt at a worse angle till her stern came out of water before taking a final plunge into the deep. Nothing now remained except a few swirling eddies, the usual indefinite debris, and the small white dots of lifeboats rowing hard towards safety. The crew of *Carmania* crowded to watch in awed silence this dramatic passing of a fine ship. And then, as if to relieve feelings so long pent up, a cheer was raised both for a gallant foe and for *Carmania's* victory.

Commander Wirth was among those of the Germans killed. Captain Barr, who was not aware of this, remarked on a later occasion : "I do not know his name, but he is the only German I would care to meet, for he put up a very gallant fight." And that was the general feeling of the vanquishers. *Carmania* was in a bad way herself, with severe wounds, nearly one quarter of her guns' crews and ammunition-supply parties now casualties. Fresh smoke was seen on the horizon, and it was thought this might be another raider : indeed, it has been stated that it was *Kronprinz Wilhelm* coming to aid *Cap Trafalgar*. That is not correct, for *Kronprinz* was (as we have seen) not as far south, though she did receive wireless news of the action. More likely the smoke was that belonging to one of *Cap Trafalgar's* colliers. At any rate Captain

CAPTAIN NOEL GRANT, R.N.
Commanding officer of armed merchant cruiser *Carmania*.

COMMANDER J. C. BARR, R.N.R.
Second-in-Command of *Carmania*

AN HISTORIC DUEL 161

Grant, with his ship in a crippled tangle, well appreciated that *Carmania* was in no condition to fight another engagement. She had been hit by 79 projectiles, and there were 304 holes in her.

All internal communications and all navigational instruments had been destroyed by the conflagration, and it remained for the commanding officer to get her away into safety as well and as soon as he could. He therefore proceeded full speed to the south, and at dusk altered course for the Abrolhos Rocks, which he reached in spite of uncertain navigation and having to steer the ship from aft. During the night *Carmania* got in wireless touch with H.M.S. *Bristol*, arranged with her a rendezvous for the morning so that under the escort of this cruiser as well as *Cornwall* the Abrolhos anchorage was attained by 8 a.m. *Carmania* had steered to the south-west by the sun and north-east wind, until such time as some remains of the navigational gear could be fixed up. This is how Captain Grant describes the situation :

"When I first looked round after the action, I found we were in a very uncomfortable position, having no effective compasses, no charts, no chronometer or sextant or wireless code. The ship had to be steered from the after lower position, the only communication from the deck being a relay of men to pass the word down the engine-room skylight by blasts on a mouth whistle. I afterwards found that two midshipmen, Mr. Coulson (who, I am sorry to say, was later on in the war killed in a submarine) and Mr. Dickens, had gone out to the burning bridge and, at great personal risk, got the bowl of the standard compass, some charts, and the remains of the much-burnt wireless code. A sextant was found in a cabin between decks, so that by fixing the compass on a long pole, and deadening the vibration by placing it on a feather pillow, we were able to steer a moderately correct course, and we were very pleased to find our signals passing through correct enough to enable the *Bristol* to take us up the next morning, and escort us to a safe anchorage where we met other ships, and with their

L

THE SEA-RAIDERS

help we were able to make the ship seaworthy for the cross-Atlantic trip to Gibraltar."

Cornwall's engineers helped to patch up her holes temporarily, some navigational instruments were borrowed, and on the evening of September 17, escorted by that other armed merchant-cruiser, *Macedonia*, *Carmania* started off for Gibraltar amid the cheering of *Cornwall* and two colliers. On the way north two days later she passed *Canopus*, whose people cheered her likewise. That same afternoon—the 19th—she touched at Pernambuco, whence Captain Grant sent his despatches to the Admiralty, and nine days later arrived at Gibraltar where she underwent a long refit. She then was again commissioned as an armed merchant-cruiser till she was returned to her owners in May 1916. When war ended this wonderful ship was again put on the Atlantic passenger service as if she had done nothing else all her life. But the duel has now become a part of naval history, and as a distinguished Admiral (since dead, one of whose ancestors fought under Nelson at Trafalgar) remarked, there never was a single-ship action which reflected greater credit both on the Royal Navy and on the Mercantile Marine. Very aptly has it been compared with the fight between *Shannon* and *Chesapeake*. Both *Carmania* and *Cap Trafalgar* were well fought, well handled, and fairly well matched, though the German had better guns.

"The action," says Captain Grant, "was the only* one throughout the war in which an equal, or as a matter of fact a slightly inferior, vessel annihilated the superior force. My contention that we were the inferior vessel is based on the fact that the *Cap Trafalgar* was a faster ship and outranged ours by 2000 yards. I am therefore thankful that the German Captain came in towards me and put up a perfectly fair fight, instead of taking advantage of these two great assets in a naval action. I shall always feel proud of the fact that it was my great good fortune to command a ship in action in which the glorious traditions of the British Navy were upheld by every soul on board."

---

* This is not quite accurate. See the incident in Chapter XVII.

AN HISTORIC DUEL

The total casualties were nine killed or mortally wounded, and twenty-six wounded. On Captain Grant and Captain Barr the King conferred the Order of the Companion of the Bath, whilst two of the crew received the Distinguished Service Medal. Had *Macedonia* whilst escorting *Carmania* met and sunk *Kronprinz Wilhelm*, German commerce raiding would have received another ugly blow, and fate might have so ordered the encounter had not *Kronprinz* remained in the Trinidada area till the end of September. But the destruction of *Cap Trafalgar* and discovery of Trinidada as a coaling base, together with the detention of so many supply colliers, came as a serious discouragement to the German Admiralty, who on September 20 sent out from Norddeich long-distance wireless station to one of their interned liners at Lisbon—and thence broadcast elsewhither—the information that all German coaling rendezvous had been compromised excepting possibly the spot where *Eber* had met *Cap Trafalgar*. Nauen sent this message to all German cruisers at sea, and thus increased their anxieties of receiving supplies.

Cap Trafalgar's survivors after having been picked up by the collier were landed at Buenos Aires, where they became interned. It was thus at last unmistakable evidence began to gather that the elaborate German Supply System was beginning to be broken up, not so much by British cruisers hunting the raiders as by trying to discover the latter's rendezvous, and by keeping a watch on ports where suspected supply ships were known to be and likely to break out. The weakness of Germany's raiding strategy, dependent as it was on the violation of neutral waters persistently, and on the secrecy of lonely rendezvous, became only too apparent after the first phase of war. Looking back calmly on this conception we can see that in spite of her usual thoroughness and detailed organization, there was a lack of penetrating imagination and there was an entirely restricted vision. Any campaign based on the snatch-and-grab principles of the common thief must inevitably fail, unless the war should be certain to conclude in a very few months.

THE SEA-RAIDERS

Later on, as we shall shortly watch, the German Admiralty having learned its lesson by bitter failure, and having scrapped this indifferent plan of raiding, found a sounder method than employing light cruisers or fast Atlantic liners. But before we come to that stage we have still to trace the exploits of one more of her liners which went raiding and after a hectic career was compelled to give up the hunt. Her voyage is particularly interesting, as it extended from one end of the world to almost the other. Indeed, except that she went the opposite way round, there is something comparable with Drake's circumnavigation, though she never completed the circle. We have to live again in the days of the notorious eighteenth-century pirates roving over Pacific, Atlantic, and other seas, before we can quite match the adventures of *Prinz Eitel Friedrich*. So far we have merely outlined her finale : let us now examine her cruise from the beginning.

CHAPTER XII

PRINZ EITEL FRIEDRICH'S VOYAGE

THE value to a nation during war of a Merchant Fleet in being—even if that fleet be scattered about the globe—was well illustrated not merely in European waters but in the Far East. At the same time the difficulty of finding crews for the specialized work of gunnery was one that had to be faced just when reservists were urgently required for regular naval vessels. The victory of *Carmania* was very largely that of the Mercantile Marine ; and the affirmations of commanding naval officers as to the indispensable work of such crews temporarily turned into fighting men are so unanimous and enthusiastic, that it shows how invaluable is this very silent navy which goes about its work in fishing trawlers, tramp steamers, and liners without anyone taking much notice of its wonderful seamanhood. Whilst the Grand Fleet was the very basis of British warlike strength, yet its commercial fleet was part of the essential structure.

"In the *Kent*," Vice-Admiral J. D. Allen, her former commanding officer, wrote to me, "my crews was composed of three-fifths Merchant Service, and five men in every gun's crew were Scotch fishermen. I have an immense admiration for what our merchant and fishing seamen did in the war. Personally, I think that, but for them, we shouldn't have won the war." When we recollect that, single-handed, the old-fashioned *Kent* by her gunnery sank *Nurnberg*—one of the crack gunnery ships in the German Navy—this is remarkable testimony. We have also just seen what Captain Noel Grant thought of the *Carmania's* crew, and it is worth putting on record that with the exception of this commanding officer, his First Lieutenant, the Acting Sub-Lieutenant, the retired Fleet-Surgeon, the three active-service ratings, every officer and man of the big ship's personnel was a reservist.

Thus, when we turn to the China Station and witness the beginning of the war in that area we find both Britain and Germany looking round to employ liners to assist. In the case of the former, Vice-Admiral Sir Thomas Jerram, Commander-in-Chief, China, could rely on several steamers belonging to the Canadian Pacific and the P. & O. Lines. As an instance of the varied work which one shipping company can alone perform, it is interesting to note that the Canadian Pacific S.S. *Caligarian* was first employed with H.M.S. *Vindictive* off the mouth of the Tagus to prevent German steamers interned at Lisbon from issuing as raiders. Next she was patrolling the Atlantic trade routes looking out for raiders, and eventually was stationed outside New York to prevent any German liners escaping on a raiding cruise. She finally ended her career when convoying a fleet of thirty vessels across the Atlantic on March 1, 1918. Four torpedoes destroyed her and forty-nine lives.

But at Hong Kong during August 1914 were those fine noble Canadian Pacific liners, *Empress of Russia*, *Empress of Asia*, and *Empress of Japan*. These with *Himalaya* were taken in hand, armed, and commissioned as armed merchant-cruisers. *Empress of Russia* had in the course of her normal trans-Pacific passenger service left Vancouver in August 1914, and on reaching Hong Kong that portion of her crew which was Chinese was replaced by British naval reservists in part. But there were not enough to go round. It was only by the further drafting of some British soldiers of the Royal Garrison Artillery, some French gun crews from Chinese river craft, and some Pathan Sepoys that a full complement could be made up. It was *Empress of Russia*, after moving west, which was to take over from H.M.S *Sydney* the crew of the raider *Emden* to be landed at Colombo. In conjunction with Indian Territorial troops, *Empress of Russia* captured the

Turkish Red Sea fort of Kamaran; and for twenty-three days this liner by her four 4·7-inch guns, with her sister *Empress of Asia*, defended the Port of Aden until relieved by British warships, and afterwards reduced to ruins the Arabian fort at Salif which the Turks had refused to surrender.

Now in the same way did Germany make use of such a liner east of Suez as might be suitable for conversion into a merchant cruiser. This was the *Prinz Eitel Friedrich*, owned by the North German Lloyd Company. She was of only moderate size—8897 tons—and the moderate speed of 15 knots, but none the worse for that. Instead of being allowed to continue a voyage just begun from China, she was recalled and received guns as well as additional crew from the two German river-gunboats *Luchs* and *Tiger* that were of negligible fighting value. She was thus able to leave Tsingtau on August 6 with a convoy of supply ships destined for the German Commander-in-Chief, Pacific Squadron, Vice-Admiral Graf von Spee. The latter had left Tsingtau at the end of June with the two cruisers *Scharnhorst* and *Gneisenau* and the tender *Titania*, but on August 12 these vessels were joined at Pagan Island (which is one of the Ladrones group in the Pacific east of the Philippines) by two more of his cruisers—*Nurnberg* and *Emden*. To this island came also *Prinz Eitel Friedrich*. *Emden* was now sent to raid the Indian Ocean, but the liner accompanied von Spee to the Marshall Islands which are still further eastward.

Pagan Island was well placed because it was on the flank of the Yokohama–Sydney trade route, but it was not healthy to remain there long, and no raiding of this track took place. There was the Japanese Fleet to the north, Admiral Jerram's Squadron to the west, and the Australian Squadron somewhere to the south. Before the end of August, von Spee had forsaken the Marshall Islands and proceeded over the Pacific further eastward still. At this stage we may leave the German Admiral and confine our attentions to the armed merchant cruiser *Prinz Eitel Friedrich*, which he now detached with orders to wage war against merchant ships in

Australian waters. With her went another raider named *Cormoran*. This was the Russian Volunteer steamer *Riasan*, 3522 tons, which had been captured by *Emden* on August 4 and taken into Tsingtau, where she received the armament and name of the German gunboat *Cormoran* that could well afford to sacrifice herself.

But these two ships, in being left to raid and obtain supplies from their victims, were awkwardly placed when no victims came along. The raiders found that they had been given a dangerous and impossible task, and it was only the contiguity of German colonies that enabled coal replenishment to be made. For at this time neither German New Guinea nor any of the German islands north of this colony had yet fallen. If the Australian seas were too well watched, there might be a chance further afield. *Cormoran* having hidden herself in the Carolines, till four days after von Spee's destruction at the Falklands, came forth at last, did a two-day steam to the Island of Guam (which lies between the Carolines and Ladrones) and again came to rest. But Guam happens to be owned by the United States, who promptly interned her next day. *Cormoran* thus had a career of complete uselessness; and German colonies having fallen into the Allies' hands she was in effect starved out. Here then is an illustration that the modern steamship raider, when once robbed of either bases or supply ships, is in such a hopeless situation that she must give in.

Prinz Eitel Friedrich, however, was able to fill up her bunkers just before the colonial collapse came, then went east across the Pacific from an area that could hold out no possibilities, and sought to rejoin her Admiral. She had a lonely voyage, but at last, on October 27, came up with the German Pacific Squadron, which had been to Easter Island and was now at Mas-a-Fuera, thankful not to have been caught by any British cruisers of the Australian Squadron. Thus far, then, the liner had done nothing but consume coal. She now kept with her Admiral till she was despatched to Valparaiso on a special mission. Von Spee's Squadron

PRINZ EITEL FRIEDRICH'S VOYAGE

needed coal, and *Prinz Eitel* was therefore sent ahead to ensure that this could be done. On October 31 she nearly made her first capture when she sighted and chased the British S.S. *Colusa*, 5732 tons. But a Chilean warship saved the latter from being molested in neutral waters.

Next day was fought the battle of Coronel, and three days later she was also in Valparaiso, her stay on November 1 having been for only a couple of hours. On November 8 *Prinz Eitel*, now well filled with coal, again joined up with von Spee, who had taken his squadron to Mas-a-Fuera after his victory over Admiral Cradock. But presently we see this much-travelled liner sent off to act independently as a commerce raider off the west coast of South America. The time was opportune, the Germans had just obtained command of the sea in this area, and Allied shipping could not hope for protection along this coast till a new squadron had taken the place of one defeated.

On December 5, when 70 miles south of Valparaiso, after four fruitless months, *Prinz Eitel* at last had a success, for in foggy weather she both surprised and captured the British S.S. *Charcas*, 5067 tons. The latter had a cargo of nitrate, was boarded, and sunk by bombs, the crew being landed the next day near Valparaiso. Now, on leaving for the south to round Cape Horn, Admiral von Spee had given Captain Thierichsens, commanding officer of *Prinz Eitel Friedrich*, orders to remain off the Chilean coast until the early part of December. The object was to bluff the British into thinking the German Pacific Squadron was still thereabouts. But the period of waiting was now passed, the raider was ready to come round into the Atlantic when, on December 10, she intercepted a strange wireless message sent from Monte Video intended for Port Stanley, Falkland Islands. It was this ominous message which induced Captain Thierichsens to guess that von Spee and the Pacific Squadron were lost.

A few days later the wireless of *Prinz Eitel* took in a message from the London *Daily Mail* asking the

Bishop of the Falkland Islands for details concerning the sinking of *Scharnhorst*, *Gneisenau*, and *Leipzig*. This not merely confirmed the worst fears, but made it obvious that for the present at least British naval forces in strength would be commanding the South Atlantic. It would be madness to rush into this trap : the time for rounding the Horn was not yet. She had got well down to the southward and now resolved to retrace her steps and even go right away north-west away from trade routes—in fact, to get within a "dead" zone to Easter Island. It would be safer to repose at this anchorage, which never had a visitor in months, than to hide in some South American bay ; for British cruisers would come searching along that coast for certain. Moreover, Easter Island is so well out towards the western Pacific that she was not badly placed if she should be compelled to retreat across the numerous undefended trade routes which extended from the Orient, Australia, and New Zealand to North and Central America. Many a lonely South Sea island would afford her shelter and some food.

Now on the north-west course towards Easter Island she soon fell in with a great slice of luck which, as we have seen, is the reward of the resolute. In crossing the sailing-ship route she captured on December 11 the French barque *Jean*, which had 3500 tons of Welsh coal for Antofagasta. This incident occurred in Lat. 44.50 S, Long. 81.40 W, or about 300 miles from the Chilean coast. One can easily imagine the great joy at this marvellous good fortune, since the raider was without supply ships and she dared not venture into a South American port for fear of giving away her presence.

Thierichsens was now like a hungry dog that has found a good meaty bone, and desires nothing in the world but some quiet corner where he can enjoy his discovery without interruption. He began taking *Jean* in tow, and on the next day only a little further towards Easter Island he had the happiness of meeting the British barque *Kildalton* coming up from Liverpool via the Horn for Callao. This was in a position about

870 miles SW of Valparaiso. *Kildalton* was a vessel of 1784 tons, but of no value to the German who sank her by bombs after the crew had been taken off, and the raider resumed towing *Jean* to the north-west.

The seamanship of a liner towing a barque for 1800 miles over the ocean intrigues one, though when once in the south-east trade winds towing was no longer necessary. On December 23 the inhabitants of Easter Island were surprised to see the *Prinz Eitel Friedrich*, apparently a peaceable liner, arrive to anchor in Cook's Bay.* As was natural enough, Mr. Edmunds the manager of the island, went aboard the stranger, and Captain Thierichsens stated that he would require thirty or forty beasts as meat after Christmas. The liner's people refused to give any account of themselves, or say anything about the war, and finally, when the Germans were presenting some theatricals aboard on Christmas Eve, Mr. Edmunds declined an invitation lest he should be made a prisoner.

About Christmas-time *Prinz Eitel* went out from the anchorage and came back with *Jean*. The barque was secured alongside after once more anchoring in Cook's Bay, and the coal was transferred to the raider. Thierichsens, however, did not commit the same mistake as the other commanding officer we witnessed. In order to prevent *Jean* from capsizing in the swell after she became light and gradually lost her ballast, he had the French vessel's masts and spars shot away, and on December 31 no further use could be made of an empty ship. *Prinz Eitel* took her out a little to sea still alongside, and then, being within the three-mile limit, cast her off. A sad sight *Jean* looked with only her mizzen standing, and then came her execution: the Germans shelled her till she sank into the ocean.

Prinz Eitel, thus furnished with all the coal and mutton she would require for some time, departed. Her people stated, indeed, that they had enough stores to last till April, which was a pretty accurate forecast. Not till the last moment before sailing did she land the

---
* Vide supra, *The Mystery of Easter Island*, by Mrs. Scoresby Routledge.

crews of *Kildalton* and *Jean*. She could be sure that these forty-eight persons would not be likely to spread news of the raider for many a long day, but actually some of these men died of dysentery, which in some curious way seized the islanders following the *Prinz Eitel's* visit. After two months it so happened that a Swedish vessel called at Easter Island who took off the English crew and part of the French ; a few of the latter preferring to remain, inasmuch as they had undertaken never to bear arms against Germany. Mrs. Routledge records the indignation which the islanders felt at the Germans' behaviour on the occasion of *Prinz Eitel's* visit. Every day the officers used to come ashore, ride over the island, and they "generally behaved as if the whole place belonged to them". Especial anger was caused both by the ship remaining over the legal twenty-four hours, and by their insolence in daring to erect on Rano Aroi—the lofty central peak of the island—a signal station whither they sent an officer with a signal party whose duty was to maintain a lookout and communicate to the raider below news of any approaching ship. When tidings reached the Chilean Government the latter were not less indignant, and formally protested to Germany at this insult.

By that time it was too late : the last of the raiders had touched at this island. But on February 26 there steamed into Coronel the British vessel *Skerries* which brought the strange intelligence that when passing Easter Island she had noticed a party ashore signalling. She therefore went into the anchorage to investigate, and there found the crews of *Jean* and *Kildalton*. When *Skerries* offered to bring them away, the marooned party refused to embark. It was therefore subsequent to this that the arrival of a Swedish ship changed their minds.

As to *Prinz Eitel*, her final departure from Easter Island was on January 6. It was now about a month since von Spee's disaster at the Falklands, and Thierichsens decided to make a gamble, round the Horn, come up the Atlantic, burst his way through the British blockade into the North Sea, and so reach

Germany. To this end he proceeded with extreme cautiousness, so that according to one authority* he went so far south in rounding the Horn as to reach Lat. 61 S. He was thus in the neighbourhood of the Antarctic, encountering much ice and terrible weather : in fact, he passed through that area known to Shackleton and many another sailor as notorious for the worst weather in all the world. But to the captain of *Prinz Eitel* this was indeed preferable to falling into the hands of British warships. He then came north by the sailing-ship route which, as we have noticed, keeps fairly well into mid-Atlantic. And then, all of a sudden, he had a remarkable windfall.

On January 26 he was in Lat. 33 S, Long. 28.30 W, or more than 1300 miles east of the Uruguayan coast, when he sighted and captured the Russian barque *Isobel Browne*; next day, a little further north and east, he captured a French barque named *Pierre Loti* and the American four-master *William P. Frye*; on the 28th he did the same with the French barque *Jacobsen*. Four sailing vessels in three days were ample compensation for his roundabout voyage, and the fate of three of them did not worry him for long ; they were speedily sunk after the crews had been transferred. The case of *William P. Frye*, however, caused him to hesitate. Her cargo consisted of wheat from Seattle for Queenstown, yet she was owned in the United States. His first intention was therefore to destroy the wheat, and release the ship subsequently.

But the task of dumping overboard from a sailing vessel's hold many thousand pounds' worth of grain took longer than the German imagined, so he gave up the task and sank the *William P. Frye*. It was an impulsive and illegal act, creating no little anger in America, the result being that eventually Germany had to pay a heavy compensation.

After these sinkings *Prinz Eitel Friedrich* somewhat modified her plans. At last she had reached an area where she could justify her character late in time as a commerce raider, and she yearned for more. It was

---

* *Seaborne Trade*, Vol. I, by C. Ernest Fayle, London, 1920, p. 374.

worth waiting about if she could find some other sailing vessels which, of all the craft that float, are the most helpless and defenceless during a period of war. The raider at the first week of February was also in easy reach of the locality where *Kronprinz Wilhelm* had arrived. About this time the German Admiralty were sending out wireless messages from Berlin to *Kronprinz Wilhelm* suggesting she should abandon her cruise and lay herself up in either a Spanish or American port. This message evidently impressed Thierichsens, for from now he gave up all idea of running the blockade and reaching Germany. He was content to steam about during a fortnight and was only little more than a couple of hundred miles north-east of where he had sunk *Jacobsen* when on February 12 he captured still another sailing vessel.

This was the British barque *Invercoe*, 1421 tons, carrying wheat from Portland, Oregon, for Great Britain. She was sunk by bombs. The position where this capture was made is not without interest. From Cape Frio (near Rio Janeiro) it is 890 miles E by S$\frac{1}{4}$S, or in Lat. 26.31 S, Long. 26.15 W : that is to say, a mere 30 miles east of the spot where nine days previously *Kronprinz Wilhelm* had captured the sailing-vessel *Semantha*. On sentimental grounds the loss of all these sailing craft is to be regretted since they were never replaced, and thus it will always be laid to Germany's account that she gave the final blow to the moribund era of canvas and spars. But these prizes, whilst wounding the Allies, did not profit the raiders themselves, and Thierichsens must have been bitterly disappointed that not one of this bunch yielded the essential commodity which *Jean* had given him.

The problem of finding coal wherewith to steam from the Antarctic to Germany by way of the Arctic, and the increasing difficulty of getting fuel from German Atlantic supply ships (concerning which *Kronprinz Wilhelm* could well inform him), may have compelled *Prinz Eitel Friedrich's* captain to realize that his first intention was impracticable. Once again the limitation of even an economical steamship for commerce raiding manifested itself. And very shortly another weakness would become equally clear.

Having exhausted the sailing-ship route, Thierichsens now adopted Thierfelder's strategy and went north to get on to that treasure area east of the normal St. Paul Rocks—Fernando Noronha line. Here he was bound to succeed, and when 400 miles east of Pernambuco captured on February 18 the British 3605-ton steamer *Mary Ada Short*, bound from Rosario towards St. Vincent with maize. She was sunk at 11 a.m. just below where *Kronprinz Wilhelm* had captured *Hemisphere* on December 28. Thierichsens may have thought himself unfortunate in again not finding a cargo of coal, yet he was really extremely lucky. It needed only just the amount of delay, which the unloading of a ship would begin to create, for his final disaster. The very next morning there passed within sight of this spot the British armed merchant cruiser *Otranto*, homeward bound with German survivors of the Falklands battle. Only by the narrowest margin were German prisoners thus prevented from seeing a duel between two converted liners.

But *Prinz Eitel* had gone away north-west till she was almost on the regular north-east track, and a little to the north-east of Fernando Noronha in Lat. 2.28 S, Long. 31.10 W, where she now captured and sank the French liner *Floride*. Thence, turning to make east of the track once more but towards St. Paul Rocks, the raider captured on February 20 the British S.S. *Willerby* 490 miles north-east of Pernambuco. As the latter was bound for the Plate in water ballast, it was another disappointment that no fuel was available. She was sunk by bombs in the usual manner.

This was the last prize which *Prinz Eitel Friedrich* ever made. She had reached the desperate stage when she could get no more coal, and now had to face another problem : her boilers and engines, after all this steaming since Tsingtau, so badly needed overhaul that they were breaking down with serious frequency. Such an accumulation of prisoners was she by this time carrying, who were fast consuming the Easter Island mutton, that the captives were as numerous as her crew. To the southward of her *Kronprinz Wilhelm* was entering on her last phase, which could not be much prolonged, and now *Prinz Eitel* must take the advice of interning herself in some neutral harbour.

She selected Newport News in Virginia and began her last 3000 miles of steaming. On the way thither she had another narrow escape, for she passed close to the British armed merchant cruiser *Edinburgh Castle* on February 21-22, which was coming south-west towards South America. On March 11 *Prinz Eitel* managed to get into Newport News and there she landed her prisoners. But how was it that she did not fall into the hands of a British cruiser off the Chesapeake before getting into neutral waters? The answer is that her whereabouts had been a mystifying secret, and the British Navy were not even aware that she was in the Atlantic; for one advantage of a raider's crowding herself up with prisoners, and not sending them away, is that silence can be preserved. Indeed, so little was known of her that on March 7 she was supposed to have been seen off Iquique in the Pacific. Her arrival in the United States was a complete surprise for everybody.

But there was a secondary reason why she safely entered Newport News. It was impossible for watching cruisers to be everywhere at one time, but it was requisite that patrols should be off New York, Halifax, and Bermuda. This meant that the approaches to the Chesapeake, Delaware, and Boston must be neglected. Furthermore, early in this month of March there was a strong rumour that German liners interned at New York were ready at any moment to rush out. The British Admiralty were anxious because there was no United States man-of-war at New York to enforce the regulations of internment: consequently special vigilance by British cruisers was imposed. But after Great Britain had made representations to the American Government this was remedied by the latter sending the old gunboat *Dolphin* (carrying two 4-inch guns) to New York, whilst another U.S.A. warship was sent to Boston.

CARMANIA READY FOR ACTION
Showing rope protection to deflect splinters.

CARMANIA'S RANGEFINDER

PRINZ EITEL FRIEDRICH'S VOYAGE

Prinz Eitel Friedrich at Newport News was allowed to dock for repairs until March 14. It was found that she was armed with four 4-inch, six 12-pounders, and ten pompom guns. During her time in dry-dock this raider effected some repairs, had her bottom anti-fouled, and Thierichsens professed his determination to go out again to sea. This caused no little uneasiness, for there was a suggestion that Germany was at last to try breaking through the barrier which now hemmed in all her raiding hopes. If the New York liners were about to escape—one of them, the S.S. *Pisa*, was reported to have already coaled by March 28 and prepared with supplies—part of the new campaign was to include the breaking forth from Germany of some powerful cruisers, and thus the Atlantic was to be cleaned up of British commercial shipping.

For a period, then, there was apprehension in Whitehall. On April 2 there fell over the Virginian scene a blizzard so fiercely as to wreck all communications with Newport News, and it was feared that *Prinz Eitel* had escaped; but three days later she was taking in stores and showing every intention of sailing. By this time however, H.M.S. *Cumberland* and *Niobe* were waiting off the Chesapeake. On April 6 news came that *Prinz Eitel* had taken her pilot aboard, and it seemed as if something interesting was about to occur. But on April 8 Thierichsens had changed his mind, for on that date he handed the Collector at Newport News an application for internment, giving as his reasons the non-arrival of expected relief, and the impossibility of dashing out when such British cruiser strength awaited him.

Thus, with von Spee's Squadron all at the bottom of the sea, *Karlsruhe* likewise, the two converted liners *Prinz Eitel Friedrich* and *Kronprinz Wilhelm* both interned by the end of April, the seas were again free of German raiders, marine business could go on as usual, passengers and cargoes could be carried all over the well-known routes in confidence and safety. With marvellous celerity had the commerce destroyers been accounted for during the first nine months of war

—a condition that meant everything to an island nation whose very life depended on seaborne commodities.

But just as Germany realized that the campaign of attacking commerce by surface ships was played out, she was instituting a more deadly war by submarine. Admiral von Pohl, Chief of the German Admiralty Staff, declared by a notice in the official *Reichsanzeiger* on February 4, 1915, a submarine blockade : the waters around Great Britain and Ireland were herewith in the war zone ; and that from February 18 every merchant ship met within that zone would be destroyed. There were only twenty-three German submarines to begin this campaign, but the craft grew in numbers and in size as officers grew in experience and extended voyages. The result was that in the last stage of the war, ocean-going submarines were going as far south as the African coast, crossing the Atlantic, and largely taking the place of commerce-raiding cruisers.

But the weakness of these big submarines lay primarily in their limited radius. They had no bases outside the Mediterranean where they could take in oil fuel ; they could not profit by meeting colliers and they could not receive on board more than a handful of prisoners. As, moreover, submarines increased in size, so they took longer to dive. This was a serious factor now that so many merchant vessels were defensively armed, and so many traps were steaming about in the form of Q-ships. Therefore raiding by surface ships was not given up entirely, but Germany adopted new methods in more suitable ships commanded by officers most carefully picked. No effort was made to send out any more genuine naval cruisers to replace *Karlsruhe*, or the Pacific Squadron : the work could not be carried on even by the *Kronprinz Wilhelm, Berlin*, or the *Kaiser Wilhelm der Grosse* type of merchant steamer. It became necessary, also, to be careful of American susceptibilities ; for, apart from the feeling of resentment caused in the United States by Germany's disregard of neutrality, German naval officers by the end of March 1916 had made three serious blunders, any one

PRINZ EITEL FRIEDRICH'S VOYAGE

of which might have brought the United States into the war on the Allies' side:

Firstly, there was the sinking by *Prinz Eitel Friedrich* of the *William P. Frye*. When prisoners landed at Newport News and they were found to include the four-master's crew, there was a howl of indignant anger. Secondly, in the following May came the *Lusitania* folly and frightfulness. Thirdly, on March 24, 1916, came the torpedoing of the British S.S. *Sussex* in the English Channel whilst American passengers were aboard. This caused such a wave of emotion that U-boat warfare in Northern Europe had to be cried off from May 8 till July 5, 1916.

Before closing this chapter it is necessary to mention the raiding voyage of that regular naval cruiser *Leipzig*, which, though of short duration, may well be considered now that the more important features of this first phase have been studied. We have to confine our attention to a comparatively limited part of the west coast of America, and see what possibilities were available. Off this coast British naval forces were very weak. On July 27, 1914, when the precautionary telegram was sent out from Whitehall, the sloop *Shearwater* was at San Diego, and the sloop *Algerine* was off Mazatlan (Gulf of California), whilst the eleven-year-old cruiser *Rainbow* was at Esquimalt. It so happened that the modern and far more able German cruiser *Leipzig* was also off Mazatlan.

Then suddenly came activity, when *Leipzig* left her anchorage on August 2; followed by *Algerine* at 2 a.m. on August 3, in the process of escaping to Esquimalt before *Leipzig* could cut her off. Thirteen hours later left *Shearwater* also for Esquimalt. The German, after departing, went north to coal at Magdalena Bay, and on the 5th steamed still further north up the coast till she arrived off San Francisco by the 11th. During the next few days she cruised about off this port, entered on the 17th, came out the day following, once more cruised up and down till she was at Ballinas Bay, Lower California, on the 28th, and then spent some weeks in concealment whilst the trend of war developed. She was alone, if not isolated, sufficiently in touch with the land to know and be communicated with, and then in September she began her brief career as raider.

It was on September 11 that she captured her first prize. This was off the Mexican coast, some eighty miles south-west of Cape Corrientes, the victim being the British S.S. *Elsinore*, 6542 tons, an oil-tanker in ballast. After the crew had been taken off, the tanker was shelled and sunk. Next, with the tactics customary among raiders, *Leipzig* used the geographical situation for her own ends and delayed as long as possible any news of her activities becoming known. For coal supplies she relied on her own tender, a steamer named *Marie*, which now accompanied her south to that lonely Galapagos group of Pacific islands which belong to Ecuador and are about 700 miles from the South American continent. In the olden days sea-rovers used to anchor off here, later on came the sailing-ship whalers, but in our own age it is rarely that a vessel calls unless she be after the reputed hidden pirate treasure, or a yacht going across between the Panama Canal and the South Sea Islands, or the still rarer ship of a naturalist.

Thus there was something of the same remoteness which belonged to Easter Island and Mas-a-Fuera, or Juan Fernandez. Certainly the Germans, for a continental nation, had a marvellous feeling for islands. Here *Elsinore's* crew were put ashore after *Leipzig* had coaled from *Marie*, and were landed next month at Guayaquil. But before they could arrive, *Leipzig* herself had proceeded into the Gulf of Guayaquil where on September 25, at the seaward side just off the Callao-Panama track, she captured the British S.S. *Bankfields*, a vessel of 3763 tons, bound for the Panama Canal, which had only recently been opened. The crew were transferred to *Marie*, and *Bankfields* was sunk by gunfire, but the former were landed a week later at Callao. In October, *Leipzig* joined Admiral von Spee at Easter Island and her independence as a raider ended : except for two chance prizes she had no further captures. On the day following the Battle of Coronel she found a victim in the French barque *Valentine*, which was carrying coal to Valparaiso, but was now brought into Mas-a-Fuera whither von Spee had temporarily withdrawn. On December 2, when von Spee's Squadron had just rounded the Horn, it fell in with the British barque *Drummuir*, 1844 tons, with a cargo of coal for San Francisco. *Leipzig* captured her whilst 70 miles east of this dread Cape, and she was taken to the back of Picton Island where two of the squadron's colliers, *Baden* and *Santa Isabel*, were secured on either side of the sailing-vessel. Four days later *Drummuir* was sunk by bombs.

Now it was this delay, caused by the greed for coal, that lost von Spee his squadron and his own life. Had *Drummuir* been ignored, he would have reached the Falklands and surprised it before Admiral Sturdee's battle-cruisers could arrive and surprise von Spee's cruisers. Moreover, *Baden* and *Santa Isabel*, which were coming up astern of the squadron and were to rendezvous in Lat. 54 S, Long. 57 W, were captured and sunk by the armed merchant cruiser *Macedonia* and H.M.S. *Bristol*. Thus *Leipzig*'s total accomplishment of four sinkings, before she herself was sent to the bottom, can hardly be counted as a brilliant performance ; and during the earlier part of her independent cruise she was too nervous of British men-of-war to display any great spirit of adventure.

But with the failure of the German raiding campaign in its primary phase there came also a political change which foreshadowed the transformation that must ultimately come over the war. We have seen the unscrupulous manner in which Germany's representatives abroad contrived, schemed, deceived, and stopped short of almost no methods for assisting the raiders. The rights of neutral countries meant nothing, the existence of the laws of nations was ignored and defied impudently. Captain Boy-Ed, the resourceful square-faced, heavy-lipped, bull-necked dominant Naval Attaché at Washington, had done his able best for Germany, but in so doing he had overstepped the bounds which hospitality required in regard to diplomatists. His machinations could not go on for ever. So in November of 1915 Mr. Lansing, the United States Secretary of State, informed the German Ambassador at Washington as follows:

"On account of what this Government considers improper activities in military and naval matters, this Government has requested the immediate recall of Captain Boy-Ed, the German Naval Attaché, and Captain von Papen, the German Military Attaché, as they are no longer acceptable to this Government."

Thus the Supply System, with all its intricacies, had first broken down, and then the head of this system had been dismissed. We therefore now pass to a totally different kind of raiding campaign, which was self-contained and had to rely not on the trickery or the subterfuge of Supply Officers, but on the personal courage and enterprise of captains whom we can afford to respect as men and regard as clever seamen. This new service corresponded more nearly to the gallant Q-ship service created within the British Navy, and in watching the fresh development of a former enemy's exploits there is still greater adventure to be found, far more romance, and certainly superior originality. The first episode is limited to the Narrow Seas, but nearly all the others were based on a wider ambition.

CHAPTER XIII

RAMSEY AND *METEOR*

FEW chapters of naval warfare so well illustrate the varied careers of ships as that series of incidents which brought to a quick end the two ships which performed such useful work until the month of August 1915. It almost seems as if some vessels are predestined for adventure from their early days.

The first of these was built in Barrow originally for the Lancashire and Yorkshire Railway Company and for some time, as the *Duke of Lancaster*, used to steam regularly across the Irish Sea between Fleetwood and Belfast. Presently, however, she was sold to the Turks and was reconditioned with new boilers; but then came the war between Greece and Turkey, so that she was prevented from being handed over. In 1912 she was purchased by the Isle of Man Steam Packet Company, who named her the *Ramsey*, and was employed in the service between Liverpool and Douglas where this single-funnel twin-screw steamer was well known to excursionists from Lancashire and Yorkshire. She fulfilled her duties as usual carrying summer visitors in 1914, and was then taken over by the British Admiralty as an armed boarding steamer to look out for suspicious ships who might approach the British Isles on mine-laying raids.

Ramsey was given a couple of 12-pounder guns mounted below the bridge to starboard and port respectively, and she carried a crew of ninety-eight. In November 1914 she was sent up to Scapa Flow and thence began her duty of patrolling off the north-east Scottish coast. Steaming at night without navigation lights, one of the marines would be sent round the ship at dusk to ensure that all scuttles were screened and not the suspicion of a light was visible anywhere. Every man was on the alert, and whenever a ship was sighted, *Ramsey* would steam up abeam of her, keeping about 50 yards away, and then illuminate with her searchlight the stranger's form whilst the latter was being questioned, "What ship?" "Where from?" "Where bound?" Assuming everything seemed correct, the stranger was allowed to proceed, and the patrol resumed her cruising.

So weeks and months in that trying North Sea weather sped by, but the summer of 1915 was a busy one. The Grand Fleet having dominated the High Sea Fleet into a state of inactivity, punctuated by occasional tip-and-run raids, it remained for Germany to rely on the operations of submarines and furtive minelaying adventures by surface craft. *Ramsey* in the last three months of her life stopped and searched quite a large number of ships, and in some cases had to put prize crews aboard them and take the suspects into port for further examination.

At last came Saturday, August 7, 1915, and it so happened that on this day Admiral Jellicoe proceeded to Cromarty in *Iron Duke* where he was to meet the Prime Minister, Mr. Asquith, who came north from London to discuss urgent matters with the Commander-in-Chief. At 5 p.m. *Ramsey*, in the ordinary course of her routine, left Scapa Flow for her patrol area off the Moray Firth, which of course has to be negotiated by all ships making for Cromarty Firth. Something out of the ordinary was happening on the night of August 7-8, for two separate patrol units—an armed yacht and an armed trawler—both sighted strange lights without being able to identify the vessel. About midnight there came through to the commanding officer of *Ramsey* a wireless message ordering him to keep a sharp lookout to the westward.

Nothing further seemed to happen, though a great deal had occurred. The night was exceptionally fine though a little hazy, and thus the conditions had been ideal for a German raider. The German Admiralty were not aware that the flagship of the British Fleet, the Commander-in-Chief, and the Prime Minister, were at the end of the Firth : that was a mere coincidence. But German naval intelligence still believed that Cromarty Firth, which in peace time had so often been used by the British Navy, was the Grand Fleet's war headquarters and base. For this reason Germany had sent out a steamer named *Meteor* for the operation of laying mines to entrap all ships passing through Moray Firth.

The selection of *Meteor* was wise. She was really the British S.S. *Vienna*, which used to trade between Leith and Hamburg, but at the beginning of hostilities chanced to be in Germany where she was arrested and taken over by the Germans. As this vessel was just the kind of steamer likely to be seen in Scottish waters, she was not likely to arouse immediate suspicion when sighted : in fact, she was somewhat similar in build to *Ramsey*, though slightly bigger and slower. It so happened that the summer haze and extent of sea combined to prevent her being observed, and she worked her time to a nicety, so that just as it was dusk she made the coast of Scotland and was able to lay her mines right up to within a mile of the southern shore of the Moray Firth. This was the new phase of raiding which for the present took the place of those abandoned ocean operations which we have just witnessed, and the strategy was sound. No fewer than 374 deadly eggs were thus laid, and the raider was able to dump her terrible cargo without interference.

Theoretically this effort should have been a huge success, for the field was laid in such a position that if the Grand Fleet were using Cromarty, and if they were shortly to proceed down the North Sea for one of their customary sweeps, they must inevitably have the same experience as happened to *Audacious* soon after *Berlin* deposited her traps. But the German enterprise failed to allow for one important fact : minesweeping trawlers next morning in the course of their usual work of towing their sweep-wires along Moray Firth's southern shore discovered these black eggs off Banff. It was thus that the enemy's secret was revealed, and this was immediately notified as a danger area. Its extent could obviously not be defined immediately, and at 6 a.m. on the 9th H.M.S. *Lynx*, a destroyer, struck one of the mines, blew up, with the loss of her commanding officer as well as all hands except three officers and twenty-one men. During the ensuing weeks sweepers carried on, so that by the first of October 280 of the then unknown number of mines had been accounted for.

But in the meanwhile, what about *Meteor*? At 5 a.m. on Sunday *Ramsey* sighted smoke on the horizon, and, in accordance with the wirelessed orders, chased after the strange ship which was eventually overtaken, so that in half an hour that which was *Meteor* was seen to be flying the Russian flag and resembled a tramp steamer. So far there was no reason to suspect her particularly, when *Ramsey* blew her whistle for *Meteor* to stop. Perfectly disguised were ship and men, and after *Meteor* had stopped, *Ramsey's* boat with a boarding party put off. Now the latter had rowed only a short distance, when suddenly the Russian flag was hauled down and up went the German Ensign. Simultaneously *Meteor* threw off the last vestige of deception, opened fire with machine-guns, as well as two 4-inch guns on disappearing mounts. *Ramsey* was taken completely by surprise, her decks being showered with bullets and shells, her commanding officer, Lieutenant-Commander Raby, R.N.R., and the officers with him on the bridge being immediately killed. *Meteor* then loosed off a torpedo which hit *Ramsey* aft where the crew's quarters in this ship were situated, thus causing heavy loss of life as most of the men were off watch and below. The stern was shattered and the steamer began to sink before a gun had been able to fire in reply.

The Chief Engineer, Mr. T. Fayle, was asleep in his cabin at the after deck-house, and the torpedo's explosion carried away the deck abaft this house, so that this officer, on finding the deck here missing, jumped into the water whence he was later rescued by the Germans with a severely crushed foot. Unfortunately that incident which always seems to accompany the

RAMSEY AND METEOR 187

loss of a merchant ship occurred on this occasion : one of the boats, in being lowered, capsized. Thus the occupants were trapped underneath, but some of the ship's personnel managed to reach the bottom of the upturned boat and were rescued by the Germans whilst still clinging to the keel. One or two boats from *Ramsey* were lowered safely, but the whole incident happened so quickly that within four minutes the 1862-ton vessel had gone down, though with colours still flying.

Meteor picked up a total of four officers and thirty-nine men, and it is a pleasure here to record that, contrary to certain unforgettable incidents connected with the U-boat campaign, the behaviour of the German rescuers was both humane and courteous. Captain von Knorr, *Meteor's* commanding officer, was in every sense of the word a gentleman. Having mustered the British prisoners on deck, he sent them below to get dry clothes and medical comforts. Afterwards he made a speech, expressing his regrets to see them in such a plight and his sorrow that so many brave men had been lost, but this was the fortune of war. He added that, as British officers had been so kind to many Germans, it behoved him to do all within his power for the British prisoners ; and anything that was asked for in reason should be granted. At the same time he inquired if they would like to have a service in memory of their lost comrades. The reply was that the offer would be gladly accepted, so this was done ; a lectern was covered with the Union Jack, Captain von Knorr and all officers not on duty attending the service.

The *Meteor* made her way south-eastwards towards Germany and the excellent treatment of prisoners was not abated. They were supplied with cigarettes and cigars, extra privileges were conceded to officers who were confined to cabins on deck, whilst the men were placed in the ship's hold with a mattress and blanket for each. Here they remained till 3 p.m. that Sunday afternoon when they were brought up on deck and exercised for an hour, after which they were sent below, given tea, and eventually went to sleep. Their slumber that night was disturbed by the firing of *Meteor's* guns; for, towards the middle of the North Sea, she encountered one of those little Norwegian schooners which at this time were making such good profits by carrying cargoes of pit-props so badly needed in England. *Meteor* sank her, brought the Norwegian crew on board and sent them down into the hold to join *Ramsey's* men.

But an interesting situation was fast developing. When the various items of news reached Admiral Jellicoe on Sunday in *Iron Duke* that a Moray Firth minefield had been discovered and that an armed steam yacht as well as a trawler had sighted strange lights during the dark hours, the Commander-in-Chief realized that the visitor had been a German surface minelayer. He therefore reasoned that this vessel would now be on her way back home and might with luck be intercepted. There were but two routes available: either up the Skagerrak and then south down the Kattegat; or south-east across the North Sea to pick up Horn Reef, and thence to the Heligoland Bight. So the Admiralty was informed, and whilst one Light Cruiser squadron was sent to the Skagerrak, other Light Cruiser squadrons were sent to the Horn Reef.

Thus we come to the afternoon of Monday, by which time Commodore Tyrwhitt's Light Cruiser force had come out of Harwich, steamed to the north-east, and about 4 p.m. was off Horn Reef. *Meteor* was some 50 miles still to the north-west of that Reef when she was warned by a German airship of the approaching British cruisers. German air scouts were patrolling north-west of the Ems, and it so happened that the German submarine U 28 was in the neighbourhood on her way home. She picked up the wireless signals likewise. When Knoor sighted those beautiful Harwich greyhounds of the sea, he realized that the game was up. Thanks to Admiral Jellicoe's foresight, retribution had arrived in due time at the right spot. The German captain decided to abandon and sink *Meteor*. That was why his British prisoners, to their surprise, were hurriedly ordered to come up out of the hold as quickly as

RAMSEY AND METEOR

possible, only to find smoke on the horizon signifying the approach of naval strength. *Meteor's* people were not a little alarmed, but a number of Danish fishing sailing craft happened to be about, and one of these was commandeered by Knorr, who packed into her both British prisoners and the Norwegians. Two German officers remained to place a time-fuse bomb in *Meteor* and then joined the rest of Knorr's crowd, so that just as the cruisers came up *Meteor* was seen to explode and sink.

Now the senior surviving officer from *Ramsey* was Acting-Lieutenant P. S. Atkins, R.N.R., and he did a smart thing. As he watched the leading cruiser—H.M.S. *Cleopatra*—come rushing along, Atkins ordered a surviving signalman to inform *Cleopatra* that *Ramsey's* survivors were aboard the fishing craft and asked to be taken off. But the picture at that moment was a complicated one, the Commodore was being attacked by aircraft and submarines, so a signal came back thus: "Steer south-west. I will return and pick you up." Atkins was also ordered to take charge of the fishing vessel.

Knorr, of course, would not allow interference with the fishing vessel's navigation, and reminded Atkins that they were under a neutral flag. But eventually British arguments prevailed, and a south-west course was steered until another fishing craft was reached. This was a Norwegian, and Knorr after consultation with his brother officers agreed to the British prisoners being transferred. By means of two dinghys Atkins and his shipmates were taken off, whilst the Germans remained in the Danish vessel; but an incident at this juncture took place which would never have happened if Knorr had not possessed the character which we have noted. Just as Atkins was leaving, the German captain inquired if he had any money. "Seeing that you picked me up in my pyjamas," answered the R.N.R. officer, "how could I have any?"

Knorr insisted on Atkins accepting money, but the latter equally insisted that this would not be necessary. In the end Atkins did as he was requested, receiving an

English £5 note together with other money. The courtesy was another instance of the statement that the German surface-raiders usually carried out warfare with clean hands and respect for the traditions of the sea ; whilst U-boat officers too often showed a total disregard for anything but frightfulness. It only remains to add that eventually this money was handed to Admiral Jellicoe, who sent it on to the British Admiralty asking that it might be returned with the thanks of the British.

Atkins and party were aboard the Norwegian only about half an hour when H.M.S. *Arethusa*, flying the broad pennant of Commodore Tyrwhitt, came along. After the latter realized the state of affairs, he lowered a boat and took his compatriots off. The latter, now full of joy at such deliverance, were mustered on the quarter-deck and addressed by the Commodore and then given a good square meal. On Tuesday afternoon they were landed at Harwich where they were sent to Shotley Barracks. Yet even now there was not immediate rest. About midnight the Germans had their revenge by an air-raid, and bombs dropped over the *Ramsey* men in such proximity as to cause the latter to wonder which was the worse : a raid from the sea, or one from the air.

To very few sailors has there ever been the experience of being at sea in one afternoon under four different flags. Possibly no other men have been guests on the same day in a German, Danish, Norwegian, and British vessel. Nor have many survivors had the rare experience of being addressed by a German officer on Sunday, and similarly mustered by a British officer on the day following.

Knorr owed his escape, after the British cruisers had departed, to the presence of U 28, which the German Commander-in-Chief, Admiral von Pohl, had sent out, by whose orders, likewise, the airship had been sent forth as escort. (Admiral Tirpitz none the less severely criticized his brother admiral by remarking : "Young Knorr has carried out a brilliant minelaying operation. Pohl had again failed to fix any rendezvous for a supporting force for Knorr's auxiliary cruiser.") Ordering the submarine to take the fishing vessel in tow, Knorr, with his crew numbering over a hundred, thus reached Lister Tief (Sylt) in safety after a brief but exceedingly adventurous raiding cruise.

This was not the first minelaying mission which *Meteor* had undertaken, for in June of that year she had been up to the White Sea and laid a series of minefields off various landmarks of the Kola Peninsula so as to entrap the steamers bringing munitions from Britain to Russia. A very tiresome series of operations followed when British minesweepers, in the face of every difficulty (not excluding Russian lethargy and pro-Germanism), were sent to locate and destroy these hidden dangers.

But the great lesson which the German Admiralty learned from the *Meteor-Ramsey* episode was this: An ordinary merchant steamer—not a big liner nor a naval cruiser—properly disguised and well armed with powerful guns as well as torpedo-tubes, possessed considerable possibilities as a raider. If she were accosted by some armed merchant cruiser and ordered to heave-to, she would have plenty of time to unmask herself and attack whilst the British patrol was lowering the boat with its boarding party. The use of some foreign flag, the perfection of disguise, would be efficacious for a temporary delay, and then would come the knock-out blow following immediately after perfect surprise.

The only weakness to Knorr's exploit had been the narrowness of the North Sea, which had enabled the Harwich cruisers to dash out and make interception across the only two possible tracks. If, therefore, the principle were applied again to the ocean with its wide area, and the right kind of vessel were chosen that had the right type of captain, then it was possible that deep-sea raids might again be launched even though the German Supply system and Captain Boy-Ed had fallen. The crux of the cruise would be how to get through the British blockade both outward and homeward bound. If this could be overcome, then the chances of doing on a big scale what Knorr had achieved in a limited sphere were quite as favourable as could be expected.

Mines must be laid at strategical points off the British Isles where they would be likely to destroy, or at least damage seriously, capital ships. But sufficient armament must be aboard the raider to cope with any likely patrol vessel, and the long nights of winter must be taken advantage of in order to allow sufficient cover for the minelaying operation. It is thus that we reach the period when the greatest possible effort was made (1) to break out of the North Sea by every artifice and daring, and (2) reach the trade routes along which for months British vessels had been bringing food, raw materials, and warlike stores with impunity, whilst the Grand Fleet was keeping the same from reaching Germany.

Looking at the problem from the Teutonic point of view, one appreciates that something had to be done. The submarines had not yet realized their full powers or radius of action, the High Sea Fleet was deteriorating slowly both in moral and popularity because it did nothing, and the German public was just becoming conscious that the British blockade was to cause them inconvenience followed by serious hardship. The time, then, was ripe to make a fresh effort at harrying British commerce on voyage, and in thus doing bring back to the German nation the confidence which was once possessed in its naval strength.

CARMANIA SINKING THE RAIDER CAP TRAFALGAR
(From the painting by C. E. Turner.)

AFTER THE FIGHT

Carmania's bridge and chart house wrecked by *Cap Trafalgar's* guns.

CHAPTER XIV

MOEWE'S FIRST VOYAGE

TOWARDS the end of 1915 Germany had completed her plans for the revival of warfare against commerce, but by means of new methods. The selected vessel was a two-masted, single-screw steamer of 4500 tons, 385 feet long, with a speed of 14 knots. She had been built at Geestemunde and launched in May 1914, the pre-war intention being to employ her to carry bananas from German African colonies to Hamburg. Fitted with electric light and refrigerating machinery, painted black, with poop, fo'c'sle, and superstructure white, she was now fitted out with clever devices whilst still presenting the appearance of a very ordinary ocean-going steamer.

Between the bridge and fo'c'sle were bulwarks to screen her guns and torpedo-tubes, but she was able within the shortest time to disguise herself by the erection of a fake funnel, the lowering or raising of false superstructures, and even by extending the upper part of her stern. Many of these items were dodges employed by the British Q-ships, and it is quite remarkable how easily the character of a vessel can be altered by a little ingenuity plus a liberal use of paint. The fake funnel was a fairly old idea and had been used long before the war by British warships during naval manœuvres. The underlying principle of disguising a man-of-war belongs, however, to the old days when sail and hemp were still ruling the sea.

Thus a slow eighteenth-century warship would sometimes entice an enemy by pretending to be a merchantman, and then suddenly open fire when the latter was within range. Pirates were also trapped in like manner. Among French sailors such mystery ships were known as *vaisseaux-trompeurs*, because they "semblent appartenir au commerce et sont armés en guerre". The old-time skippers of warships could effectively deceive their victims by painting out gun-ports or giving a slovenly impression as to sails and yards, quite apart from the very obvious use of false colours. In 1778 the French considered a scheme for rigging decoy ships as coasters, and sending them with concealed guns to cruise about in certain areas where the probability of decoying British ships was almost a certainty. British frigates in the time of William Pitt, the younger, used so to disguise themselves as to lure French privateers right alongside and then treat the latter to a violent broadside. Even in the seventeenth century British commanding officers by housing guns, showing no colours, and working their warships in a clumsy manner, were able to deceive such able seafarers as the Dutch. In the time of Charles II one naval vessel, named the *Kingfisher*, was specially built to resemble the most usual type of large merchantman, and furthermore she was given collapsible bulwarks, as well as a detachable head. She was then employed in the Mediterranean against the Barbary pirates. Coming down to more recent times, Lord Cochrane disguised his brig *Speedy* to resemble a certain Danish brig well known to the Spaniards, and even provided himself with a Danish quarter-master to do the necessary hailing. When Admiral Mahan was a midshipman in 1861 he suggested the employment of decoy ships to capture the steamer *Sumter*. And (if I may be permitted to add a small personal instance) I remember so disguising the vessel which I happened to be commanding in December 1915, that we deceived by our paint, faked lettering, and other items, even those who had for months been patrolling the same bit of Atlantic coast.

So, when Germany relied, for the success of her raiding, on deception rather than speed, she was using a well-established and very sound method. The abovementioned banana steamer was originally named the *Pugno*, but she now changed that to *Moewe*, which means "seagull". She was armed with two 4·1-inch

MOEWE'S FIRST VOYAGE 195

guns mounted under the fo'c'sle, two other guns of the same calibre mounted abaft the break of the fo'c'sle, one 22-pounder mounted on the poop disguised as hand-steering gear (a favourite Q-ship device); and two above-water torpedo-tubes placed between the bridge and foremast. This, of course, was inspired by the success of *Meteor* in having torpedoed *Ramsey*. But *Moewe* was also fitted so as to carry a few hundred mines and to have the ability of laying them.

We have, then, not an exceptional ship such as a fast liner or rakish cruiser, but a quite ordinary steamer with moderate speed and size, just the type which was likely to be seen on almost any trade route and would not excite suspicion. It was a return from the early war months of a complicated supply system and uneconomical ships to extreme simplicity and independence. But for that reason this new manner required a personnel as carefully selected as the British Q-ship service insisted for its own requirements. As commanding officer of *Moewe* the German Admiralty chose a keen, zealous, courageous and adventurous officer from the regular navy, old enough to temper daring with prudence, yet not so stereotyped by age as to flinch from original tactics. He who commands a British or German decoy ship can spoil the whole preparation of months by one act of rash impetuosity: the discipline of self and crew, the patience, the coolness, the penetrative imagination for seeing into an opponent's mind, are just as important as the ability to fight gloriously till a finish. In Korvetten-Kapitän (i.e. Commander) Burggraf Graf Nikolaus zu Dohna-Schlodien was found an extremely able officer for *Moewe's* special service, and his skill no less than his considerable success as a raider cannot be questioned.

Before setting out from Germany in December 1915 he received the following instructions: "Lay mines in various places along the enemy's coast; then carry on cruiser warfare." Just before Christmas everything was ready, and in thick weather this apparently innocent cargo steamer set forth up the North Sea. After approaching so close to the Norwegian coast as to sight the snow-clad mountains, she took advantage of the long dark hours of winter's night to avoid the British blockade, and then arrived at the area where her first minefield was to be laid. This was off the north coast of Scotland east of Cape Wrath. Sule Skerry Lighthouse (west of the Orkneys), whose light was visible for 13 miles, assisted her in fixing her position, and on New Year's Day *Moewe* deposited her terrible mines. The latter had been stowed in long rows in her hold, and were then run on rails to a lift which conveyed them to the upper deck, where they were again placed in rows on rails. To ensure the mines dropping into the sea clear of the stern, these rails projected about three feet out board.

The operation took from 6 p.m. to 11.30 p.m., the prescribed intervals being regulated by an officer with a stop-watch, and the minefield was over a wide region. But Cape Wrath light (visible 27 miles) was a further assistance in *Moewe's* navigation. Thus, in spite of a heavy gale—force 10 to 12—which usually blows at this time of the year, the raider was able to lay 252 mines in eleven different lines. The intention of this exploit was to entrap deep-draught ships in waters where British men-of-war were known to carry out fleet exercises or to pass when going to a port for refit. The night was exceptionally dark, with heavy seas, and the "seagull's" dangerous "eggs" had been set to float at a depth from the surface of from 3·7 to 4·7 metres. With the western approach to Pentland Firth thus fouled, it could only be a little while before disaster came. At 7 a.m. on January 6, H.M.S. *Edward VII*, the well-known battleship, was on her way to Belfast from Scapa Flow to refit, and it happened to be low water. She steamed unsuspectingly over the south-east corner of the field, and when in Lat. 58.43 N, Long. 4.4 W there came a violent explosion beneath her starboard engine-room which sent the water pouring in so that she heeled over to starboard. There was still a heavy sea running, but she was taken in tow till she finally had to be abandoned. Happily there was no loss of life, but the battleship turned over and sank the same evening.

MOEWE'S FIRST VOYAGE

Nor was this the only vessel to suffer. Next day the Norwegian S.S. *Bonheur* foundered, and another battleship, H.M.S. *Africa*, on her way from Belfast to Scapa had the marvellous good fortune of having passed through this area untouched only a few hours before *Edward VII* was mined. The sweepers got to work, capital ships were sent by a route well north of the Orkneys, and the mined area was partially cleared, but eventually avoided altogether till shortly after the war. By that time the bad weather of three winters in those rough waters had cleared all the other mines away.

From the German point of view this Whiten Head Bank minefield, as it was officially known, had been a great success. But it was even more harmful than appeared by the loss of an old battleship. The weather for weeks was too bad for the minesweeping vessels to do their job, and this raid showed the grave danger of the Grand Fleet being mined in at its base, whilst likewise it pointed to the necessity of having more minesweepers built as soon as the shipyards could deliver them. Still the only efficient protection was the paravane, which could be attached to the ships themselves, and this invention was now being perfected though it would be a long while before it would be ready as a reliable aid and defence.

Count zu Dohna-Schlodien had chosen the locality of his first minefield well, and long before its existence was discovered he was hundreds of miles away down the Atlantic, having gone away westward of Ireland and so into the Bay of Biscay till he closed the French coast. In the meantime his wireless intercepted news that *Edward VII* had struck a mine, though he did not know that it was one of *Moewe's* "eggs". About January 9 he laid the rest of his mines off La Rochelle, not far from where it had been suggested in the eighteenth century that French decoy ships should hang about to entrap British privateers. The first of these mines was reported off Rochefort on January 10, and three days later the Spanish S.S. *Bayo* (Huelva for Pallice) struck one of them 40 miles west of La Rochelle, so that she went down. On January 15 another Spanish steamer, *Belgica* (Clyde for Bordeaux), also sank on a mine in about the same spot. Presently a large number of other "eggs" was found off Pertius d'Antioche, Ile d'Oleron, and Ile d'Yeu.

Having now got rid of all her dangerous cargo, *Moewe* was free to carry out the second part of her instructions. She had shown that she could do the work of *Berlin* and *Meteor*: it remained for the Count to begin his warfare against that commerce which had been so regularly carried on since April between Britain and overseas ports to the intense annoyance of Germany. At 10 a.m. on January 11 he sighted smoke on his starboard bow, having by this time reached a position some 150 miles west of Cape Finisterre. He made all possible speed, and at 3 p.m. was abreast of this steamer when he sighted a second vessel's smoke to port. *Moewe* accordingly reduced speed, and when close enough signalled the latter: "What is your name?" The steamer, perceiving nothing extraordinary in this single-funnelled "cargo" ship, replied by hoisting her flags that she was the *Farringford*. The raider then disclosed her true character by signalling *Farringford* to stop, by hoisting the German ensign, and by firing a shot across *Farringford's* bows. Approaching to within 50 yards, *Moewe* next signalled: "Abandon ship at once."

There was a heavy Atlantic sea running, the crew were taken aboard, but during this interval the second ship escaped in dense rain. *Moewe* wasted little time, fired a few rounds to sink *Farringford*, and left her moribund. She was a British ship of 3146 tons.

Now most unfortunately the ship that had been first sighted, instead of sheering off in another direction, held on her original course, so that she was overhauled gradually and then had to endure *Moewe's* shelling. She turned out to be the British S.S. *Corbridge*, 3687 tons, Cardiff to Brazil, with 4000 tons of coal. Her master put up a brave defence by sending out a heavy smoke screen and trying to get away; but the raider was slightly superior in speed and a second shell caused *Corbridge* to heave-to. Still the collier had given *Moewe* a run of two hours before being compelled to yield. We

MOEWE'S FIRST VOYAGE 199

now have a repetition of the practice inaugurated by the previous ocean raiders. *Corbridge* was too useful to be sunk, and she was sent off under a German crew with special orders to meet *Moewe* at a certain rendezvous. Such a splendid supply of coal would be invaluable when the raider's bunkers presently became more empty.

The accompanying photograph enables one to imagine oneself aboard *Moewe*. On the upper bridge at sea was stationed the Navigating Petty Officer, whose duty was to watch the ship's speed and course. A signalman was always ready to signal passing vessels, and a look-out man was placed up the mast whence he could see 5 miles further than anyone on the bridge. He was carefully selected for his excellent eyesight. The Officer-of-the-Watch was always on the navigating bridge, and on either side of him was placed a look-out with a large prismatic telescope. Keen alertness was encouraged, for the first of the look-outs to report a prize was allowed to choose something for himself from the loot—a pot of jam, for instance, or cigarettes.

Ships with two funnels were usually avoided, since they were for the most part passenger steamers and would be a nuisance. Neutral steamers could also be generally avoided since they had either light funnels, or bore the owners' mark painted in red, yellow, or blue rings. But if a vessel were seen with a plain black single funnel, it was always a hopeful sign that here was another British victim coming into the trap. The prize crew was ever prepared to go off in the boarding boat and consisted of the following : two officers, with four seamen as guard armed with pistols and side-arms ; one signalman to communicate such details as her name and nature of her cargo. It was then easy enough for an officer in *Moewe* to check her from the alphabetical list in Lloyd's Register and to signal further instructions as to how she should be dealt with. A torpedo officer and two ratings also were included among the prize crew, for the purpose of placing explosive charges. Thus the Count had everything arranged in the most efficient manner.

He was steaming down the route well to the seaward of the Cape Finisterre–Canaries line, and could be sure that this busy thoroughfare—so long accustomed to immunity—would yield a regular amount of traffic. So, only a couple of days after sinking *Farringford*, and being now 220 miles west of Lisbon, *Moewe* cautiously approached a 3627-ton steamer which was seen to have no wireless and therefore unable to bleat for help. The stranger took alarm, tried to escape, was signalled to stop, and brought-to by a shot across her bows. The prize crew were sent aboard and found her to be the British *Dromonby* carrying coal to South America for the British Squadron in those waters. The crew were taken off, explosive charges were distributed as widely as possible along her sides, the fuse was then lit, and the demolition party hurried into their boat only a few minutes before the explosion occurred that sent the ship to destruction.

This was to be a memorable day, for now some more smoke was observed, and only five miles from this spot *Moewe* at 3.30 p.m. captured the British S.S. *Author*, 3496 tons, which had left London on January 8 for Durban and Delagoa Bay with general cargo. There was a light north-east breeze, the weather was fine and clear, when *Author* sighted the raider approaching with the British Red Ensign flying. As soon as *Moewe* came abreast, the latter hauled this down and ran up the German naval ensign. With torpedo-tubes showing, and two guns trained on *Author*, the German signalled, "Stop immediately. Abandon ship." *Author's* master complied, three boats with armed crews came off, took possession, and began loading up with stores. Sea-cocks were opened, bombs with time fuses placed in the hold, and about 5.50 p.m. the steamer sank, the captain and crew of fifty-seven being removed to *Moewe*. There was no secrecy of the raider's name or nature, for the name *Moewe* was on the sailor's cap ribbons, and when *Corbridge* had been stopped *Moewe* had signalled by Morse lamp that she was a German cruiser.

On this same day and to the same spot came shortly afterwards another steamer who suspected nothing till

MOEWE'S FIRST VOYAGE

Moewe gave her the usual peremptory order. This was the 3608-ton British S.S. *Trader* on her way to Liverpool with a cargo of raw sugar. Within fifteen minutes the vessel was sunk by opening the sea-cocks and by bombs. In one day, then, three steamers each of nearly *Moewe's* size had been destroyed within a 5-mile area, and already there were about 150 prisoners on board. Crowded below in the badly ventilated and unpleasantly hot forward mine-deck, the white crews were accommodated with some difficulty whilst the lascars were located aft. The Count realized that the time was near when he must get rid of all this colony.

He was still lying just along that busy route where shipping, making to or from the Canaries, must inevitably be sighted. On January 14 nothing was seen, but on the following day two more British steamers fell into his hands. The first was the *Ariadne*, 3055 tons, with a cargo of maize, which was captured at 7 a.m. After transferring the crew, the raider sunk her by shell fire and the expenditure of a torpedo. *Moewe* had reached so far south as to be only 140 miles east and slightly north of Madeira, therefore well placed for trapping ships coming up from south-east America or the West Coast of Africa. Scarcely had *Ariadne* been disposed of than a fine passenger liner of 7781 tons was observed coming north. *Moewe* was steered to cross her bows and read her name, and then a reference to Lloyd's Register soon gave the raider all the information he required. This was the Elder-Dempster liner *Appam*, which at first refused to stop and called up help on her wireless. But a shell across her bows brought her to, for, defensively armed as she was, there were passengers' lives to think of. It was one thing to shell from aft a submarine, but it would be an impossible duel with women and children on board to fight a much better armed surface raider. *Moewe* jambed the wireless signals, so that they could not have meant much had they been picked up by any of Rear-Admiral Sir Archibald Moore's units.

This flag-officer in charge of the Madeira-Canaries area had under him H.M.S. *King Alfred* and *Essex* (both cruisers) and two armed merchant cruisers *Carmania* and *Ophir*; whilst further south, off the Cape Verdes, were the cruiser *Highflyer* as well as the armed merchant cruiser *Marmora*. *Moewe* was taking a great risk in visiting this region, and her sole hope of safety lay in her quick-change capabilities whilst keeping a perfect look-out for anything that resembled a warship. It was only when a fairly fast and biggish steamer had to be approached that a nervous tension was felt by the raider, who could not be sure whether this were a potential victim or an armed merchant cruiser like herself. *Appam*, by her high masts and wireless and absence of ensign, at first created such uneasiness, but this soon passed, and when *Moewe's* naval ensign revealed a hidden nature there was a strange welcome from one section of *Appam's* passengers to the number of about a score. For this little bunch consisted of German subjects who were being sent from West Africa for internment in England, but now to their intense surprise found rescue at hand.

Appam was captured about 135 miles east of Madeira, and was a notable prize. She was carrying about £50,000 worth of gold in bars and dust, besides the rest of a valuable cargo. She also had 160 passengers, amongst whom were Sir Edward Merewether, Mr. Frederick Seton James, C.M.G., and Mr. F. C. Fuller, C.M.G. Sir Edward was the retiring Governor of Sierra Leone homeward bound. Mr. James was Administrator of Lagos (Nigeria), whilst Mr. Fuller was Chief Commissioner for Ashanti. *Appam* was a comparatively new ship, having been launched in 1913, and her arrival on the scene was valuable to the Germans for the additional reason that by her all the accumulated prisoners could be sent away.

The time, however, was not yet. She was placed under the command of Sub-Lieutenant Berg, of the German Naval Reserve, one of *Moewe's* officers, and at first was ordered to remain with the raider. Berg was a Schleswig-Holsteiner, aged thirty-nine, a disciplinarian but not of the harsh Prussian brutal type. A German prize crew was placed permanently aboard, and every man of the prisoners capable of military service was

MOEWE'S FIRST VOYAGE

compelled to sign a declaration undertaking not to bear arms against Germany.

It was on the following night (January 16) that the two vessels had steamed further down the track till they were 120 miles south by west of Madeira, when they came up with a steamer of 5816 tons. The following dialogue by Morse lamp then took place between *Moewe* and the stranger :

"What is the name of your ship ?"

"Tell us your name first," replied the stranger with justifiable caution.

"*Author*," answered *Moewe* with subtle deception.

(Followed a brief period of hesitation, and then finally the stranger morsed :)

"*Clan Mactavish.*"

Having been convinced that this was a British ship, *Moewe* cleared for action, trained her guns on *Clan Mactavish*, and morsed :

"German cruiser here. Stop immediately."

"We have stopped," came the reply.

But, just because *Clan Mactavish* was thought to be trying to escape, and sending out wireless calls, *Moewe*, fearing that British men-of-war might be about, felt justified in opening fire. Only 450 yards separated raider from British steamer, and now the darkness of the Atlantic night was made ghastly by German shells fired almost point-blank at the *Clan Mactavish's* bridge. But there came a surprise. The steamer was one of those which were armed defensively against submarines, and in spite of this great inferiority of gun power against a confessed cruiser, *Clan Mactavish* did not hesitate to reply with his weapon. "Suddenly," related Count zu Dohna-Schlodien, "there is a flash from the other steamer, and I hear something whistle through the air over our heads. At first I think that I must have been mistaken, but when one of her shells strikes the water close to the *Moewe* there is no further room for doubt : the steamer has actually accepted action with us."

But obviously such a contest was too unequal to last long. The range came down to only 330 yards, and in spite of the merchantman's courage the cruiser quickly had the best of it, so that *Clan Mactavish* was burning with thick smoke issuing from her hull. It was useless to fight any longer, and too many lives had been lost, so the steamer flashed from her lamp: "We have stopped altogether." *Moewe* therefore ceased fire. In that short space of time seventeen men had been killed, five wounded, whilst the damage to captured ship had been considerable. The bridge had been knocked about, the second officer's cabin penetrated, the hull hit at the waterline, and one shell had entered the engine-room. Rarely have spectators representing both nationalities watched a naval engagement under such circumstances as the British and Germans witnessed from aboard *Appam*. It was impossible for the captors to do much with their prize. Although *Clan Mactavish* had a cargo of wool, gum, leather, and other commodities from Australia worth about half a million sterling, her engines were now ruined, and she had to be sunk by gunfire forthwith lest the dreaded British cruisers might too suddenly appear.

When, presently, the Count had the Scottish skipper brought before him, and the latter manfully stated that he had received orders to bring *Clan Mactavish* to England, that he had been provided with a gun for that express purpose, and regarded it as his duty to fight his way thither, the Count shook hands and admitted that he would probably have acted in the same manner had he been so placed. Nevertheless this skipper and the two British gunners were taken prisoners for the rest of the war and duly interned.

Moewe continued further to the south-west and on the next day dismissed *Appam*, Berg being ordered to take her into a United States port, the distance being long enough to prevent news of the raider being made known for days. In that prize went the crews of the seven steamers, so that enough room might be left aboard *Moewe* for further prisoners. But three British military officers, some naval ratings and marines, the master and gunners of *Clan Mactavish*, and the two gunners of *Appam*, as well as a hundred lascars, were retained in *Moewe*. Eventually *Appam* safely crossed the Atlantic and on February 16 landed her people at Newport News, that favourite last resort of German raiders. The voyage was not too pleasant, for *Appam's* food ran short with all those mouths to feed. Some anxiety had been felt as to her fate when she became overdue, and one of her lifeboats had been sighted empty on January 16, some 39 miles north of Tenerife. *Moewe* had cleverly mystified the British authorities by ingenious secrecy, but the time came when *Appam* again regained freedom, for by order of the United States Court she was released.

Moewe by means of her wireless learned of *Appam's* arrival at Newport News, and it was only after this captured ship had reached the United States that the British Admiralty became aware of *Moewe's* existence. Meanwhile, of course, the Count had moved away to a different area : indeed, his technique was such that always he kept moving on to a different sphere, not criss-crossing a lucrative region, but steaming from one trade route to another so that always there was an element of surprise where security had been for long customary. He became a kind of phantom pirate, his *Moewe* a bird of mystery which would swoop suddenly to destroy and then vanish into space, only to be heard of weeks later in a totally different part of the Atlantic. By this kind of tactics he left astern the slenderest of clues and became a master of evasiveness.

Having rid himself of *Appam*, and well realizing that the latter might fall into the hands of a British cruiser before reaching America—thus divulging the last position of *Moewe*—the Count had shifted his hunting to the south-west to reach that rich area where a few months previously *Karlsruhe*, *Kronprinz Wilhelm* and the others had found such excellent prizes up and down the north-east trade route. So valuable and busy had the Cape Verdes–Pernambuco section proved itself to his predecessors that he could not possibly afford to omit a visit, and thereby attack British commerce at one of its most sensitive parts.

But before that could be done it would be necessary

THE SEA-RAIDERS

to coal. *Corbridge*, as we have noted, had been sent off to a secret rendezvous. Here the prize with all her fuel awaited the raider, who had managed quite comfortably with her not uneconomical engines to carry on independently of any supply ships or captured colliers. We know to-day that the anchorage to which *Corbridge* steamed was Maraca Island, at the mouth of the River Amazon, where *Karlsruhe* and *Patagonia* had met for a similar purpose in August 1914, as already mentioned. The Count was thus making use of a valuable tip brought home by *Karlsruhe's* survivors.

Now on the voyage towards Maraca and whilst only 700 miles W by S of St. Vincent, Cape Verdes, *Moewe* came up with the British three-masted barque *Edinburgh*, 1473 tons, bound for Liverpool. After taking off the 67-year-old skipper and crew this beautiful ship was destroyed on January 20 by means of explosives. In the passing of yet another vessel belonging to the now defunct sailing-ship brotherhood there was something reminiscent of a Viking's burial. Flames leapt high over hull and spars, making a weird effect all red and crude yellow against the brilliant tropical moonlight, and *Moewe's* captain himself was moved to remark of *Edinburgh* that "she was beautiful even in death". One may well sympathize with her old skipper that this chance meeting of a helpless vessel with a most modern warship should have ended so sadly.

A week later *Moewe* reached Maraca, having picked *Corbridge* up on January 27 as arranged, and for the next three days coaling went on vigorously day as well as night amid all the heat and dust. The raider, having replenished bunkers to their utmost capacity, towed *Corbridge* out to sea and sank her. The reader will not fail to notice that *Moewe* had thus cruised about for over a month between Germany and South America before coaling; she had neither been supplied by any shore organisation nor been accompanied by tenders; yet her successes had already been as real as they were concealed.

But during this second part of her cruise *Moewe* began by being disappointed: those north-east approaches towards Pernambuco seemed to be devoid of shipping. Steamers had gone right off the normal tracks, become both evasive and extremely cautious. She saw that the British arrangements for warning were effective, so she was compelled to keep altering her appearance by paint and device frequently. On one occasion she was seen in the distance by H.M.S. *Glasgow*, who gave chase, but just when it seemed as if the cruiser had captured the raider there came a sudden rain squall which enveloped both vessels. The *Glasgow* presently passed another steamer but with three instead of two masts, and assumed that this was *Moewe* after one of her quick-change acts. Unfortunately it was a perfectly innocent ship, and the delay caused by this mistake enabled *Moewe* to escape.

On February 4, however, a victim was at last found when *Moewe* captured and sank the 4322-ton Belgian S.S. *Luxembourg*, which was carrying 5900 tons of coal for the railway at Buenos Aires. Two days later, when 310 miles NE by N of Pernambuco, she captured and destroyed by bombs the British S.S. *Flamenco*, a vessel of 4629 tons. Thus the Rocas Reef area was at last able to reward the raider, but she was to understand that a great risk was being run and she had better clear out. The light cruiser *Amethyst* was seeking her, so too was *Glasgow*, whilst the armed merchant cruisers *Orama*, *Macedonia* and *Edinburgh Castle* were all on the southeast American station. On the night of February 5 *Glasgow* must have passed extraordinarily near to *Moewe*, and *Flamenco* tried to wireless for cruiser aid. One of the neutrals brought from the latter informed the raider that *Glasgow* on February 5 had even stopped *Flamenco* and warned her of *Moewe*.

At first the Germans were disinclined to believe that story, but some of the prisoners happened to have taken photographs of *Glasgow*. These plates were now developed and left no doubt: there was *Glasgow*. The Count was wise enough to get away whilst the going was possible, and up that old north-east trade route he steamed till two days later—February 8—he was 530 miles NNE of Pernambuco. He had passed the

Norwegian S.S. *Estrella* and noticed that she had wireless; so the Count again changed *Moewe's* appearance. On the evening of the date mentioned a steamer of 3300 tons was chased and reached, but she was old and slow, with a cargo of coal. She turned out to be the British-owned *Westburn* and became an easy prize. At 5 a.m. next day the British S.S. *Horace*, 3335 tons, was captured another 80 miles further up this route and destroyed by explosives.

Westburn was not sunk, but to her were transferred 180 prisoners of war, excluding *Westburn's* master and second officer who were retained. Under Acting Officer Badewitz, with a prize crew of eight men, *Westburn* was now dismissed and on the afternoon of February 22 reached Santa Cruz, Tenerife, where the captives regained their liberty. Next day *Westburn* came out again to avoid being interned, but H.M.S. *Sutlej*, a cruiser, was awaiting her as soon as she should pass the three-mile limit. *Westburn* therefore blew herself up.

As to *Moewe*, she had a narrow escape from encountering H.M.S. *Highflyer* which was on her way from St. Vincent to St. Paul Rocks. It would have been fitting if the cruiser which sank *Kaiser Wilhelm der Grosse* should also have met *Moewe*, but these incidents of elusiveness and almost fatal gambling with fate could not be kept up indefinitely. The raider knew that the trade routes could no longer be regarded as happy hunting areas. "It must be admitted," confessed the Count, "that the British system of warning and reporting works most admirably." That fact, combined with the realisation that cruisers were tracking him with sure destiny, convinced him that it was time to quit. There was a further consideration which weighed with him decisively—how was he to reach Germany through that dreaded British blockade?

He remembered that outward bound he had succeeded in running it by taking full advantage of the long dark nights and the heavy weather of deepest winter. But it was now well on into February, and by the time *Moewe* could reach the north of Europe the days would be longer, the nights shorter, and the gales less frequent:

ARMED BOARDING STEAMER *RAMSEY*
As she appeared in pre-war days when an excursion steamer running to the Isle of Man.

GERMAN MINELAYER *METEOR*
On fire just before she sank as the British light cruisers came up.

MOEWE'S FIRST VOYAGE

he could not afford any more to tarry in these hot latitudes. We therefore find the Count taking his ship straight up mid-Atlantic, not following the routes from South America north-eastward, but proceeding northward so that he actually crossed athwart the numerous lanes which lead between the Old World and the New. He was in wireless communication with Berlin, able to inform his Admiralty of the successes, to recommend members of his crew for awards, and to learn that fifty of them had been awarded the Iron Cross.

Between February 9 and 23 he made no captures, and this was scarcely surprising since he was following no route of traffic: the most he could expect would be an odd ship or two that chanced to be met with at right angles to his own course. On the last date mentioned, when he was well out into the Atlantic north-west of Finisterre, he had the luck to meet the French S.S. *Maroni*, 3109 tons, which was on her way from Bordeaux to New York with general cargo. After transferring her crew of thirty-three, *Moewe* sank her.

Still steaming northward, and still cutting across the North American tracks, *Moewe* aimed to pass several hundred miles west of the British Isles and therefore right away from all likely patrols. Thus it was that on February 25 when 620 miles west of the Fastnet, on crossing the homeward track of ships from the United States to England, she encountered and sank the British S.S. *Saxon Prince*, 3471 tons, bound from America with such articles as explosives, cotton, and grain. The captain and crew were all made prisoners.

If ever there should be another naval war—which may God forbid—it is highly to be desired that before a merchantman allows herself to be captured, her master should destroy not merely such obvious documents as log-book, charts showing his daily positions, secret sailing instructions, and all confidential papers which indicate minefields or other secret information; but also the less obvious yet invaluable newspapers whether of Allied or neutral countries; since a raider is able to obtain valuable data after collating even the most ordinary paragraphs. *Moewe*, it will be recollected, had

o

been away from land for two months, but *Maroni* and *Saxon Prince* were fresh out of harbour with the latest press intelligence up to date of sailing. Consequently these news sheets gave the Count most acceptable facts as to the general effect of *Moewe's* activities on the shipping world of owners and insurance companies ; as to the arrival of *Appam* at Newport News, where she was of course welcomed by the officers of *Kronprinz Wilhelm* and *Prinz Eitel Friedrich*. Other details were afforded, such as the values of ships and cargoes sunk by *Moewe*, the theories held as to the nature of *Moewe*, the rumours that she was a genuine naval cruiser, that she had been sunk off the Bermudas by H.M.S. *Drake* —and so on.

Now, as the raider passed upwards giving the coasts of Ireland and Scotland a very wide berth, so the nervousness on board proportionately increased ; for British cruiser patrols enforcing the blockade south of Iceland would not be less on the alert than hitherto. But a combination of resource, courage, and good luck did wonders for *Moewe*. By day she kept a good lookout for smoke on the horizon, and avoided any suggestion of a steamer carefully. On February 28, having gone well north, she had the fortune to get into dense snow squalls and a heavy gale. The Count had chosen his date well, for the ensuing night was not moonlit but dark. South at last he came till again he sighted the snow-clad coast of Norway.

The last twenty-four hours of this memorable cruise were thrilling alike for *Moewe* and the German naval authorities. They were mutually in communication by wireless, but always there was the possibility of some British armed merchant cruiser, some armed boarding steamer, some destroyer or a cruiser—perhaps the whole Grand Fleet in making one of its periodical sweeps down the North Sea—rounding up *Moewe* and sinking her within a few minutes. For this reason, when the raider had got within a short distance of Germany, the Commander-in-Chief of the High Sea Fleet sent out as escort and cover not merely destroyers, but three cruisers and four battleships. Nature sent forth a still more useful protection in a thick fog. At length, however, the island of Amrum (one of the North Friesian group off Schleswig-Holstein) was picked up to the eastward, and that day with the house-flags of all her captured victims flying from her masthead like a racing yacht displaying her winning burgees at the end of the season, *Moewe* steamed into Wilhelmshaven accompanied by hovering seaplanes and the rousing cheers of her country's seamen whom the Grand Fleet was confining to harbour.

This was March 4 : the next day came a telegram of thanks from the Kaiser at the Army's General Headquarters, conferring the Iron Cross on the entire crew, and summoning the Count to report himself to the Emperor as soon as possible. There can be no denying the brilliance, the daring, and good luck of this cruise. It was well planned, the selected period and its duration were perfect, the time spent in each area was not overdone, the ship and its personnel were ideal. With only one coaling—though more than one collier was captured—the entire voyage had been accomplished and no reliance had been placed on overseas organisation. The gross loss had been that of Berg and Badewitz and their skeleton prize crews apparently prevented from further participation in the war. On the other hand, she had inflicted on the Allied nations the loss of fifteen ships, of which one—*Appam*—was eventually released.

One can afford to admire Count zu Dohna-Schlodien's technique and undoubted bravery, no less than one can respect his humanity and even courtesy to prisoners. But he had instituted a new form of campaign which would be very hard to check. The weak feature was the necessity of having to land most of his prisoners before reaching Germany. Except for this he would have been able to retain the mysteriousness of his voyage for months. As it was, however, the news flashed from America concerning *Moewe* after *Appam's* survivors had been released, caused both anxiety and the promulgation of new measures on the part of the British Admiralty as well as Admiral

Jellicoe. The grave danger to seaborne trade through such raiders suggested two antidotes : (1) the employment of similar decoy ships, fitted with torpedo-tubes and sent to steam along the trade routes, on the principle of setting a detective disguised as a thief to catch a thief, (2) the use of the historic convoy system which proved so valuable in previous wars. This, I believe, was the first time that the convoy idea was seriously considered during the war of 1914–18, though it was not actually adopted for some months later, subsequent to the date when Admiral Jellicoe on leaving the Grand Fleet and taking up office at the Admiralty was able to work with a free hand.

But with regard to (1), the British Admiralty by the end of February at once set going a new scheme for making the ocean trade routes more extensively patrolled than previously. It was a most difficult thing trying to perform such a task, having regard to the immense extent of even those limited tracks into which shipping could be confined. Looking back on events, one feels that it would have been the wisest move to have started the convoy method right away, and Admiral Jellicoe was wholly in favour of this. But a great effort was made by taking up ten colliers, fitted with wireless, and sending them to work as a combination of scout and bait in conjunction with cruisers. On a small scale this had been attempted in 1915, but now the scheme was elaborated, and it was worked out as follows.

Of the ten colliers *Bellucia*, *Prophet*, and *Pretoria* were allocated to the south-east American coast ; *Maresfield* and *Willow Branch* to work off St. Vincent, Cape Verdes ; *Horngarth*, *Portsea*, and *Djerissa* to work with the 9th Cruiser Squadron ; whilst the *Competitor* and *Norman Monarch* were to cruise in the Pacific. For the Atlantic colliers there would be fuel at Sierra Leone and Gibraltar on one side, and the Abrolhos Rocks at the other ; whilst Esquimalt would provide for the Pacific units. These ten steamers were to change their names and external markings, to be provided with false papers—in fact, to employ all those subterfuges which Germany made use of for deception. Their speed was no better than 10 knots, but that would mean economy, and their tactical employment would be akin to that of the tenders which used to accompany the German raiders, and thus form a kind of arm extended from the cruiser. But besides increasing the cruiser's vision, these colliers would be able to carry the cruiser's fuel. It was hoped that some raider would make one such collier a victim, begin unloading the coal, but would be caught by a British cruiser in this very act.

CHAPTER XV

LOOKING OUT FOR RAIDERS

BY reason of the minefields which had been laid from surface ships off Orfordness, the Humber, Tyne, Tory Island, Moray Firth, and Whiten Head Bank; in consequence, too, of the *Ramsey* disaster, together with the breaking through of *Moewe*, stringent orders were impressed on all patrols round the British Isles to be on the alert for suspicious ships which might be raiders. Trawler patrols, armed boarding steamers, armed merchant cruisers were never more vigilant and ready.

This was bound to lead to a few cases where friend was taken for foe, just as often enough British submarines were fired on in mistake for U-boats. As early as July 3, 1915 (that is to say, only a month before *Meteor's* visit), the armed trawler *Granuweal* was to the north-east of Moray Firth in Lat. 58.20 N, Long. 2.48 W (25 miles from Noss Head) when her commanding officer, Skipper Fred Paley, R.N.R., sighted a two-funnelled ship whose appearance seemed to him so unusual and warlike that he was convinced she was nothing else but a German minelayer. *Granuweal*, in spite of being of inferior size and armament, shelled her. The fisherman's gunnery was excellent and did serious damage, killing one of the stranger's engine-room staff and wounding a stoker.

Unfortunately the strange steamer was H.M.S. *Lilac*, a sloop, one of that new class of British war vessels rather like a small cruiser but quite different from all existing naval types. Not many people had yet seen this sloop species, and the minesweeping gallows with which they were fitted, together with the two funnels and general appearance, quite naturally created

LOOKING OUT FOR RAIDERS 215

Skipper Paley's suspicion. *Lilac* was on her way to Scapa Flow before beginning her duties, and the incident, whilst sad and regrettable, was a proof that if vigilance could hinder raiders then German visitors could expect a hot reception. Similarly in other parts of the Narrow Seas Q-ships were sometimes subjected to narrow escapes of being fired on through unsatisfactory answers after being hailed. One memorable moonlit night I was on the verge of making the same horrible mistake against a most distinguished and gallant ship which shortly afterwards won for her captain the Victoria Cross. Later on a sloop, whose captain happened to be one of my best friends, made an error during a misty afternoon and dropped two shells straight at my ship, but fortunately about ten yards short.

But it was exactly such mistakes of identity which German patrols in Heligoland Bight made in regard to German outward-bound raiders; whilst ashore commanding officers of the latter were more than once taken for spies in their own country. Such inconvenient happenings are inevitable when deception and mutual distrust are part of war's conditions.

All the valuable work of the British patrols, from destroyers and converted liners down to the smallest commissioned craft, was based on and the expression of the Grand Fleet's dominance. The armed boarding steamers, for example, by reason of this freedom were able in a quite efficient manner to render excellent service that has not been generally realised. Those employed in the Dover Straits, for example, where there was a steady stream of neutral traffic, had a most onerous duty. It was necessary to employ vessels which possessed adequate speed for overtaking passenger liners not too willing to stop and be examined. Boarding parties and prize crews were kept pretty busy in that section of the Dover Patrol known as the Downs Boarding Flotilla, which was the counterpart of those armed merchant cruisers of the 10th Cruiser Squadron operating between the north of Scotland and Iceland.

The risk which these Dover Straits armed boarding

steamers ran was not small. To this day one marvels that no German raider or cruiser squadron ever even attempted to rush the Straits, as German destroyers did successfully on several occasions. Had a disguised raider of the *Moewe* sort timed her advent to coincide with a feint by a destroyer flotilla, she would under the cover of night have had a good chance of getting clear away down Channel. Any boarding steamer would have been sunk at the first interference.

For it was such steamers as those engaged in the cross-Channel trade which were especially found suitable in this boarding work. The *Peel Castle*, another of the Isle of Man packets, may be cited to illustrate the risky yet essential work which was being carried on in that stretch of water between the Goodwins and the English coast. Throughout the war there was an average of over a hundred merchant vessels a *day* passing in and out of this examination area, and it required only a little daring enterprise for a disguised raider heavily armed to have been one of the daily hundred and sunk any of the examination craft that chanced to be on duty. I believe there was only one German ship which got through. This was during the night of November 7–8, 1916. She made the mistake of trying to proceed east of the Goodwins, whereas all traffic was compelled by regulations to pass first through the Downs for examination. She was sighted at 7.30 that autumn morning by the armed drifter *Paramount* 16 miles east of the South Goodwin lightship, was ordered to stop, but finally had to be shelled into obedience and captured. She was the schooner *Virgen del Socorro* which had been obtained at Corunna, and was full of Germans who had been interned aboard German liners at Lisbon or had been interned in Spain. She was trying to reach Germany, or at least Zeebrugge, but was towed by the drifter into Ramsgate.

On May 1, 1915, a boarding party from *Peel Castle* was examining a Dutch liner, and a gang of stokers was sent to make a search of the engine-room. Presently one of the latter on going through a coal bunker noticed a pair of eyes glaring at him from a mound of coal. The

LOOKING OUT FOR RAIDERS 217

stowaway was found to be a well-known German business man from New York and was transferred to internment ashore. Only a few weeks later—June 11— a boarding party from *Peel Castle* on searching the Dutch S.S. *Rotterdam* found a most interesting man disguised as one of the ship's greasers. He turned out to be the second engineer from the raider *Prinz Eitel Friedrich*, whose internment by the United States we have already noticed.

Similarly there was the incident when a Holland-American liner arrived from New York, and aboard her were found two Germans who were travelling under assumed names. One was proved to be a notorious agent who organised a campaign in the United States against Great Britain, set fire to factories, placed bombs in ships, or was instrumental in these events taking place. The second man pretended to be a railway magnate from Mexico, but in reality was chief assistant to the first.

But it was the German submarines which at once increased the utility and peril of the boarding steamers both in the English Channel and the North Sea. The policy of the British Admiralty after the loss of such warships as *Cressy, Aboukir, Hogue, Hawke*, and *Pathfinder* was not to risk regular naval cruisers too freely in the North Sea at the mercy of submarines, but rather to rely on the armed boarding steamers in regard to look-out duties. The inevitable happened. On July 13, 1916, the armed boarding steamer *Duke of Cornwall* was engaged south-east of the Pentland Skerries examining a vessel, when a submarine fired two torpedoes. Fortunately they missed, but it was a narrow escape. On August 24 of that year the armed boarding steamer *Duke of Albany* was 20 miles east of the Skerries when a submarine sank her and caused considerable loss of life, including Commander G. N. Ramage, R.N.R., who in peace-time was captain of a liner running to India.

As the reader will in due course appreciate from harsh example, the risk of intercepting, single-handed, any strange ship that might be a neutral or disguised

German had to be accepted. At the discretion of the boarding steamer's commanding officer (who in almost every case was an experienced master mariner) any ship sighted might be sent into Lerwick or some other port with an armed party; especially was this so if the stranger happened to be a big vessel, or disobeyed instructions, or the weather was too bad for boarding. Not one of these armed boarding steamers had been designed for carrying in the bunkers coal sufficient for the long periods which were necessarily imposed on these cross-Channel steamers accustomed to making a short, quick run. War consequently required that winter and summer they left port for patrol so overburdened with coal that they were not in a satisfactorily seaworthy condition. Furthermore, they were inferior to any raider both in lightness of construction and armament. After the loss of *Ramsey* 12-pounders were replaced by a couple of 4-inch guns in the boarding steamer *King Orry* (one more of the Manx Fleet), but she would hardly have been a match for a raider.

The onerous boat work was necessary alike for raider and armed boarding steamer, and called for high skill. Anyone who has been alongside a big steamer in an oared boat during even moderately bad weather knows the risks which are endured of being smashed to matchwood any moment. But the enthusiastic admiration for these boatmen drawn from the Mercantile Marine is still on the lips of commanding officers. Of these boat-crews Captain Selwyn M. Day, who commanded *King Orry* for some time, tells me that "their skill excelled any that you would be likely to discover nowadays except that healthy young volunteers were again given an opportunity".

But the Northern Patrol of armed merchant cruisers with their areas north and south of the Faroes, west of the Hebrides, north and east of the Shetlands, was always a source of keenest anxiety to raiders whether outward or homeward bound. It was the mine-laying voyage of *Berlin* which had shown the absolute necessity of such a movable bulwark. It could never be completely raider-proof, yet, in spite of the vile northern

LOOKING OUT FOR RAIDERS 219

weather and the expanse of sea, this was a formidable preventive barrier. Steamers were taken up from such lines as the Royal Mail, Furness Withy, Elders & Fyffes, Pacific Steam Navigation Company, Anchor, and Clan lines. These vessels had little homogeneity, their size varying from 7000 to 2876 tons and the speed from 17 to 11 knots. It was on December 3, 1914, that Rear-Admiral Dudley de Chair hoisted his flag in the armed liner *Alsatian* in command of these merchant-cruisers, which constituted the new 10th Cruiser Squadron.

One of the mysteries of the war is concerned with the small unit of that squadron named *Viknor*. She was the well-known popular tourist steamer *Viking* which used to run excursions in the summer months to Norway, but modified her name on becoming a warship. Now in January 1915 every effort was being made to intercept the Norwegian S.S. *Bergensfjord*, which was suspected of unneutral action. She was thought to be carrying German reservists to Europe with neutral passports. Next, on January 10 at 6.30 a.m. the *Bergensfjord* was heard faintly on the wireless communicating with Bergen, and two hours later *Viknor* intercepted her in Lat. 60.10 N, Long 2.24 W, that is to say 90 miles NNW of the Shetlands.

Viknor's boarding party had discovered in *Bergensfjord* a Baron von Wedel travelling with a neutral passport in the name of Spero. He, together with six stowaways and a sexagenarian passenger thought to be a German reservist, was transferred to *Viknor*, which was never seen again. She was last heard of at 4 p.m. on January 13 off the north Irish coast in Lat. 56.18 N, Long. 9 W, when she was steaming at 10½ knots to pass south of Tory Island for Liverpool. But then her wireless signals ceased suddenly and permanently; nothing else except bodies as well as wreckage was ever found. She had evidently been another victim to the minefield laid by *Berlin* the previous autumn.

Such risks were part of the routine which had to be experienced by the armed boarding steamers and armed merchant cruisers on whom especially rested the duty of preventing German raiders from breaking through on to the high seas. By the end of February 1916 the 10th Cruiser Squadron had lost one ship through stress of weather, two through mines, and three owing to submarines. But at this time, when *Moewe* slipped through the blockade, information was reaching the British Admiralty that a German armed merchant cruiser, which had recently been working in the Baltic as decoy ship with a submarine, was on her way to attempt penetrating the blockade; that she was off the Skaw at 7 a.m. on February 28, and was coming along at 10 knots. At 8.20 that evening a suspicious steamer's position was fixed by directional wireless as being off the south-west Norwegian coast, so it looked as if it were certain that a raider might be coming up the North Sea.

February 28 was a beautiful spring day at first but a gale sprang up in the afternoon, and it is interesting to note that just as *Moewe* was approaching the Atlantic end of the blockade, another German raider was making for the eastern end. The German planning was clever: if the look-out vessels of the British forces should catch one raider, perhaps they might not expect a second. As early as February 25 careful precautions had been made to intercept every kind of vessel passing the Butt of Lewis and Cape Wrath, so that if a raider should attempt steaming close to likely landfalls and evade the armed merchant cruisers further out, she would be spotted. An endless chain of armed trawlers was at work between the Butt of Lewis and Sulisker, each trawler 10 miles apart and steaming at 7 knots, with an armed yacht supervising; two more trawlers were off Cape Wrath, and two more off North Rona with a supervising yacht.

It was at 11.38 a.m. on February 28 that the Admiralty telegraphed to Admiral Jellicoe warning of the Skaw ship, so he ordered two light cruisers—*Inconstant* and *Cordelia*—and four destroyers from Rosyth to patrol the area enclosed by lines drawn from the Skaw across the North Sea to the British

LOOKING OUT FOR RAIDERS 221

coast at the Farne Islands, and from the Naze to May Island (Firth of Forth). Other light cruisers, *Calliope*, *Comus*, and *Blanche*, each with a destroyer, were sent from Scapa Flow to search the middle of the North Sea between Lat. 57.20 and 60 N, and Long. 2 to 4 E by day, but by night to patrol along the meridian of Greenwich. When, however, the directional wireless fixed the mysterious steamer as being near Ekersund at 8.20 p.m. Admiral Jellicoe signalled *Calliope*, *Comus*, and *Blanche* to be on an imaginary circle whose radius was 200 miles from this stranger's last position. The armed merchant cruisers *Columbella* and *Patia*, both of the 10th Cruiser Squadron, were ordered to patrol 30 miles apart in line-ahead.

Now in the neighbourhood also were the two armed merchant cruisers *Andes* (Captain G. B. W. Young, R.N.) and the *Alcantara* (Captain T. E. Wardle, R.N.). The latter had been taken up from the Royal Mail Line and commissioned on April 16, 1915. In November 1914 she was still carrying on her usual passenger trade off the east coast of South America during the first phase of the German raiders, and for a time had to remain in Santos. But now she was as much a warship as *Kronprinz Wilhelm* had been. These 10th Cruiser Squadron converted liners used to go south into Liverpool at regular intervals to coal, and *Alcantara* was due to leave her area for that purpose on the afternoon of February 29 : but soon after 8 a.m. she was ordered by wireless as follows :

Alcantara not to leave patrol pending further orders. Armed disguised enemy merchant auxiliary from the southward may pass patrol line to-day.

Captain Wardle, instead of preparing to depart, therefore got ready for action, and shifted his men into clean underclothing in accordance with accepted naval practice. His ship was one of the single-funnel, multiple-deck type of liners, and at 8.45 a.m. on February 29 *Alcantara* was steaming to the NNE, where he sighted smoke on the port beam. His position at this moment was near to Lat. 61.45 N,

Long. 0.58 E, that is to say, to the north-east of the Shetlands between the Faroes and the coast of Norway. Ten minutes later *Alcantara* received a signal from *Andes* (which was north of Captain Wardle, but not visible):

Enemy in sight steering NE 15 knots.

At 9.10 a.m. *Andes* again signalled:

Vessel steering north when sighted then altered to NE. Painted black, black funnel, two masts. Speed about 15 knots.

It was at this time that *Alcantara* sighted *Andes*, hull down, to the north and steering to the north-east. Captain Wardle increased speed to full, and altered course to the north-west and so came between *Andes* and the stranger's smoke. Before long Captain Wardle made the latter to be a one-funnelled steamer flying Norwegian colours, and these were likewise painted on the vessel's sides as was the custom of neutrals at this time. *Andes* was seen to be hurrying away to the north-east and at 9.35 a.m. signalled:

This is the suspicious ship.

But before proceeding to assist *Andes*, Captain Wardle considered it his duty first to examine the Norwegian, so the boarding party was in readiness to do its job. "At 9.40", reported Captain Wardle, "the boat was being swung out, and I was closing stranger on her port quarter, when I noticed her ensign staff drop over the stern, and men clearing away a gun on the poop. At the same moment stranger fired a shell at our bridge, which put the telemotor steering gear, engine-room telegraph, and all telephones on the bridge out of action, besides killing and wounding men."

Thus with little enough delay the stranger had disclosed her true character, for the preliminaries had been of the briefest. *Alcantara* when approaching had hoisted "M N" of the International Code ("Stop Instantly") and fired two rounds of blank. Thereupon the pretended Norwegian had obeyed and signalled

LOOKING OUT FOR RAIDERS 223

that she was from Rio de Janeiro for Trondhjem, and she bore on her hull the name *Rena* of *Tonsberg*. The enemy on coming into action and abandoning further disguise let down the gun flaps on the ship's side, but not in such a manner as to obscure the flags there painted: consequently the engagement was fought under Norwegian and German colours.

Here, then, at last a raider trying to break through the blockade had been discovered, and the latter knew that she must fight to a finish: no other alternative was possible. A duel, rivalled only by the *Carmania-Cap Trafalgar* affair, was now beginning, the range this time being from 2500 to 3500 yards. In addition to the first few shells which wrecked the boarding boat, cutting *Alcantara's* electrical communications and pipes of the steering gear, there came a terrible spray of machine-gun bullets on to the bridge. Captain Wardle sent his messenger to order the after steering gear to be connected up, but the man was killed on the way, so that for ten critical minutes *Alcantara* was not under control yet continued to close the German, who was now going ahead, and turned to starboard.

Firing high-explosive shell, *Rena* kept holing *Alcantara* near the waterline amidships and penetrating the stokehold bunkers. At 10.2 the German fired a torpedo, but *Alcantara* starboarded helm and the missile passed under the stern. *Alcantara* had not altogether been taken by surprise: on the contrary, she had opened fire immediately after the attack began and did tremendous execution with her guns, the first round from her after 6-inch gun on the port side hitting the *Rena's* ammunition of the latter's after gun, and sealing her fate. By 10.15, indeed, *Rena* was seen to be on fire at the bridge, and seven minutes later boatloads of men were leaving her.

It was an awe-inspiring spectacle this cold morning in that dull, drab atmosphere, as clouds of smoke enveloped the raider in her death-shroud. She had become so suddenly silent, with not one gun barking defiance. But *Alcantara* was in a very bad way too, and with a serious list to port. Nor is it surprising that two merchant ships with ordinary steel plating should so speedily succumb to the rough usage of war. By 10.45 it was evident to Captain Wardle that his vessel was sinking, and that he must abandon her. He therefore gave orders for his men to go to boat stations. By 11 a.m. she had listed ninety degrees, and two minutes later she sank at this angle, finally turning right over.

Inasmuch as *Rena* had opened fire just when the armed guard were about to enter the hoisted-out boat, some of the first shots had been responsible for killing a few of the *Alcantara's* crew. The most obviously striking feature of this engagement was the celerity with which a decision had come to both combatants, each of which was a blazing conflagration and being fiercely destroyed within an hour of exchanging shots. In the olden days of wooden hulls the fighting would have been prolonged, and there would have been a much more pronounced suspense. If at the very first Captain Wardle had been deceived by *Rena's* appearance for one short interlude, no time had been lost after the enemy manifested her real nature, and Captain Wardle paid an enthusiastic tribute to the great gallantry with which his men fought, their coolness and perfect discipline.

At the time of abandoning ship there was no headlong rush, no sort of panic: but the men who were making their way up to the deck just stood aside to let the wounded pass ahead or else helped to carry these afflicted to the boats; thus most of the casualties were able to get away. But two officers and sixty-seven men were lost. *Alcantara* was certainly torpedoed, and according to some of *Rena's* survivors two torpedoes had been fired. Germany had by these tactics not failed to profit from the lesson learned in the sinking of *Ramsey*.

Now when the action began, *Andes* was 7500 yards away and had come up at exceptionally fast speed to succour her sister. The sea was calm, the wind SW, and the visibility 12 to 15 miles. Whenever not screened by *Alcantara*, *Andes* was able to shell the German with 6-inch guns so frequently that 98 rounds were fired.

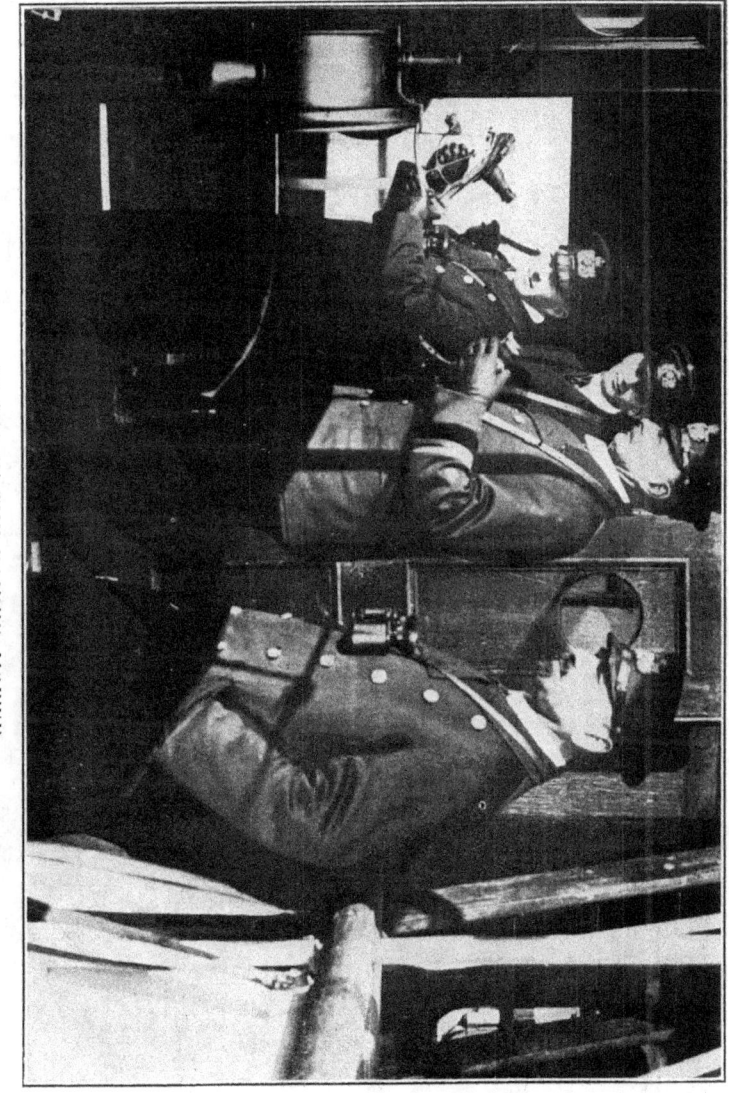

AT SEA IN THE RAIDER *MOEVE*
Count Nikolaus zu Dohna-Schlodien with some of his officers on the *Moeve's* bridge.

ABOARD THE RAIDER *MOEWE*
Count Nikolaus zu Dohna-Schlodien making a speech to his crew.

In order to keep out of torpedo range, she never approached more closely to *Rena* than 6000 yards. One of the first shots from *Andes* hit the enemy's bridge, destroying his steering gear, and disabling every officer on that part of the ship. About the same time another shell exploded in the German's engine-room and put out of action, by gas fumes, all who were in that section.

But also there had arrived on the scene the cruiser *Comus* with her destroyer *Munster*. The former (under the command of Captain Alan Hotham, R.N.) had taken in *Andes*' signal announcing that the enemy had been sighted. *Comus* had then steamed towards her at 27 knots, but arrived only after *Alcantara* had sunk. *Rena*, however, was still afloat, so the cruiser assisted *Andes* to finish off the raider, who sank at 1 p.m. with the German ensign still flying. *Munster* was able to rescue Captain Wardle and some of his crew, whilst *Andes* picked up both British and German survivors. Of the latter there were taken prisoners five officers and 115 men, who were brought into the Firth of Forth. It was then that the whole story of the raider began to be straightened out.

Rena was not her true name, but she had assumed the appellation of a genuine ship about whom and her voyage particulars were known to the British Navy. Certainly the raider (whose name really was *Greif*) answered to the Norwegian's description, and it was part of the German planning on such occasions that the raider should be supplied not only with an external similarity to a definite ship, which might be expected to be sighted in the North Sea on a specified date, but with even forged ships' papers. *Greif* had left Kiel fifty-six hours previously, escorted for part of the way by U-boats. Before starting off on what was to have been as memorable a voyage as had been *Moewe's*, the Kaiser had come aboard and made a speech to the crew. *Greif* was intended to do no raiding in the Atlantic, but to begin operations only when she had reached the other side of the Cape of Good Hope, and she was to render aid to German forces in East Africa. Thus at a time when *Moewe* (whom she somewhat resembled in appearance) was ending one raiding voyage, *Greif* was setting out on another just before the nights would be too short to hope for luck in getting through the blockade. *Moewe* having made the Atlantic too much on the alert for some time, it was not advisable to attack commerce in that ocean just yet awhile.

Greif had been built in 1914 as *Guben* for the German–Australian line. She was an ordinary trader, and not likely to arouse suspicion if seen between Australia and Africa. The success of *Moewe's* technique had caused *Guben's* selection, and early in the New Year she had been secretly fitted out at Hamburg. After leaving Kiel on February 25, she had again been to Hamburg and left there on February 27, thence proceeding up the Norwegian coast with the intention of being on the line Faroes–Shetland during the forenoon of March 1. Her course was then to take her round the north of Iceland, and thus she was to reach the Atlantic by those safe and extremely high latitudes which had been successfully tried by other German adventurers.

Greif's deck had been a veritable shambles, and her captain was one of the slain. Her death-agony was not unlike that of *Alcantara*, for at 1 p.m. she listed heavily to port, her stern went down, and then she disappeared into the sea amid a cloud of smoke and steam. Her complement consisted of over 300 men. Like *Alcantara* and *Andes*, nearly all her crew consisted of reservists, with the exception of the captain and torpedo-lieutenant, who were active service officers. She was armed with four 15-centimetre guns and two 19·7-inch torpedo-tubes, besides one 28-pounder gun. She had a speed of 16 knots, and her cargo holds were full of coal, so that she could have been independent of fuelling facilities for quite a long period. Her crew had been drafted without warning from depot hulks in Kiel on Sunday evening, February 27, just before she came through the Kiel Canal. Not one of these ratings had any idea of the service on which she was bound, and they had not yet had time to settle down aboard before they were in action. Some of the crew had not yet even been allotted General Quarters Stations.

Greif hoped after her raiding voyage to reach Germany again, but if British warships in the Indian Ocean should make it too hot for her she was to make for German East Africa. Having been provisioned for nine months, she could afford to sink merchant vessels without waiting to transfer consumable stores. After the brilliant send-off which *Greif* received and *Moewe* was to be given a week later, it was a serious disappointment to Germany that this blockade-running by raiders should have received a sudden check, and it was not till March 25 that Berlin broadcast the news.

But the interesting and amusing fact has to be mentioned that *Greif* was not the mysterious steamer which had been sighted at the Skaw: that vessel had gone back. And at 11.35 a.m. (just as *Greif* was *in extremis*) the British Admiralty had been able to flash this revised intelligence to Admiral Jellicoe. Nor could *Greif* have been the vessel mentioned as being off Ekersund. The whole incident was just a logical conclusion resulting from plans and counterplans: the raider was attempting to break through by a well-thought-out route, whilst the patrols had been so skilfully and meticulously arranged as to have a scientific rather than a sporting chance of waylaying her. It was a mere coincidence that the snare was laid for one culprit, whilst it caught a second instead.

Another coincidence is concerned with Rear-Admiral Sir Dudley de Chair, who was in command of the 10th Cruiser Squadron and flew his flag in the armed merchant-cruiser *Alsatian*. On his shoulders rested the responsibility of these converted merchant liners for thwarting raiders who sought to slip through the blockade. The Germans were well aware that he was the human representation of this British blockading patrol that caused them so much anxiety. To them he was the personification of the big sea-barrier. So it is curious to note that after *Moewe* had made her successful cruise and evaded the British armed merchant-cruisers, Germany had a medal struck to commemorate the event. It was dedicated to Admiral de Chair and showed a seagull ("moewe") with a fish in its mouth flying over a chain guarded by two sleeping sea-lions. Now it so happened that the British Foreign Office required a naval adviser in connection with the newly appointed Minister of Blockade, and no officer had so much practical blockade experience afloat as Admiral de Chair. He had just been appointed to this shore advisory job, and during the time when *Greif* was being sunk and *Moewe* was nearing Germany, the Admiral was actually steaming in *Alsatian* towards Liverpool on his way up to London.

Of this fight between *Greif* and *Alcantara* Admiral Jellicoe remarked concerning the latter's officers and men: "Their conduct was worthy of the best traditions of the Service, and is one more instance of the exceedingly gallant and valuable services which have been rendered to the Empire by the officers and men of the Mercantile Marine during the present war." But in another place he remarked also that "the incident showed the great difficulty of carrying out blockade work under modern conditions. . . . A raider disguised as a neutral, and armed with torpedo-tubes, is a most difficult customer to deal with, and every neutral vessel had perforce to be treated as 'suspect' after an incident of this nature."

During the year 1915 these converted merchant steamers of the 10th Cruiser Squadron intercepted no fewer than 3098 vessels of various nationalities. But the torpedoing of *Alcantara* showed the danger of coming close to a ship that is to be boarded. Not very different was the risk which a U-boat encountered when she stopped a tramp steamer who might suddenly reveal herself as one of the British Q-ships. War is a horrible, if perhaps inevitable, affair, and I submit that all these losses of brave and clever men, of beautiful ships that were never intended for resisting shells, show the utter futility of wasting lives, brains, time, and money in seeing how much damage the one combatant could inflict on the other. To-day much of the mutual hatred belonging to the previous decade is giving way to a mutual respect between officers who fought each other afloat, in the air, on land, for their respective countries.

I have before me a letter from one of the ablest U-boat commanders who writes to me of the "purgatory" which he suffered during those strenuous months when he was sinking British shipping, and was in turn being attacked by Q-ships. And this is but typical of the new spirit which is going to spread.

From survivors of *Greif* we know that *Alcantara* was able to give the raider undiluted hell. About the second or third salvo from Captain Wardle's ship pierced the enemy's main steam-pipe, blew up the crews of *Greif's* two forward guns, and set on fire the large oil tanks above the engine-room. *Greif's* captain and boatswain abandoned the ship simultaneously, and as the latter was sliding down a rope over the port quarter a shell splinter struck the former carrying half his head away.

The fascinating feature among all this sad slaughter is that drama of man versus man, with the sea as a background: the adventure of living dangerously, the delight in taking big risks, the joy of achieving. From the raider's point of view there certainly was something exhilarating in the great gamble of trying to steal through the blockade. *Greif's* skipper appreciated all that. Just before dawn on February 29 he had passed quite close to one of the 10th Cruiser Squadron; and as the raider was not observed, the German imagined he had got through the last of the patrols. But next along came *Andes*, and from now it was realized that the game was up. *Greif* tried ineffectually to torpedo her, and then started off to make a run for the Norwegian coast. But *Andes* kept ahead of *Greif*, outmanœuvred her, and by the time that the raider was being threatened from *Alcantara*, it was too late for anything but a straight fight.

CHAPTER XVI

THE RAIDERS RESUME

WITH the advent of Spring the time for raiders had passed, till the long wintry nights should again bring their opportunities for evasion. In the meanwhile certain important events were combining to make highly desirable a fresh era for raiding.

For, firstly, the entry of Portugal into the war on the Allies' side came as a nasty blow to German sea pride. All those German steamers, which had been lying interned up the Tagus, were during February 1916 seized, in addition to others at Oporto, the Azores, and St. Vincent. Further and further had receded those times when there were supply bases, and interned ships could hope ere long to rush out into the ocean. Secondly, there was the Sinn Fein trouble in Ireland fast ripening into an opportunity for Germany to profit thereby. Thirdly, on March 24 came that colossal blunder when a German submarine torpedoed the cross-Channel passenger steamer *Sussex*. So great and noisy was the outcry, especially in the United States, that U-boat warfare in Northern Europe stopped, as we have mentioned, altogether from May 8 to July 5, 1916. And fourthly, came the battle of Jutland on May 31, which had a direct influence on the raiding campaign.

The active connection between Germany and the Sinn Fein movement was even in September 1914 as important as it was secret, and during the ensuing months considerable intrigue was being carried on through the German Embassy in Washington. It will be recollected that the notorious German spy Carl Lody was arrested in Ireland, at Killarney, on October 2,

THE RAIDERS RESUME 231

1914, and executed in the Tower of London on the following November 20 : but that extraordinary character Sir Roger Casement reached Berlin from the United States and worked in close association with Germany to attack Britain through an Irish rising. By the spring of 1916 matters had so far progressed that it was arranged for rifles, machine-guns, ammunition, and explosives to be landed on the west of Ireland at Fenit Pier, Tralee Bay, between the 20th and 23rd of April. These warlike stores were to come from Germany and be at the disposal of the plotters in Ireland.

In the United States a sub-bureau of the German Washington Embassy was by an ingenious subterfuge established at 60 Wall Street, New York, where one Wolf von Igel had in the autumn of 1914 started what was ostensibly an advertising agency. That alleged business was mere eye-wash : Von Igel was one of the Embassy's staff specially detailed to carry on German-Irish plotting, and (according to an intercepted despatch from the German Ambassador Bernstorff) had been engaged in conducting the "War Intelligence Centre" in the United States in addition to "the various matters started by von Papen", who had been already given his passport, as we have seen. The American Government, following a seizure of documents at Von Igel's Wall Street office, arrested the latter.

Now Casement left Keil about April 12, 1916, in a German submarine and landed on the coast of Kerry from U 22 during the early hours of Good Friday, April 21, and the Irish rebellion broke out in Dublin on Easter Monday. Those of us who were patrolling off the south-west Irish coast at this time had been warned that the landing of arms might be expected even as early as St. Patrick's Day, March 17. All likely bays were being watched carefully by trawlers, drifters, and other small armed craft, whilst sloops were to seaward ready to examine any strange vessel.

It was the S.S. *Castro*, 1228 tons, which the Germans chose to carry these essential arms to the Irish, and we here have an adventure whose plan was largely based on the success of previous German raiders though carried out after the raider season. *Castro* was originally a British ship of the Wilson Line, and used to trade between Hull and Germany. Built in 1911, she had one deck, was 250 feet long, 35 feet in beam, and 15.9 feet deep. She was detained with a cargo of coal in a German port at the beginning of war and made a prize. In March 1916 she was thought to be just the handy little ship for getting through the blockade and into a small Irish harbour of the west coast. She was therefore specially fitted out at Wilhelmshaven alongside the recently returned *Moewe*.

On March 21 Lieutenant Karl Spindler, an officer of the German Naval Reserve, was given command of this mystery ship and her name was changed to *Libau*. Spindler had been fourth officer in one of the North German Lloyd liners, and with him were now appointed two warrant officers together with nineteen petty officers and men—all these twenty-two having been drafted from German armed trawlers based on Wilhelmshaven. Before leaving port she dropped her dockyard name of *Libau* and changed it to *Aud*, assuming also Norwegian nationality. She was provided with faked documents, in case she should be stopped and examined by British patrols. For this reason she was given two separate manifests—one for Cardiff, one for Genoa and Leghorn. Very ingeniously a purely fictitious log was written up indicating an imaginary voyage to England, so that the boarding officer might be inclined to believe all that she pretended to be.

From Wilhelmshaven she passed through the Kiel Canal and reached Lübeck as a merchant ship. Here she took on board a cargo of arms, munitions, bombs, supplies for six months, coal enough to last forty-five days, but also a camouflage cargo consisting of pit-props and other goods which were placed on top of the real freight. Having now her Norwegian certificates and bills of lading comprising an apparently perfect set of ship's papers; having also both port and starboard sides painted with the lettering *"Aud . . . Norge"*, she finally set forth from Lübeck at 6 p.m. on Sunday,

April 9, in the hope that the pit-props, wooden window-frames, tin goods, beneath her hatches might bear out her pretended story. The rifles, trench tools, and bombs had been largely obtained from the Russian armies which collapsed on the Eastern Front. Spindler, being an experienced Mercantile Marine officer, had omitted no item which ought to complete the character of a small trader. For instance, the chalked tally-marks which one sees on a tramp's hatches after loading were all carefully added. Altogether this ex-Wilson liner was a pretty good piece of deception.

Before setting out, Spindler had various interviews with Casement, and arrangements were made for the arrival of U 22 to synchronize with that of *Aud*. Rather than let his steamer fall into British hands, Spindler could blow his ship up by a large quantity of explosives, which had been placed in a suitable position with a 3-foot casing of cement built round it, and the detonating wire carried to the upper deck.

His course was by the Kattegat and Skagerrak, then up the North Sea till he was 75 miles east of the Shetlands, thence northward to where the Polar Circle intersects the meridian of Greenwich, where *Aud* lay-to a whole day with engines stopped to kill time. For the weather was too calm, the atmosphere too clear, it was nearing full moon, and in those high latitudes at that time of the year there was practically no night : in other words, the conditions for penetrating the blockade were anything but favourable. But now bad weather followed a falling barometer, and the misty atmosphere with heavy showers came as the greatest blessing : *Aud* slipped away to the south-west.

On Sunday, April 16, at 7.15 p.m., *Aud* sighted one of the British blockade armed merchant cruisers, which steamed parallel with the alleged Norwegian for some time at a distance of about 200 yards. This worried Spindler. "I must confess", he afterwards wrote, "that the conduct of this English auxiliary cruiser—whose name, unfortunately, we could not make out, as it had been painted over—was one of the greatest puzzles of my life, and has remained so to this day." But

Spindler was making the old mistake of assuming that the enemy has not an ability as high as oneself. The German never seems to have suspected that it was quite possible the British Navy knew all about the *Aud*, yet this was the case. "We knew he was coming," Admiral Sir Reginald Hall, then Director of Naval Intelligence at the Admiralty, has since remarked, "and watched him most of the way. There was no object in sinking him in the North Sea; we wanted to make certain that he intended to carry out the object with which he was credited—namely, to carry supplies to Ireland—and this could only be proved by the arrival of the ship at her destination." So *Aud* was carefully noted, and allowed to carry on.

After proceeding so far to the west of the British Isles that she was off Rockall, that lonely Atlantic islet between two and three hundred miles west of the Outer Hebrides, *Aud* was again scrutinized by an armed merchant cruiser and, on April 20, having changed her disguise and jettisoned most of her camouflage cargo, was off Inishtooskert, that uninhabited island on the north-west end of Tralee Bay, where the rendezvous was to be kept with Casement coming in U 22. Now *Aud* steamed around without any luck that night. She made towards Fenit Pier in Tralee Bay, then along the south Kerry coast for two hours, and displayed the green light which was to be the signal for the Sinn Feiners. But nothing happened, there was no response, and there was no U 22 then to be seen. Therefore at 1.30 a.m. on the 21st *Aud* let go anchor under Inishtooskert.

Four and a half hours later she was visited by one of the armed trawlers based on Galway. This was *Setter II*, but the warrant officer in command, a skipper who in peace-time was a fisherman, did not make more than a cursory examination; however, at 1 p.m. *Aud* became nervous, weighed anchor, and proceeded southwest. Her fate was sealed. Before the evening was over she was encircled by sloops whose smoke clouds could be seen in the distance. At 7 p.m. H.M.S. *Bluebell*, one of those flower-class sloops, ordered her to stop at once

THE RAIDERS RESUME

and asked: "What ship?" "Where bound?" Spindler must have been very simple and extraordinarily stupid, for he replied, "Genoa."

That settled matters. A cargo ship of mysterious character, off the Sinn Fein centre, pretending she was bound for Italy! And these sloops on the look-out for a steamer due off the Irish coast about this time! It needed a shell from *Bluebell's* forward gun to burst ahead of the German before the latter obeyed the order to follow. During the night *Bluebell* escorted the prize towards Queenstown, but on Easter morning, April 23, when off Daunt's Rock lightship, by Queenstown, *Bluebell* was seen from the Commander-in-Chief's house with *Aud* suddenly stopped, the German White Ensign hoisted, and the crew going off in boats. A flash, an explosion, a cloud of smoke, some red-yellow flames, and *Aud* disappeared into fragments, together with all the munitions which should have reached the Irish rebels. Spindler and crew were picked up and taken prisoners, but he had blown his ship up to prevent her being taken into Queenstown.

Casement and two other men from U 22 had landed in a collapsible boat on the beach to the north of Fenit not till 4 a.m. on Good Friday. The U-boat had reached Tralee Bay late on the evening of April 20 and had seen from a distance in the dark the outline of a ship at anchor off Inishtooskert. She mistook this for a British destroyer, though actually it was *Aud*. Casement, despairing of *Aud's* arrival, went ashore as stated, was arrested, subsequently tried, and—as everyone knows—executed. The historic collapsible boat was in due course sent as a present to His Majesty King George. It had been found with revolvers near by in Ballyheighe Bay.

Setter II had soon retrieved her mistake. When it was realized that this was the wanted *Aud*, *Setter* and another armed trawler *Lord Heneage* went in pursuit of the German, and the signal station at Sybil Point saw these two auxiliaries chasing as hard as they could go, flying the signal to stop at once. *Aud* took no notice and was hurrying off as best she could, expecting to get right away. It was now about 4 p.m. on Thursday, but into *Bluebell's* wireless office came the patrol trawler's signal that a suspicious steamer was steering to the south-west, and at 5.40 p.m. *Bluebell* intercepted her.

So *Aud's* voyage had been a complete failure. She had been watched and allowed to get through patrol after patrol, and her efforts at deception had been the cause of no little amusement. Spindler was taken to Donington Hall camp, escaped, but was recaptured; and in the meantime *Aud's* White Ensign was hanging suitably framed in the wardroom of *Bluebell* as a memento of an interesting naval occasion.

Now on April 20 the German Embassy, Washington, had sent the following telegram to the Foreign Office, Berlin :

> Cohalan requests me to send on the following :
> The Irish revolt can only succeed if assisted by Germany, otherwise England will be able to crush it, although after a severe struggle. Assistance required. There would be an air raid on England and a naval attack timed to coincide with the rising. . . .

Actually a Zeppelin raid was made on East Anglia during April 24 (the day the rebellion broke out in Dublin), and on April 25 a naval raid was made on Lowestoft and Yarmouth whilst a Zeppelin raid was made on Essex and Kent. But the United States, in consequence of the *Sussex* incident on March 24, sent a very sharp note to Germany, threatening to break off diplomatic relations. This note was dated April 20, Germany decided to yield, and sent orders to the Naval Staff that henceforth submarine warfare was to be carried on in accordance with Prize Law. This order reached the High Sea Fleet on April 25 by wireless whilst on their way towards Lowestoft, and in effect stopped U-boat warfare for a few weeks as stated. It was this restriction of German naval operations, combined with the injury and lessons learned at Jutland, that were to make raiding overseas this coming winter more essential than before. The German Navy must

THE RAIDERS RESUME

do something, and British commerce must be attacked on the ocean whatever might be done by submarines in the Narrow Seas.

After the German surrendered fleet was scuttled at Scapa Flow following the Armistice, there was discovered in an officer's cabin aboard one of the ships an interim report dated July 4, 1916, addressed by Admiral Scheer, Commander-in-Chief of the High Sea Fleet, to the Kaiser touching the Battle of Jutland. He concluded this report by submitting the opinion that even the most favourable issue of a "battle on the high seas will not compel England to make peace in this war", but "a victorious termination of the war within measurable time can only be attained by destroying the economic existence of Great Britain". Scheer was thinking of the submarine campaign, but the surface raiders were part of the scheme for destroying Britain's means of keeping alive.

When the late autumn set in, and the season for deep-sea raiders to leave Germany was once more at hand, Admiral Jellicoe was already anticipating events and issuing fresh orders for preventing these disguised vessels from breaking through into the Atlantic. Portugal having declared war against Germany that spring, British cruisers were able to use Funchal and the Cape Verde Islands which were denied to raiders. Count zu Dohna-Schlodien still remained Germany's chief expert in this armed merchant cruiser warfare against British commerce, and whilst he was resting these summer months, his ship *Moewe* was being refitted in the dockyard for her second cruise. He himself had been decorated with the Iron Cross of both the first and second class, but he had also received the Order Pour le Mérite.

This keen officer with the short imperial beard and moustache, which made him appear extraordinarily like the well-known illustrations of that fictitious character "Captain Kettle", was far too valuable to his own country to be wasted on enterprises other than raids. On November 22, 1916, he steamed away from Germany for his second voyage, to be followed a week later by the *Wolf*, and on December 21 by the *Seeadler*. The last two raiders developed on a much bolder scale the general idea which *Moewe* had initiated, and their remarkable voyages will be duly considered. It is noteworthy that Germany should have shown her belief in this war against commerce by risking three ships through the blockade within a month, notwithstanding the fate which had befallen *Greif* and *Aud*. There was, moreover, a fourth which was to come very much into the limelight during the next March.

Again proceeding by the North Sea route and hugging the Norwegian coast, favoured by fog and then by heavy weather as well as bad visibility, passing through the danger zone at night, but not going right up to Arctic north this time, the Count saved five days, so that by November 26 he was well through the blockade into the boisterous Atlantic. Dirty weather compelled him to heave-to, but by November 30 this moderated and *Moewe* went south giving the west coast of Ireland a berth of several hundred miles. She was thus well clear of all patrols. On December 2 she was cutting across the North Atlantic steamer track and had reached a point 650 miles west of the Fastnet, that is to say only about 30 miles away from where she had captured the *Saxon Prince* at the end of her previous cruise; and now she captured and sank the British S.S. *Voltaire*, 8618 tons, bound to America in ballast.

Having thus begun by attacking the North Atlantic trade route, and taken as prisoners *Voltaire's* crew of ninety-five, *Moewe* elected to remain hereabouts with a view to trapping others. Here, almost half-way between Ireland and Newfoundland, she could be sure of finding victims and of not being interrupted. Two days later *Moewe* had the misfortune to meet with the Belgian Relief S.S. *Samland* with 9000 tons of meat for Belgium and a permit from the German Embassy. A Norwegian steamer with machine parts and steel tubes (thought to be intended for the manufacture of rifle barrels) for England was sunk, and then on December 6 the British 9792-ton S.S. *Mount Temple* was captured and destroyed by bombs 620 miles west of the Fastnet, after having been shelled. She was bound for Brest with horses, wheat, and other cargo. Three lives were lost and the rest of the crew taken prisoners.

On the same day and at about the same spot the little British sailing-vessel *Duchess of Cornwall*, 152 tons, bound for Gibraltar with salt meat, was also sunk. On December 8 *Moewe* had moved along the track till she was 700 miles east of Cape Race, Newfoundland, where she captured the British S.S. *King George*, 3852 tons, having 600 tons of gunpowder as well as other cargo ; next morning another British steamer, *Cambrian Grange*, of 4234 tons, carrying wheat, was taken and destroyed, the position being 90 miles nearer to Cape Race. But *Moewe's* captain had now reason to become apprehensive, for the Belgian Relief ship had naturally made known the fact that *Moewe* was again at sea, and the tidings were flashed far and wide to all British merchant ships. Thus *Moewe* intercepted from Bermuda wireless station on December 9 :

> Government war warning begins : Enemy raider sighted 7 a.m., 4 December . . . take all precautions.

To the Count this meeting had been particularly annoying since it broke down that secrecy and mysteriousness which were essential parts of his tactics, but he was in too busy a locality to move far away from these North American sea-lanes immediately. Was he not on the very highway, along which were being borne so many cargoes from America wherewith to win the war ? He was thus in the most direct manner striking violent blows not merely at Britain's munition factories and her armies, but at the nation's food supplies and that economic existence concerning which Admiral Scheer had correctly reasoned. *Moewe* therefore held on, came across the British S.S. *Georgic* 590 miles ESE of Cape Race early on December 10, and shelled her because the latter was defensively armed with a gun. One life was lost, and *Georgic* was finally destroyed by a torpedo. This was a 10,000-ton vessel with 1200 horses, wheat, oil, and other commodities all very necessary for Britain just now ; and this is a perfect instance of the great havoc which can be done to an island nation by disguised cruisers allowed to roam about the seas. The person who in time of strikes and internal disputes motors across country cutting telegraph wires does on a small scale that which *Moewe* was achieving in a larger manner when she severed the communications between Britain and America.

On the 11th, only 50 miles nearer towards the American continent, *Moewe* made another valuable haul, when she captured the British 4652-ton S.S. *Yarrowdale*. For a reason that will subsequently appear, this vessel was an important capture, quite apart from the fact that she was carrying 100 motor-cars and 3200 tons of steel for the Allies. As she had enough coal for a month, it was decided to transfer to her all the accumulated prisoners and send them into Germany. This was a modification of the Count's practice during his first cruise, and it would preserve his later movements from becoming known. He therefore put in charge of *Yarrowdale* that officer named Badewitz who will be remembered as having in the previous year taken the *Westburn* with prisoners into Santa Cruz where he was subsequently interned. But such was the slackness of the Spanish authorities that he escaped, got back to Germany, and joined *Moewe* for her second cruise. To attempt rushing the blockade with *Yarrowdale* was taking a risk that was desirable though hardly necessary. The aim was not merely to prevent all these merchant crews from informing the British Admiralty where and by whom the steamers had been sunk; it was also to rob Britain of seafarers at a time when she could not afford to lose master mariners, marine engineers, and junior officers for the rest of the war period. But the transference could not be made immediately. *Moewe* in the meantime steamed about 150 miles to the southeast, thus crossing one of the more southerly tracks, and on December 12 when 520 miles west of Flores in the Azores captured the British S.S. *St. Theodore*, a vessel of 4992 tons with 7000 tons of American coal.

Because of her cargo this was too valuable a ship to be sunk, and ensured fuel for *Moewe* during a long time

ARMED MERCHANT CRUISER *ANDES*

Which assisted in sinking the German raider *Greif*. *Andes* is seen in the familiar war-time dazzle paint.

THE RAIDER REWARDED

Count Nikolaus zu Dohna-Schlodien, Captain of *Möwe*, leaving his hotel after being decorated by the Kaiser with the Order Pour le Mérite after a successful cruise.

THE RAIDERS RESUME

to come. It was on the next day that Badewitz with 440 prisoners from all the prizes was dismissed to take *Yarrowdale* round the north of Scotland and down the North Sea, whilst Sub-Lieutenant Köhler was put in command of *St. Theodore*, which was sent to a secret rendezvous as had been customary for a captured collier in the previous cruise. But *Moewe* now changed her area from north of the Azores to the south and went still further south-east till she reached a point 490 miles south-west of Flores, intersecting the track from the Panama Canal to the English Channel via St. Thomas (West Indies) and the Azores.

It was thus that on December 18 she captured and destroyed the 5415-ton British steamer *Dramatist*, carrying, besides explosives, Californian fruit. The latter was, of course, taken aboard the raider, who then continued further south still, so that the next day she was in another of those "dead" zones away from traffic, where three days were spent cleaning boilers which had been in continuous use for just a month. Two days before Christmas the rendezvous was kept with *St. Theodore*, which was now armed with guns, fitted with wireless, provisioned for a month, renamed *Geier*, and sent off on December 28 under Lieutenant-Commander Wolf to waylay sailing vessels. In the meanwhile *Moewe* herself on Christmas Day had stopped and sunk the French sailing-ship *Nantes*, 2600 tons, that was bringing 3300 tons of saltpetre to the London river for the manufacture of gunpowder.

Moewe was now to operate for some time in that most attractive region which has been so frequently mentioned in these pages as the raiders' paradise and contains the tracks which run north-eastwards from Brazil. It is worth noting that, except for occasions when atmospherics were bad, *Moewe* was able to keep in wireless touch with the German Admiralty, and now the news reached the Count that *Yarrowdale* was to be added to the list of German ships which had evaded the British blockade. On the last day of 1916 she got safely into Germany, and, however regrettable this incident is to record, there can be no denying that it was a brave bit of work. Nor was this the last time that *Yarrowdale* should venture into forbidden waters.

On January 2 *Moewe* was able to sink another French sailing-vessel, the four-master *Asnières*, 3000 tons, bound for Bordeaux with 4200 tons of wheat, and this capture was followed shortly afterwards by that of the Japanese small steamer *Hudson Maru*, which was not sunk but kept going with a prize crew. It is, however, noteworthy that *Moewe*, in spite of searching this South American trade route with keen diligence, was finding it singularly barren : shipping was now being warned and controlled with great efficacy. But on January 7, when 110 miles east of Pernambuco, that is to say by the track leading from Brazil to St. Paul Rocks, the raider made another British capture. This was the S.S. *Radnorshire*, 4310 tons, with a valuable cargo of coffee from Santos, and from her *Moewe* obtained large quantities of provisions before the prize was destroyed by bombs. After this incident the German steamed north-eastward up the track, and two days later sank the British collier *Minieh*,* 3806 tons, which had recently coaled H.M.S. *Amethyst*, the light cruiser that was patrolling the South American coast.

Thus warned of his peril, the Count left the Rocas area for the safer central Atlantic, and in so doing captured the British S.S. *Netherby Hall* next day, 300 miles from Pernambuco. The latter was a vessel of 4461 tons. But by now *Moewe* had again a congregation of 250 prisoners, so it was necessary to send them off in the *Hudson Maru* on January 10, and they duly reached Pernambuco. A week after these two ships had separated, *Moewe* met *St. Theodore* (alias *Geier*) and coaled from her at sea, with the usual difficulties under the circumstances of a heaving swell, and the death of a stoker. The cruise of *St. Theodore* had been singularly unproductive : she had made only the insignificant capture of the small Canadian sailing-vessel *Jean* (215 tons) 60 miles east of St. Paul Rocks.

---

* S.S. *Minieh* was actually trying, on behalf of the *Amethyst*, to decoy the raider.

THE RAIDERS RESUME 243

On January 19 coaling had to be concluded, as *St. Theodore* tore open several of *Moewe's* plates. Again the two raiders went their separate ways, and the latter now chose an entirely new route. Between January 22 and February 2 she was operating on the track to the Cape of Good Hope between Lat. 15 and 30 S. By the former date news of *Yarrowdale's* arrival in Germany was known in England.

The Count's decision to try the Cape route proved entirely abortive, so that again he returned towards the Brazilian coast, and on February 11 met *St. Theodore* near the island of Trinidada, where *Carmania* had many months ago sunk *Cap Trafalgar*. Once more *St. Theodore* had failed : she had sunk but one sailing-ship again. On February 14, after transference of crew, *Moewe*, not having destroyed a ship since January 10, sank *St. Theodore*.

The raider's next area was well away from the South American coast, roughly 500 miles E by N from Cape Frio, Brazil, where it was not likely that armed merchant cruisers might interrupt her. On February 15 she sank the British S.S. *Brecknockshire*, 8423 tons, a fine ship on her maiden voyage with 7000 tons of coal. From her were obtained English newspapers dated January 23, which provided interesting war information including references to *Moewe* herself : one more instance of the necessity to destroy such items before capture by the enemy. Next day the British 4766-ton steamer *French Prince* was also captured and sunk, a similar fate meeting the British S.S. *Eddie* on the day following, this being a smaller craft of 2652 tons. But *Moewe* at last was close to danger : the armed merchant cruiser *Edinburgh Castle* sighted and chased her, incidentally preventing the raider from capturing another cargo steamer. In order to get right away, the Count took his vessel eastwards, having been favoured with a rain squall which enabled him to alter course. He got off the frequented track and from about February 17-23 was on a northerly course up the Atlantic, three days being spent repairing one of his boilers which had been unable to bear the strain caused by the exceptional speed which the chase had necessitated. As usual he had been lucky, but it was a new experience for the hunter to have been hunted by another converted merchantman.

His aim now was to find his way back to Germany, crossing the trade routes in mid-ocean, and to attack whatever should be seen on the way. Thus a whole week elapsed before he had another capture; but on February 23 when 200 miles north-east of St. Paul Rocks he found a victim in the British S.S. *Katherine*, 2926 tons, bringing 4500 tons of wheat from Rosario. No more good fortune could be found on the South American routes, and from February 27 to March 3 he again overhauled boilers in readiness for the last stages of his voyage when he would need the highest engine-room efficiency. On March 4 he was athwart the track from the West Indies and sank the British S.S. *Rhodanthe*, 3061 tons, when 330 miles NNW of the Cape Verdes. *Rhodanthe* was in ballast bound to Cuba for sugar.

After molesting but releasing a Norwegian sailing-vessel next day, nothing further happened till March 10, by which time *Moewe* was 420 miles to the westward of Lisbon. The Count was both disappointed and surprised at the paucity of British traffic now to be seen, but had to content himself with sinking the 4678-ton British steamer *Esmeraldas* on the track for Baltimore whither she was to fetch horses for the Army.

On this same day and at about the same spot she shelled the British S.S. *Otaki*, 9575 tons, but the fire was returned with gallantry, *Otaki* being armed defensively though with very considerably inferior strength. *Otaki's* shells exploded under *Moewe's* bridge with serious effect, but the duel was uneven. The British merchantman developed a heavy list to starboard and became on fire till she sank. The master and five others had been killed, and the rest were taken prisoners, but this was one of the many glorious episodes of the British Mercantile Marine during the war. Not every master mariner with a small single gun considered it prudent to fight a heavily armed raider:

THE RAIDERS RESUME

some held the opinion that against such odds it were foolish to throw away the lives entrusted to their care, and with this argument it is possible to agree. But *Otaki's* captain in his brave self-sacrifice was doing service to the rest of the Allies' seaborne commerce. He made some nasty holes in the raider's hull, which had to be plugged, and he caused her some serious leaks, besides several deaths among *Moewe's* engine-room staff.

Had this incident occurred earlier in *Moewe's* voyage, and further to the south, the raider would have been so crippled that she could not have afforded to risk another action. If only a second *Otaki* had stood up to her, the cruise against trade would have ended. As it was, however, *Moewe* with a plucky and determined skipper was every day getting nearer home and could afford to take on a few more risks. She had been sent forth to sink and fight, whilst the primary duty of every merchant vessel in peace or war is not to fight but to get safely over the ocean.

It was on December 13 that *Moewe*, in her northward progress and still keeping cautiously in mid-Atlantic, encountered the British S.S. *Demeterton*, 6048 tons, in a position 730 miles east of Cape Race. *Demeterton* had a cargo of timber and was defensively armed, but before she could open fire, *Moewe* shelled her into submission. She was destroyed by bombs, but as usual it was most difficult to sink a timber-laden vessel. Next day *Moewe* had got as far north as 930 miles west of the Fastnet when she came across another defensively armed steamer of British nationality, *Governor*, of 5524 tons, who did her best to escape until shelled by salvo after salvo. After four men had been killed, she did surrender, one officer standing by the master on the bridge being blown to pieces. *Governor* was finally destroyed by torpedo. Already part of her navigating bridge had been shot away and her decks shattered.

This was the last victim that *Moewe* ever made. By March 16 she was steaming at utmost speed through the blockade with a total of 800 people on board, of whom about half were prisoners. March 18 found the raider steering south from the Iceland neighbourhood, but she had left the time for returning somewhat late ; the nights were dangerously light had she not gone to such lonely and unpatrolled latitudes. The Norwegian coast was passed after sunset, and on March 22 she reached Kiel, having had an adventurous four months of cruising.

It was her last voyage. Neither *Moewe* nor her captain made a further attempt, and the *Otaki* incident emphasized that surface raiding even by the ablest of commanding officers with the ideal ship had its limitations. Just as British Q-ships reached the peak of their usefulness and were not immediately abolished, so the German surface raiders even after the height of their success still continued for a while. But from February 1, 1917, a change had come over the situation when Germany began her campaign of unrestricted submarine warfare. She now possessed under-water craft that could cross the Atlantic and do the work of surface raiders with even greater surprise. Instead of U-boats sinking 42 merchant ships a month—which was the highest rate at the time when *Moewe* started her second cruise—the figures by March 1917 had reached 103, to be followed in April by 155, which was the highest during the whole war. Germany was hoping by this intense concentrated activity against commerce to force Britain into peace, and very nearly succeeded. The real difficulty of these ocean-going submarines was (1) that they were slow in submerging, and (2) had not the space for taking captured crews as prisoners. Therefore they selected as captives the best brains and most valuable persons, such as the master and the chief engineer.

The strain on the officers and crew of German raiders was comparable only with that on men in Q-ships. That Count zu Dohna-Schlodien was able to make two long voyages each of several months, and four times to run the blockade, shows the extraordinarily strong nerve which a man in the prime of life possesses. But it could not be tested indefinitely. Both he and his subordinates suffered from the strain, and rheumatism

THE RAIDERS RESUME

was not the only penalty for having flitted about from Arctic regions to tropics. He still remains the greatest of all these raiders by steamship, and it was his brains which enabled him to outwit difficulties. This is to be appreciated only by comparing his blockade running with the efforts of those who failed. As Captain (now Admiral) Gordon Campbell stamped his own character on the British Q-ship service, so *Moewe's* captain raised the art of blockade running and raiding to such a high standard of efficiency that it became a model for others ; and a study of his technique cannot be neglected if one has in mind the possibility of future attacks on seaborne trade.

CHAPTER XVII

SINKING THE RAIDER

WE approach now an extremely interesting sequel to *Moewe's* second raid, and it illustrates the working of the German Admiralty's mind in its endeavour to assist the returning Count. Already we have seen that just as he was coming back through the blockade at the end of his first voyage Germany sent out *Greif*, hoping that this diversion would enable at least one if not both ships to succeed.

Before the end of 1916 Admiral Beatty had succeeded Admiral Jellicoe as Commander-in-Chief, and the possibility of raiders attempting to pass north of Scotland during the long nights caused further detailed instructions to be issued for the Grand Fleet, 10th Cruiser Squadron, and Armed Boarding Steamers. In the meanwhile, however, *Yarrowdale*, which had reached Swinemunde on December 31, was taken in hand, fitted out as a raider, and sent forth from Germany so that on March 16—the very day that *Moewe* was in the middle of the blockade area—she also was passing through that forbidden region. This twin-screw British-built steamer of 4652 tons had been armed by the Germans with nine guns and disguised as a Norwegian. She had also changed her name to *Rena* and pretended to be one of the many ships which at this time were trading from Norway. She was painted black with some white about her upper works, and she had one black funnel.

Her masts were two, with cross-trees on each, and she had long derricks. Two white bands were painted on the funnel. One of her guns was concealed in the house astern, and she had torpedo-tubes on each side: altogether she was a formidable warship ingeniously

SINKING THE RAIDER 249

disguised. Whilst the words *Rena . . . Norge* were painted conspicuously on her sides, her naval name given by the Germans was *Leopard*, and she was so well laden as to have the appearance of carrying a full cargo.

The sixteenth of March was one of those biting days with a south-east wind (force 4 to 5) accompanied by squalls of rain and snow, and there was a moderate sea. The locality to be considered may be fixed in Lat. 64.62 N, Long. 0.56 W, that is to say over 200 miles north-east of the Faroes, between Iceland and Norway; a most likely track for a blockade-runner bound to or from Germany. Still, what with northern mists and endless expanse of waves this was no sort of guarantee that an intruder might be sighted. Patrolling about here was H.M.S. *Achilles*, a light cruiser, and the armed boarding steamer *Dundee*. For as far back as March 9 of the previous year this dual type of patrol had been instituted to cover the tracks of vessels *en route* between the north of Iceland and Norway. At 11.45 a.m. a steamer was sighted bearing N 84 E some nine miles away and steering about ENE, whilst *Achilles* was heading N 15 W but altered course to N 84 E with the intention of closing her, and directed *Dundee* to conform. The speed of advance was 15 knots.

The commanding officer of *Achilles* was Captain F. M. Leake, R.N., who had been torpedoed whilst in command of the flotilla-leader *Pathfinder* by U 21 when that submarine succeeded in sinking her off May Island at the beginning of the war. This charming and courteous English gentleman—now, alas, gone aloft— was an old *Worcester* boy before entering the Royal Navy, and died an Admiral. *Dundee* was commanded by Commander Selwyn M. Day, R.N.R., who also had received his early training in *Worcester*, but later on in the well-known sailing-vessel *Macquarie*. Captain Day's experience of merchant ships both in peace and war was already exceptional, and we shall presently note how valuable this was to be. In the previous August whilst in command of the armed boarding steamer *King Orry*, Captain Day had taken the latter across the North Sea from Scapa Flow disguised as a merchant ship and operated for a short while off Stadlandet, Norway, to intercept vessels which were carrying contraband.

King Orry was another of the Isle of Man steamers which had been taken up in the first autumn of war, and originally carried nothing heavier than a 12-pounder till the loss of *Ramsey* brought the decision to fit a couple of 4-inch guns. For the Norwegian venture she was made to look the perfectly peaceful trader. Breaks in her sides were filled up with canvas and painted black, derricks were fitted to masts, guns were covered by temporary superstructures, the funnel painted yellow with a black top, and the embossed name on her bows transformed to *Viking Orry*—*Viking* being a very usual name for a ship of Norwegian waters. The net result of Captain Day's exploit was that he came across a large cargo steamer carrying ore for Germany. As soon as the stranger had emerged from the mist, a couple of 4-inch shells across the bows caused her to stop, whilst a boarding party was sent from *King Orry*. A prize crew was put in charge and the magnetic iron ore was brought into Kirkwall. Under various captains *King Orry* survived the four war winters of vile weather in north Europe, yet she had been designed as a pleasure steamer for carrying summer passengers.

The armed boarding steamer *Dundee*, which Captain Day was commanding on March 16, was a single-funnelled coasting steamer belonging to the Dundee, Perth, and London Shipping Company. She was built in 1911 and was of 2187 tons. Her armament consisted of two 4-inch guns (throwing a weight of 80 lbs.) and two 3-pounders.

Now it was some time before the strange steamer sighted by *Achilles* and *Dundee* could be approached. *Achilles* increased speed to 18 knots at 1 p.m. and three-quarters of an hour later altered course to S 87 E to avoid following directly astern, lest the stranger should be up to any tricks. By 2 p.m. the latter had been overtaken and signalled to stop. She obeyed the cruiser's order, and was seen to have the Norwegian

SINKING THE RAIDER

flag painted on her quarter, with "*Rena . . . Norge*" on each side.

Captain Leake next directed her to steer W by S and at 2.35 she was again stopped for *Dundee* to make an examination of her. This method of employing an armed merchant ship to do the actual boarding work, whilst her companion the naval cruiser stood by, was employed to lessen the risk of the latter being torpedoed. In plain language the nation could better afford—at the worst—to lose a converted merchant steamer than a costly four-funnelled lithe cruiser of the regular service. Whilst *Achilles* was manœuvring some $2\frac{1}{2}$ to 3 miles away, *Dundee* at 2.42 lowered a boat containing Lieutenant F. H. Lawson, R.N.R., four R.N.R. seamen (all named Anderson), and one R.N.V.R. seaman named Birchall. These six comprised the boarding and boat party, who were rowing towards the intercepted *Rena* (alias *Yarrowdale*, alias *Leopard*) that was about a couple of miles off but steaming slowly towards them.

During the interval the following signals were being exchanged:

Time.	Signal made by "*Dundee*".	Reply by "*Rena*".
2.40	What ship is that?	No reply.
2.45	Stop instantly.	A.P. [Answering Pendant.]
2.50	Pay attention to my signals.	No reply.

No reply being forthcoming, *Dundee* now fired a blank round. This woke *Rena* up.

2.59	What is your cargo?	General.
3.10	Where are you from?	Mobile.
3.30	When did you leave?	No reply.

These extremely unsatisfactory answers of course pointed to one conclusion. Captain Day was now convinced that here was an enemy, and her motions were more than suspicious. "Her size, manœuvres, and the information in confidential books supplied, convinced me eventually she was a raider," wrote Captain Day, "and it was obvious he was trying to defeat my object of maintaining a position (for attack) close up to the weather quarter and heading across his stern, and he constantly moved the propellers, slewing to port or starboard. Keeping station thus, we awaited some sign from the boarding officer or the boat, which was, of course, on the lee side, and could not be seen by us.

"At 3.40 I heard the noise of the large Norwegian flag painted on her port quarter fall outboard, being hinged on the lower side, and I gave the orders, 'Fire' and 'Half-speed ahead' to keep station, the raider now slewing rapidly to port with slight, if any, headway. Two torpedoes followed from her in quick succession, passing from 20 to 50 feet astern. The Norwegian flag remained hoisted on the ensign staff throughout, and no other flag was seen. Our guns were already firing, and every shot was a hit. The first (from our aft 4-inch) raked the port battery deck, causing an explosion and volumes of smoke. The fore gun fired through the deck into her engine-room and volumes of steam spread with intense smoke and flames, caused by further hits, so as to completely hide the ship from us from bridge to stern. The 3-pounder gun fired at her bridge . . .

"Forty-four 4-inch and twenty-five 3-pounder rounds were fired at about 1000 yards range before the raider fired her first gun. *Dundee* was then in the smoke (wind SE, force 4 to 5) to leeward, and both ships practically obscured from each other in consequence.

"Observing *Achilles* on almost opposite bearing, I turned, and went full speed down the lane of smoke so as to clear the range for the cruiser. On turning one torpedo was fired at us, and also three salvos, two short and one over, of three or four guns by her port broadside. Then followed some very wild single shots, including shrapnel, fragments of the latter only hitting the ship. The aft gun was bearing the whole time, and

SINKING THE RAIDER

made consistently excellent hitting on any visible part of the enemy. Ignited oil was observed streaming from her port beam.

"At 4.10, when out of torpedo range, we again engaged the enemy in company with *Achilles* already firing, and ceased fire at 4.15, having no more ammunition. The raider was a mass of flame, and obviously a doomed ship, although she continued to fight with apparently but one gun. Enemy sank whilst under fire of *Achilles*, 4.35 p.m."

It was at a range of 5300 yards that *Achilles* joined in the engagement, *Rena* firing both at her and *Dundee*, though principally at the latter. Captain Day's tactics throughout were brilliantly effective. He had answered *Rena's* first hostile act with remarkable promptitude and thus saved *Dundee* from destruction. In obtaining those raking hits, he had gained a considerable initial success; and in extricating *Dundee* from a dangerous position he had shown himself a most able tactician. When *Achilles* joined in, there was no masking of fire: *Dundee* went full speed down the lane of smoke so as to afford Captain Leake a clear range for his guns.

Rena on opening fire at once enveloped herself in light-coloured smoke, and fired a torpedo at *Achilles*, which broke surface off the port quarter. *Achilles* replied not merely with shells but by firing a torpedo which struck *Rena* at the bows. When the raider finally sank almost horizontally she presented an appalling sight: just one mass of flames and red-hot forward, and then disappeared into the sea leaving not a single visible survivor. Continuous rain had been falling throughout the action, and occasional explosions had been going on aboard her. The position of her foundering was approximately Lat. 64.54 N, Long. 0.22 E. Not a British life had been lost, with the exception of the entire boarding and boat party.

This was virtually a single-ship action, for *Dundee* had done decisive damage to *Rena* before *Achilles* could co-operate. In a private letter to me Captain Day acknowledged, as a brave warrior does, the courage of his opponents. "Gallantry on both sides: no hesitation: no compromise . . . the German raider went down firing defiance up to the moment of extinction beneath the waves." And this in spite of the fact that about 4 p.m. she had the opportunity of surrendering.

On the other hand, it must be stressed that Captain Day was fighting an enemy of superior strength. There can be no doubt as to that fact, for Captain Day subsequent to the war was given by no less an authority than Count zu Dohna-Schlodien (of *Moewe*) the following details which have been courteously passed on to me. *Rena* had five 5·9-inch, four 3·4-inch guns, and two 21-inch torpedo-tubes. The 5·9-inch weapons fired 100-lb. shells, she was able to present a broadside of three such guns and two of the smaller calibre, whilst *Dundee's* broadside amounted to only 43 lbs.

This was therefore an action where seamanship, penetrative imagination, and forthright pluck combined with alertness, triumphed in spite of being (on paper at least) hopelessly outmatched. Indeed, the incident is fit to be ranked with the finest achievements which belong to the old days of frigate actions. It has now passed into British naval history as an epic, but it is doubly memorable, since it is probably the last time that an officer who once went to sea in a sailing-ship will ever live to command a steamship in battle.

It seems almost incredible that *Dundee* suffered no casualties to her crew, nor was herself damaged: that could have been only through clever handling. It is good also to have the opportunity of paying admiration to those Royal Fleet Reserve, Royal Naval Reserve, and Royal Naval Volunteer Reserve gunlayers of *Dundee*, who with calmness and skill controlled the guns' crews and their own firing, doing their own spotting, and judging the point of aim at the most vital places about the raider's decks and hull. There were no Officers of Quarters available, inasmuch as two were absent on duty.

These keen men, brought into duel from their peaceful avocations by the advent of war, had tackled and defeated an enemy twice the size of their own ship.

SINKING THE RAIDER 255

Their marksmanship had made *Rena* incapable of inflicting the smallest injury, but on the contrary had so disabled the raider that the latter would have been consumed by the raging conflagration had she now been left to herself. The fight had begun with *Dundee* at right angles across *Rena's* stern, the range gradually dropping from 1200 to 800 and even 500 yards. It should be put on record that the raider flagrantly defied the law of the sea in firing her torpedoes when flying Norwegian colours : for the torpedo-tubes on each side came through ports covered by the Norwegian flag. She had clearly intended by subtle manœuvring, both during the chase and the time of being boarded, to torpedo *Achilles* and *Dundee* : only skilful seamanship had turned the fortune of war against herself.

Captain Day had been suspicious of *Rena* quite early in the proceedings, and he allowed his officers to know his suspicions. His First Lieutenant was Lieutenant F. H. Lawson, R.N.R., who volunteered for the job of boarding, for the reason that the officer whose duty it really was had till now no great experience. Lieutenant Lawson performed a deliberate act of quiet courage in going off to the stranger. When the action commenced, this boarding boat was within a few feet of the German's ladder, and the whole party must have been forced into *Rena* ; but the boat, being on the lee side, could not be seen by *Dundee*. It was whilst Captain Day was waiting some sign from Lieutenant Lawson that noise was heard of the large Norwegian flag, painted on *Rena's* port quarter and hinged on the lower side, falling outboard. When next the boarding boat was seen, the little craft was empty.

The value of common sense, observation of details, and quick reasoning was well proved in the preliminaries to this action, and deserves to be emphasised. For some eyes might have omitted to take in certain essential items. When the German had announced herself as *Rena* by the visible sign on her hull, Captain Day on looking up her name in Lloyd's Register was unable to reconcile her appearance with the printed particulars ; and, incidentally, we have here a weak link in the carefully wrought chain of German pretence. If one is to succeed by deception, the masquerading must be complete. The carelessness of the dockyard official who allowed the painted words to pass may be held by any impartial jury largely responsible for *Rena's* loss. Whilst Captain Day was becoming more, rather than less, suspicious, Lance-Corporal G. Short, of the Royal Marine Light Infantry, noticed, and called Captain Day's attention to, the curious detail that the letter "N" in *Norge* and *Rena* was upside down ; thus—И. And it was this information, coming at the psychological moment, when split seconds were the equivalent of an era, that gave the final confirmation to Captain Day's forebodings, and prevented the enemy surprising *Dundee*. Another of the *Dundee's* crew, Leading Signalman A. E. Martin, did excellent observation work by keeping his eyes concentrated on the raider's rudder and propeller, thus being able to inform Captain Day of the slightest enemy motion. Both Short and Martin thus won the Distinguished Service Medal.

Commander Day was awarded a D.S.O. and noted for early promotion, as a reward for his vigilance, judgment, promptness, ability, and splendid tactics. Promotion soon came to him and also the Order of Commander of the Bath. Captain Leake, who had been two years in command of *Achilles* and missed the good fortune of being present at the Battle of Jutland, was another recipient of the D.S.O., for his promptitude in opening a heavy fire and averting or helping to avert the loss of *Dundee*. These honours were well earned. During the last five months the search for raiders had involved constant steaming and relentless looking out, to say nothing of arduous coaling. One may gain some idea of the activity of these patrols by stating that since September 1, 1916, *Achilles* had steamed a total of 27,722 miles, or the equivalent of voyaging most of the way round the world.

But it was the work of lowering boats and boarding tall steel hulls in that vile, cheerless part of Europe that always deserved to be rewarded. Oarsmanship

CAPTAIN SELWYN M. DAY, R.N.R., C.B., D.S.O.
Who commanded *Dundee* at the sinking of the raider *Leopard.*

H.M.S. *ACHILLES*

Which assisted in sinking *Leopard*.

SINKING THE RAIDER

and seamanship were tested, and courage with endurance tried to the uttermost. Indeed, as Admiral Beatty remarked, the boarding parties "throughout the war displayed the greatest skill and fearlessness in carrying out their hazardous work in all weathers". For ten whole months both *Achilles* and *Dundee* had been patrolling to the north of the Shetlands, but the latter was not to end her days in that depressing locality : she finally was sunk by a U-boat at the entrance to the English Channel on September 3, 1917.

Thus the vendetta of raiders, armed merchant cruisers, regular naval cruisers, decoy ships, and submarines went on in the contest concerned with seaborne commerce. As recently as June 1930 there was unveiled at Kiel a memorial column to the "5132 heroes and 199 U-boats that did not return during the World War, 1914–18". These figures are interesting as giving the official German statement regarding the number of submarines lost. But this U-boat warfare was only a part of the whole campaign against cargoes, crews, and ships which were the means of keeping alike the British nation and its fighting forces supplied with necessaries. There never was any attempt at surface raiding on a large scale : compared with submarine attacks, the art of surface raiding is something rarer. The chances of breaking through the blockade, or of harassing the trade routes successfully, would certainly have increased as more *Moewe* types were sent out ; yet there would have been more *Greif* and *Rena* losses to Germany had she attempted to make any wide use of her idle merchant steamers and sent them forth in disguise as cruisers. But the extremely limited number of raiders which achieved their object shows that they belonged to a class even more specialised than was the British Q-ship service, which in itself was the most individualistic section of the entire British naval strength.

There is, however, one extremely original mode of raiding which was tried and never repeated. We have seen that, however carefully these *Moewes* filled their bunkers and even their holds with coal, it was always necessary to capture at least one collier. Germany had,

R

years before the year 1914, lost all possible chance of maintaining a victory by means of her *surface* raiders. She could inflict serious losses, she could and did disorganise traffic, but never *persistently* by means of cruisers disguised or undisguised. It was the lack of coaling bases which made this form of commerce attack doomed to fail. The strategical keys of cruiser warfare were in the hands of Germany's enemies.

It was for this reason that a sailing-ship was chosen to be one of the three raiders which left Germany for the high seas in the late autumn of 1916. She possessed the independence of the olden times; she could roam wherever there was wind, without having to overhaul boilers or repair engines; she need not endanger herself by keeping rendezvous with colliers at secret positions that might become compromised. She could remain away from home indefinitely, so long as fresh water and food were procurable; and, moreover, the very fact of her being under canvas would be her greatest protection in getting through the blockade, besides affording the most perfect form of disguise when springing to attack some other ocean-going vessel. In the British Q-ship service a number of ketches and topsail schooners certainly were employed with distinction and success, though in comparatively restricted areas. Germany in sending forth a three-masted barque to the other end of the world was more ambitious: yet this was merely an isolated act and would not readily be repeated. Why? For the reason that so very few officers or men could be found who had the slightest experience of handling ships under sail.

The person whom the German Admiralty selected was Count Felix von Luckner, who had passed through no end of adventures in different parts of the globe, including serving before the mast in sail to becoming an officer in the Imperial Navy. After being present at the Battle of Jutland as Lieutenant-Commander, he was some months later appointed to the *Seeadler* for the reason that he was the only German naval officer who possessed the requisite experience of sailing-vessels. This vigorous, bronzed, six-foot stalwart, with

SINKING THE RAIDER 259

fair hair, blue eyes, and immense courage, was born on June 9, 1885. His maternal grandmother was English; before the war he used to visit Cowes in Herr Krupp's crack racing schooner *Germania*, and enjoyed the hospitality of the Royal Yacht Squadron. In the raids on Yarmouth and the Yorkshire coast, as well as the Heligoland action, he had tasted actual attack. During the Jutland battle he was gunnery officer in the *Kronprinz* which was in the van led by *Konig*—this squadron of the latest German battleships being in action with the British 5th Battle Squadron.

Seeadler was three years younger than himself. She was one of a few very fine sailing-vessels that had been built at Port Glasgow, and represented the final phase that followed the clipper-ship period. She had been launched as the *Pass of Balmaha*, was of 1571 tons, and eventually was sold out of the British Merchant Service to the United States. In June 1915 she sailed from New York with cotton for Archangel, but in July was stopped by the British blockading force north-west of Cape Wrath, and was on her way into a Scottish port to be examined, when she was molested by a U-boat who put a prize crew aboard, and actually managed to get through the blockade with her, so that she arrived safely at Cuxhaven. Incidentally the U-boat was sunk by a Q-ship. After the Jutland battle this beautiful sailing-vessel was fitted out with great secrecy, and the crew were picked from the German Naval Reserve, who did not know whither they were bound till the night they went aboard.

The skill, inventiveness and ambitious enterprise with which this prize was fitted out had no rivals during the whole war except in the most ingeniously fitted Q-ships of the year 1918. *Seeadler's* orders were to "proceed to the Pacific Ocean, to destroy as many enemy ships as possible, principally enemy sailing craft bringing food and raw war material to Europe from South Pacific and Australasian ports". She was given two 4·2-inch guns, which were at first stored in concealment between decks in the hold. Bombs, explosives, two machine-guns, carbines, and a powerful wireless plant were also carried. Two Diesel motors gave her auxiliary power in the case of calms, or when extra speed was required. At Bremerhaven the entire floor of the after saloon was cut out and reconstructed so as to form the platform of an hydraulic lift. This could be lowered 14 feet by the pressure of a button, and the intention was that if a prize crew should have come on board, Luckner had only to wait till the latter were having a meal. Then by means of an electric button in the chart-room the visitors would find themselves lowered to the next deck as prisoners.

In order to evade the blockade, *Seeadler* adopted the usual custom of raiders in pretending to be Norwegian, but with keener respect for detail than was shown by the *Leopard*. And it is as a master of detail that Luckner earns our respect, apart from his other achievements. He himself had the physical appearance of a Norwegian; he chose as his officers those who could speak Norwegian; the ship had Norwegian papers, the log-book was stolen from a Norwegian ship named *Maleta*, the navigational instruments were all made in Norway, Norwegian books and photographs were brought on board: even the labels of Norwegian tailors were sewn inside coats to replace German names. Norwegian letters were specially written to give the appearance of having been received by the crew; and the hands were chosen to fit the description given in a genuine list that had already been obtained. A carefully prepared rubber stamp, forging the British Consul's impression, endorsed a document that the ship was bound for Melbourne.

The crew numbered sixty-four, there were seven officers, and supplies for three years were carried. Under sail alone *Seeadler* (which means "Sea Eagle") could do her 14 knots, but under motors in calm weather she was good for 10 knots. Her chief officer, Lieutenant Kling, had served in Polar expeditions, whilst Ludermann (another officer) had served in British sailing-vessels. Two torpedo-tubes were fitted in case she was held up by a cruiser, and motor lifeboats were supplied so that goods and passengers might

SINKING THE RAIDER

be transhipped without wasting the time necessitated by oared craft. Just before setting out, German spies in Norway provided information concerning the movements of all sailing-ships, and it was finally decided that *Seeadler's* faked name should be *Irma*, which was painted now on the hull.

On December 21, 1916, *Seeadler* at last left German waters astern, having come out of the Weser. The customary south-west gale gave place to one of almost hurricane force, as most of us engaged in patrolling off the British Isles well remember : but it enabled the raider to go roaring up the North Sea past the coast of Norway, thence in a north-westerly direction towards Iceland, and then, from a high latitude, south-west. Thus the stereotyped raider course was followed, so that advantage was taken of darkness and there was only a four-hour day. By 9.30 on Christmas morning *Seeadler* was about 180 miles south-west of Iceland, when one of the blockade patrol steamers stopped her, lowered a boat, and sent a boarding party ; but after some delay the cleverly disguised raider was allowed to proceed. The ingeniousness and the daring, the acting on the part of her skipper, had enabled the raider to get through the one big trial, and then there awaited her the freedom of the ocean.

On January 9, having made an exceptionally quick passage in very bad weather down the Atlantic, *Seeadler* was 120 miles S$\frac{1}{4}$W of the Azores when she made her first capture, the British S.S. *Gladys Royle*, 3268 tons, bound from Cardiff to Buenos Aires with coal, and destroyed her by explosives. On the next day the British S.S. *Lundy Island*, 3095 tons, was sunk by gunfire about 70 miles further south. Luckner's voyage was to take him fairly straight down the Atlantic, so in due course he arrived at the area which lies between Brazil and West Africa. Not only would it have been difficult for him to resist visiting the "raiders' paradise", but he would have the opportunity to spend some time criss-crossing these north-eastern trade routes. On January 21 he sank the French barque *Charles Gounod* (2199 tons), and by studying the latter's log-book Luckner was able to find the course along which sailing-ships were now coming. He therefore had no difficulty in victimising other sailing-vessels. Thus on January 28 he captured and sank the *Perce*. This was a Canadian three-masted auxiliary schooner of 364 tons bound from Halifax with salt fish and lumber, but she was now 150 miles north-east of St. Paul Rocks.

The next capture in this region was the French four-masted barque *Antonin* (3071 tons) with nitrate for France, the position of their meeting being Lat. 7 N, Long. 36 W. Each of *Seeadler's* guns was camouflaged by a canvas cover painted to represent a pig pen: shirts and other seamen's clothing were also sewn to the canvas as if put there to dry. Under cover of the poop deck machine-guns were mounted, whilst fifty men with carbines were concealed and ready for action. It was not to be wondered that shipping could so easily be surprised and then overawed into submission.

No more shipping was sighted till February 9, when in Lat. 5 N, Long. 31 W she sank the Italian sailing-vessel *Buenos Ayres* (1811 tons) with a cargo of saltpetre, and ten days later the British sailing-vessel *Pinmore*, 2431 tons, 540 miles north-west of St. Paul Rocks. The latter was carrying grain, and it so happened that during 1902 Luckner had served in her. On February 25 he molested but released the Danish *Viking*, a four-master. *Moewe*, it will be recollected, was also operating not very far from this area and on February 23 was 200 miles north-east of St. Paul Rocks. It was on February 26 that *Seeadler* when 230 miles north-west of those same rocks sank the *British Yeoman*, a British sailing-vessel of 1953 tons, next day treating the French barque *La Rochefoucauld* in the same manner, followed by another French barque *Dupleix* on March 5.

On March 11 she was 220 miles ENE of St. Paul Rocks when she captured and destroyed her next Atlantic victim. This was the 3609-ton British steamer *Horngarth*, which she had to chase before the surprised merchantman gave in. The latter's wireless was shot

SINKING THE RAIDER 263

away, her boats damaged as well as her steam-pipe. But surely it was an amazing campaign that witnessed an ex-British barque shelling a British steamer ! Well may some of the crew have wondered if the world had gone completely mad. Ten days later *Seeadler* captured yet another French barque, *Cambronne*, but she was not destroyed. Luckner was embarrassed, as were his predecessors in raiding, by an accumulation of prisoners, and the time had come when he must clear out of the Atlantic. If *Moewe* were off back to Germany, *Seeadler* was bound the opposite way—to the Pacific. Between them they had created alarm and disaster, so they could afford to vacate this ocean and leave their opponents guessing.

There was, however, the same caution to be displayed in delaying the arrival of prisoners as had been always the care of other raiders who dismissed their captives. Luckner could not afford to send any of his own people as prize crew to be interned for the remainder of the war, so he hit upon a clever device. Having tran-shipped 286 prisoners aboard *Cambronne*, he had her topgallant masts sawn off, her spare sails and spars thrown overboard. Then, having supplied her with a month's provisions and navigating instruments, he sent her off with orders to make for Rio. She had been captured in Lat. 20.10 N, Long. 25.50 W, i.e. to the east of Trinidada Island, and had therefore little difficulty in making the slow passage to safety.

Seeadler now hurried south, rounded Cape Horn on April 18 and then went north up the Pacific, keeping four miles away from the coast. Luckner had been getting nervous of enemy warships in the Atlantic ; he heard a good deal of wireless talk near the Falklands and inferred that he was being pursued. In rounding the Horn he went so far south as to sight icebergs, and encountered the customary notorious weather. But he also sighted a big British armed merchant cruiser and ran for his life, taking every advantage of a squall. No more captures occurred till June 14, by which time the raider was to the east of Christmas Island in Lat. 1 N, Long. 150 W. She had been waiting some time to trap vessels between American and Australasian ports, and in the meanwhile the United States had now entered the war: more potential prizes would thus be available. On the date mentioned the U.S.A. schooner *A. B. Johnson* was set on fire, three days later the *R. C. Slade* of the same nationality was similarly treated in Lat. 2 N, Long. 150 W; and on July 8 another American schooner *Manila* in the same longitude, but in Lat. 9 N, was likewise destroyed.

These were the last vessels which *Seeadler* ever sank, for by this time her crew were weary, and the ship was very foul with barnacles after being at sea for over six months; so Luckner after beating about the Doldrums for three weeks reached Mopelia (one of the Society Islands) on July 31. Here he anchored, but at the beginning of August a tidal wave picked up *Seeadler*, threw her on to the reef, where she pounded herself to pieces till she became a total wreck. In this manner ended dramatically a cruise that might have continued to annoy the Allies for many more months.

Luckner on August 23 with five companions, leaving the rest on the island, sailed away in one of the 32-foot lifeboats rigged as a sloop and still retaining her motor. But the party were taken prisoners on September 21 at Wakaya Island (one of the Fiji group). After being interned in New Zealand, Luckner escaped but was again captured and detained till after the war. Those on Mopelia Island got away in a French turtle schooner which chanced to visit that lonely atoll, but on reaching Easter Island—the other lonely isle so much visited by German raiders—the schooner hit a rock during the first week of October and foundered. The Germans succeeded in getting ashore, remained till the end of November, and then were taken by steamer to Chile where they remained till after peace ended the war.

CHAPTER XVIII

A MODERN SEA ROVER

IT remains now to consider the third of the three raiders which departed from Germany during the autumn of 1917. We have here a steamer, yet there was so much imagination expended in her fitting out, her cruising area, and her actual tactics, that she deserves close attention. In some respects this is indeed the most romantic voyage of all the raiders, and many a boy's book of fiction has contained far less glamour or adventure.

The ship selected was one of the Hansa liners, a single-screw steamer of 5809 tons gross and 3627 tons net. Launched as the *Wachtfels*, she measured 419 feet long, with a beam of 56·2 feet, and a depth of 29·6 feet. She had two decks, the upper deck being of steel and teak-sheathed; a poop 60 feet long, and a fo'c'sle 54 feet long. Built at Flensburg in 1913, she had triple-expansion engines, electric light, and a small refrigerating plant. Her speed was exceedingly moderate—10½ knots —and she could keep this up burning 60 tons of coal a day: but at 8 knots she consumed only 35 tons. She was thus an economical ship and therefore suited for the job. Her holds and bunkers were filled with 6000 tons of coal, so that they assured her over three months of fuel independence.

Her appearance was just as it should be for a raider: she looked an ordinary cargo vessel, with one medium-sized black funnel, two slightly raked masts, though exceptionally tall topmasts could be raised and lowered for assisting in changing her disguise. She was fitted with wireless, the aerial leading down to the bridge. The latter, together with the upper bridge, was painted a very dark grey, but everything else was black. Her armament was the equivalent of a light cruiser, and consisted of two 5·9-inch, two 4·1-inch guns, two 4-pounders, two machine-guns on the fore end of the bridge-deck, one field-gun stowed below (in case assistance could be rendered in the East African campaign), and there were two pairs of above-water torpedo-tubes. One pair was placed forward and one aft, which had dropping doors. Immediately abaft the funnel was a searchlight on a collapsible platform, whilst another but smaller and movable one was placed at the after end of the boat-deck.

On the boat-deck also was the range-finder. A cask could be hoisted up the foretopmast head to enable a good look out to be maintained, but her own armament was ingeniously hidden by dummy erections, canvas screens, collapsible boxes and doors, whilst the dummy handwheel aft was another feature for concealing. She carried eleven boats, of which one was a motor-boat with which she used to do her boarding. Her crew numbered about 380, and she was commanded by Korvetten-Kapitän (Commander) Karl August Nerger, who spoke no English. He had formerly been in command of the *Stettin*. His chief officer, Kapitän-Leutnant Schmehl, of the Imperial Naval Reserve, spoke English fluently and had once been awarded a medal by the British Government for an act of bravery in going down into the burning hold of a merchant vessel at Calcutta that was carrying explosives. And it is to be remarked that in all these raiders the personnel of men as well as officers was of an exceptionally high standard.

This ship carried also a gunnery officer, a navigator, as well as two prize officers. Of the latter, one, Kapitän-Leutnant Rose, had been staying in England during the last four years preceding war, and was a member of the Richmond Tennis Club. A mining officer, doctors, and a paymaster were included. The chief engineer had formerly been the Hamburg-Amerika Line's Engineer-Superintendent at Hamburg.

This raider, like *Moewe* in her first voyage, carried mines : but, unlike any other raider, she also carried

A MODERN SEA ROVER 267

a seaplane to enable her to scout miles ahead. Nowadays we have so rapidly advanced that little would be thought of such an innovation : yet in 1916 the addition of this small flying craft was something memorable. During bad weather the seaplane was stowed out of the way in the hold, but normally it was rested on a staging built over No. 3 hold and ready for service. Two derricks on the mainmast were used for hoisting out both seaplane and mines : it required only fifteen minutes to transfer the seaplane from deck to water. Fitted with a 150 horse-power engine, the latter was capable of carrying pilot, observer, and four small bombs. On one occasion it soared to the remarkable height of 13,000 feet.

The raider during the first part of her voyage gave all shipping a wide berth, and this was scarcely imprudent considering she had 500 mines ready to be touched off. Day and night the poop gun's crew stood by their weapon, yet the rest of the armament was not kept manned till the ship reached such dangerous waters as between Australia and New Zealand, or in the Java Sea ; but a torpedo was always ready in each tube. Her wireless installation was so efficient that when steaming along the Indian Ocean she could receive messages from Berlin. The dangerous mines, after being hoisted from the holds, were slid along rails to mine doors on each side under the poop. These "eggs" were painted a light grey to make them less easily visible, and had five horns. The rails were dismantled after the last mines had been laid.

Before leaving Germany, the original name of *Wachtfels* was changed to *Wolf*, and the seaplane was named *Wolfchen* ("Wolf cub"). Nerger's instructions were to interfere with enemy shipping in distant seas, but especially the Indian Ocean where *Emden* had once distinguished herself ; to wage war against commerce, and to lay mines. *Wolf* made two false starts. The first was on a Friday, when she had to turn back owing to a fire in her coal bunkers. On the last day of November she made another effort yet was held up by a fog. During that same evening she steamed away for good, going at full speed up the North Sea and disguised as a neutral. Bad weather caused her to heave-to, but by December 2 she had run the blockade and was near Rockall.

Proceeding down the Atlantic, she made no attempt at molestation. She had started up the North Sea with a submarine in tow, but heavy weather soon made that impossible, and on January 16, 1917, *Wolf* was off South Africa. She saw an English convoy with an armoured cruiser in the distance, and this same night laid her first mines off the Cape of Good Hope. Thence *Wolf* proceeded to the Indian Ocean to lay mines off Bombay and Colombo, being off Ceylon by mid-February. It was thus that on February 17 the British S.S. *Worcestershire* (7175 tons) foundered on a mine 10 miles southwest of Colombo with the loss of two lives, and the British S.S. *Perseus* (6728 tons) four days later went down in about the same place with the loss of three lives.

Wolf then cleared right away from the land till she was in a position to cut the tracks South Africa–Bombay and Aden–Sunda Straits. On February 27, being in Lat. 7 N, Long. 63 E (or roughly 6000 miles west of Minikoi) she captured the S.S. *Turritella*, 5528 tons. This was a British vessel, but originally had been the German *Gutenfels*, which at the beginning of the war was lying at Alexandria. A prize crew was now put aboard and *Wolf* also transhipped twenty-five mines. *Turritella* was then sent off to the north-west and laid twenty-four of these off Aden, but at daylight on March 5 sank herself in that locality (Lat. 12.30 N, Long. 43.48 E), the prize crew being taken prisoners by H.M.S. *Odin*, though not immediately did *Wolf* learn of this capture. It was only when she intercepted a wireless message, giving an exact description of *Wolf* to the smallest detail, that Nerger realised *Turritella* had been accounted for.

From now onwards *Wolf* began a long ocean voyage commencing at a position north-east of the Seychelles, roughly midway between Cape Guardafui and Minikoi, and steaming in the direction of south-west Australia.

At first, then, she was still where the traffic routes crossed and she might expect to make captures. On the first of March, not far from the locality which had given her *Turritella*, *Wolf* made a prize of the British S.S. *Jumna*, 4152 tons, the exact position being Lat. 8.9 N, Long. 62 E, or about 650 miles west of Minikoi. Some excitement was caused in this operation, and illustrated Nerger's nervousness. He thought that *Jumna* was about to ram the raider, and in the confusion the port after gun of *Wolf* was fired before it was trained outboard, with the result that five Germans were accidentally killed and twenty-three wounded. In addition to this, a torpedo was damaged.

For three days *Jumna* was made to follow astern, but having been robbed of her coal and stores, she was then destroyed by bombs. Still steaming to the south-east, *Wolf* on March 11 had now arrived at a spot 680 miles east of the Seychelles and was in Lat. 4.30 S, Long. 67 E, when she captured the British S.S. *Wordsworth*, 3509 tons, with a cargo of rice. Of this commodity *Wolf* helped herself to 15 tons, and a week later sank the victim by bombs. This track between Somaliland and southern Australia is a lonely one : consequently the prizes were few and there was an absence of patrols. Not till March 31 did another incident occur when she overtook the British barque *Dee*, 1169 tons, which was on her way to Western Australia with a crew of Mauritius niggers. Her master, Captain John Rugg, had been skipper of his vessel for twenty-two years, and unfortunately he had never expected that this innocent-looking steamer might be a German warship. Captain Rugg hoisted his British ensign and number, signalling, "Report me all well." And then came the surprise. His ship was taken and sunk by bombs 410 miles W by S of Cape Leeuwin (SW Australia) and he found himself a prisoner.

Wolf's voyage, by its varied scenes and length, is much more akin to that of the old pirates than any we have yet witnessed. It had not the concentrated effectiveness of *Moewe*, yet its very diffuseness created such a sense of uncertainty and mystery that it was impossible to cope with her. The only clue had come through *Turritella* : yet the raider had long since vanished from her last reported area into the widest of oceans. The amount of steaming and time spent at sea were in total disproportion to the net results : yet there is a real fascination when we contemplate this long sea roving in an age that is all stereotype and strict routine.

Weeks passed without the slightest success. *Wolf* went south of the Australian continent, hoping to trap grain ships and colliers : yet never a vessel would be sighted. In June she was at Sunday Island, in the Kermadec group. These uninhabited islands are about 600 miles north-north-east of New Zealand and most conveniently situated for attacking the trade route from New Zealand to San Francisco. Having anchored under the land of this volcanic spot, she sent up her seaplane and on June 2 the latter flew over the British S.S. *Wairuna*, 3947 tons, bound from Auckland for San Francisco with 1200 tons of coal and other cargo, including meat, milk, and cheeses.

The *Wolfchen* swooped low over the surprised merchantman, dropped a canvas bag on the latter's deck and still hovered about. Within the bag was the following message :

Stop immediately. Take orders from German cruiser. Do not use your wireless, or I will bomb you.

Wairuna eased her engines, but did not stop until the seaplane dropped a bomb just ahead. Meanwhile *Wolf* herself had weighed and now proceeded to head *Wairuna* off. The capture was completed by the arrival of a prize crew at 4.5 p.m., who brought her under the lee of the island and anchored her there, all officers excepting the master being sent aboard the raider. Next day, owing to a shift of wind, *Wolf* steamed round to the other side of the island to anchor, *Wairuna* following and securing alongside. Then were transferred coal, fresh water, ship's stores, 42 live sheep, 14 bags of mails, and other items ; this work taking up the time till June 7, when bad weather

A MODERN SEA ROVER

caused them to change berth to the other side of the island.

Now on the night of June 5 the chief officer and second engineer of the *Turritella*, prisoners on board, resolved to escape and let themselves down over the raider's side to swim ashore. The extraordinary fact arises that they were not missed during twenty days, but they were never seen again and it is believed that they never reached land ; for a heavy surf was running and the sea was full of sharks. *Wolf* used this anchorage for overhauling her engines and making good defects. Here also crew and prisoners were allowed to fish, but baskets full of oranges and other fruit were obtained from the island where also wild goats and very large rats had their being. It was indeed a strange, deserted, end-of-the-world kind of place.

Work went on till June 12, when the two ships proceeded to sea but returned two days later, and again the transhipment of cargo went on. On June 16 preparations were made for sinking *Wairuna*, so hatches were battened down, cabin doors nailed up, lifeboats smashed, tanks holed, and at 6 p.m. both steamers got under way. But they had not gone more than 3 miles from the land when a sailing-vessel was sighted. *Wairuna* was therefore sent back to her anchorage and the seaplane sent after the stranger, which turned out to be the American schooner *Winslow*, bound from Sydney to Samoa with 500 tons of coal.

And here it is interesting to note once more the important part which wireless took in assisting the raider. On May 14 *Wolf* had intercepted an aerial message for a firm at Apia which signified that *Winslow* was ready to accept orders for loading at Sydney. Later *Wolf* intercepted a message that *Winslow* had left with her cargo : this signal being flashed from Australia to Samoa. It was therefore no surprise when this American vessel came along, and of course she was captured. At 7.45 a.m. on June 17 *Wairuna* was at last sunk, but it needed bombs as well as sixteen rounds to destroy her.

During the next three days *Wolf*, with *Winslow* as a

THE SEA-RAIDERS

potential decoy, remained at sea, but on the 20th *Wolf* towed the schooner under the lee of the island and spent a couple of days stripping her. Finally on June 22 *Winslow* was towed out, set on fire by four bombs, but thirty-nine rounds had to be fired before bringing her masts down. She was left still burning whilst *Wolf* steamed off that evening towards the setting sun. The next activity occurred on June 25, by which time she had arrived further south and then laid twenty-five mines between Three Kings' Island, New Zealand, and the mainland. This operation took place under cover of night between 10 p.m. of June 25 and 2.30 a.m. of the next day. She then made for Cook Strait, where between the hours of 10.30 p.m. of June 27 and 2 a.m. of the day following she laid fifty more mines. From there she steamed across to the south-east coast of Australia, and during the period of 9 p.m. to 10 p.m. on July 3 she laid another seventeen mines off Gabo Island. The proceedings were interrupted by *Wolf* sighting ships without lights, and it was believed that the vessels consisted of H.M.S. *Encounter* with a convoy. This interruption prevented eight more mines being laid. On July 6 the British S.S. *Cumberland*, 9471 tons, foundered on one of these mines 16 miles south-west of Gabo Island, and on the same day wireless news of the fact reached the raider.

Wolf steamed north-east past Lord Howe Island, making a big detour so as to get well away from the Australian coast. On July 9 she was in Lat. 26.42 S, Long. 166.40 E, that is to say between Samoa and New Zealand, when she captured the American barque *Beluga* with a cargo of case oil. *Beluga* had once been a whaler, but now was carrying benzine and gasolene. The former was most welcome to *Wolf*, and the other was helpful in setting *Beluga* on fire. At daybreak of the next day *Wolfchen* was sent up to reconnoitre the ocean as smoke had been sighted, but nothing followed, and on July 11 *Beluga* was destroyed by gunfire. Two more days passed and on July 13 the raider came across the four-masted sailing craft *Encore*, which was bound from Colombia River to Sydney with lumber. Oil

CAPTAIN K. A. NERGER

Being welcomed back to Kiel aboard the raider *Wolf* by Admiral Scheer.

CAPTAIN K. A. NERGER
Aboard the raider *Wolf* on her return to Kiel after a record voyage.

A MODERN SEA ROVER 273

was presently poured over her and she was set on fire. The capture took place in Lat. 21 S, Long. 169 E, that is to say in the neighbourhood of New Caledonia.

Away to the north-west continued *Wolf*, past Fiji and the Solomon Islands and close to what had once been German New Guinea, the seaplane being sent up to scout daily from July 25 till August 6, for the raider was waiting about to find a victim. On the 27th she was already close to this former German possession, that had passed into British hands in September 1914 when Rabaul in Neu Pommern was occupied by British forces. It was impossible now to avail himself of what had once been a German colony, but Nerger was able to pick up on the 28th the following interesting message by his wireless :

Burns Philp Rabaul. Donaldson left Sydney on the 27th via Newcastle–Brisbane with 340 tons piece goods, 500 tons Westport coal for Rabaul, and 236 tons piece goods for Madang. Signed Burns.

This was delightful information for *Wolf*. Messrs. Burns, Philp were the well-known Pacific shipowners telegraphing from Sydney to their Rabaul agent, where an English Governor had been appointed instead of a German. For some time Nerger wondered who Donaldson might be, but then came another intercepted wireless message :

29th July, 8 p.m. Steamer *Matunga* at Brisbane. Next Monday we are off Cape Moreton.

Still further encouraged by this intelligence gratuitously received, Nerger kept the *Wolfchen* frequently up in the air searching over the sea, and on August 5 yet another message was picked up which informed the Rabaul agents that *Donaldson* would arrive next day at 7 a.m. But the arrival never took place, for on August 6 when 300 miles east of Riche Island, New Guinea, the S.S. *Matunga*, 1608 tons, was sighted by the seaplane at 7.45 a.m. and *Wolf* made the British steamer stop. The prize officer on going aboard

S

greeted the master with the following salutation that caused no little surprise :

"Hello, Captain Donaldson, where are your 500 tons of Westport coal ?"

But coal was not the only really important item aboard : *Matunga* happened to be carrying the Acting-Governor to Rabaul, and among the cargo were provisions intended for the British troops at Rabaul, together with a number of bicycles : all of which were subsequently put aboard *Wolf*. At first the two ships proceeded in company to the north-west and west, past the north New Guinea coast, and eventually on August 14 came to a landlocked harbour previously reconnoitred by the seaplane.

In this lonely spot the Germans erected a wireless station, placed look-outs, and tried to frighten the prisoners by saying it were useless for them to seek escape, as the natives were cannibals and the water full of crocodiles. Ten days were now spent in this seclusion transhipping coal and cargo, whilst a diver went down to scrub *Wolf's* bottom that had become very foul. Nerger also took the opportunity to fire a couple of torpedoes which were afterwards recovered, and finally on August 26 both ships proceeded to sea till they were twelve miles off shore. *Matunga* was then sunk by bombs, whilst *Wolf* resumed her voyage westward, passing Celebes on August 29, and next day she was in the Java Sea. With amazing intrepidity she carried on till she was off Singapore on September 2, and under cover of night laid 108 mines between 10 p.m and 4 a.m. of the next day. She had now got rid of the last of these dangerous "eggs" and was free to return home.

September 26 found her in Lat. 0.20 N, Long. 74.30 E, when she sighted among the atolls of the Maldive Islands the Japanese S.S. *Hitachi Maru*. The raider closed her, hoisted the signal : "Stop and do not use your wireless." At first the Japanese continued on his course, but a couple of rounds were fired across the bows of *Hitachi Maru* followed by fourteen more, which brought about the deaths of sixteen among the Japanese crew. *Hitachi Maru* began calling up on her wireless, but *Wolf* jambed that, and another victim was added to Nerger's list, the passengers (among whom were ladies) being taken aboard *Wolf*.

Hitachi Maru was not now destroyed, but followed in charge of a prize crew. After steaming to the westward, the vessels secured alongside each other on September 27 at an atoll north of the equator. This was off Dewadu Island, in the centre of the Suvadiva Atoll (south of the Maldives), and till the 29th the prize coal was being transferred, together with cargo, stores, and mails, whilst every day for a couple of hours *Wolfchen* scouted from the skies. Not till October 3 did *Wolf* leave this atoll, but three days later the Japanese ship was ordered by seaplane to follow, the two ships proceeding to the west and south-west. They reached Coco Island to the west of the Cargados Carajos group, anchored and secured alongside each other for coal and cargo again to be transferred, though bad weather caused them to cast off. On November 1 everyone was inoculated against typhoid and the voyage resumed six days later, when the *Hitachi Maru* was sunk 16 miles off the shore in deep water, by means of bombs.

Wolf was once more alone, and she had been able to repair the wings of *Wolfchen* (which had been damaged) from the raw silk and white satin that had been part of *Hitachi Maru's* cargo. No fewer than sixty flights did this seaplane make during the voyage, alighting sometimes on waters that were shark-infested. On November 10 at daybreak the *Wolf* was in Lat. 21 S, Long 53.30 E, that is to say between Madagascar and Mauritius, when she sighted the Spanish S.S. *Igotz Mendi* steaming along with all lights burning. The Spaniard had left Lorenzo Marques on November 4, and inasmuch as she was carrying 5500 tons of coal for Colombo she was taken prisoner. A prize crew then brought her to Coco Island, as before, where the two steamers secured alongside and by working all night *Wolf* was again partially coaled. By the 17th the raider had taken in as much as a thousand tons.

But *Igotz Mendi* was not sunk. After having been painted grey, the two vessels now cruised about together for a time. *Wolf* then separated and sank the American sailing-vessel *John H. Kirby* bound from New York for Port Natal ; and on December 2 when about 150 miles south of Capetown *Igotz Mendi* was still alone. Three days later, however, raider and Spaniard joined forces, rounded the Cape and proceeded across the South Atlantic towards that oft-mentioned Brazilian island of Trinidada, and *Wolf* sank the French sailing-vessel *Maréchal Davout*, which was bound from Melbourne to Dakar with wheat.

It must not be supposed that in traversing all these seas the raider felt herself to be the happy, irresponsible rover. There were times of considerable anxiety and suspense, such as when the wireless of a Japanese cruiser was heard on November 14 off the East African coast, so that at 10.30 p.m. the seaplane had to be sent up scouting for an hour. Similarly when now off the east coast of South America she intercepted the wireless of British cruisers, so that on December 19 both raider and Spanish prize quickly altered course and went full speed away from the locality.

On the day after Christmas both steamers were about 700 miles east of Monte Video, when they secured alongside each other for the raider again to coal. The heavy Atlantic swell as usual caused them to bump badly, so that *Wolf* was seriously damaged and leaking more than a little. On December 30, with the raider keeping eight miles ahead, both ships continued their sweep northwards up the Atlantic, and on January 4, 1918, *Wolf* sank by bombs the Norwegian barque *Storebror* (Beira to Monte Video in ballast). The sinking of this neutral was because *Storebror* had once been owned by the British County Shipping Company before the war—an excuse that seems extraordinarily high-handed.

This was the last prize *Wolf* ever made, her total amounting to seven British ships, three American, one Japanese, one Spanish, one French, and one Norwegian. But additional to these losses must be mentioned the

A MODERN SEA ROVER

following vessels which were sunk or seriously damaged by *Wolf's* mines : five off the Cape of Good Hope, two off Colombo, five off Bombay, one off Gabo Island, and one in Cook Strait.

Aboard *Igotz Mendi* had been transferred all married prisoners, a few neutrals, and others. There was none of the old intention to put these people ashore and let out the well-kept secret of *Wolf's* wanderings : the Spanish ship was being taken to Germany. Now towards the end of January one afternoon, as the *Igotz Mendi* was reaching more northerly European latitudes, she suffered some nervousness when she sighted two large two-funnelled steamers painted light grey steering WSW and passing a couple of miles ahead. No signals were exchanged, and these big vessels were believed to be transports for the American Army in France. The Germans feared that *Igotz Mendi* might any minute be boarded ; but the Spanish chief officer, under the impression that these were Allies' ships of war who would challenge and then open fire, saw matters in a different light. He was not inclined to let the Germans sink the ship before capture—as he well knew they certainly would attempt in the last resort.

The Spanish officer therefore rushed into the chart house, seized the eight bombs which were always kept ready for blowing up the ship if capture seemed imminent, and threw these dangerous articles over the side. The two American transports passed on and nothing occurred in respect of these ships : but so infuriated was the German prize officer with the Spaniard that he sentenced the latter to three years' penal servitude to be spent in Germany. A few days later the incident was passed over and the man regained his usual liberty, but a further supply of bombs was fetched over from *Wolf*.

During the first week of February—that ideal time for the return of raiders—*Igotz Mendi* tackled the blockade, and passing by the north-west of Iceland entered the Arctic Circle on February 7, but was turned back by ice. The foggy weather afforded her at once concealment but also navigational anxiety, so that five days later she was still in Iceland waters. She then steamed south-east towards the Norwegian coast, which she picked up on February 21. Coming south, she hugged this neutral shore, entered the Skaggerak with the aim of rounding the Skaw and so down the Kattegat to Germany.

But foggy weather this time intervened with considerable effect, so that on February 24 at 3.30 in the afternoon *Igotz Mendi* ran ashore and came to a sudden stop. This placed the Germans in a most unenviable position, and an officer went off in a boat. He had taken the precaution of changing from uniform into plain clothes and discovered that the position was near the Skaw. So here was a German prize ship in Denmark and full of prisoners. About eight that evening arrived a Danish gunboat, and it was useless to try bluffing the latter's captain for long. It took only a short while for the Dane to perceive the true character of *Igotz Mendi* and the passengers whom the German was trying so hard to conceal.

The result was that the whole German pretence broke down, the passengers were landed next day in lifeboats, and taken care of by the British Consul. The weather became very bad, as so often is the case following fog, and did not ease up till February 28, when it moderated sufficiently for the passengers to recover their baggage. But there the *Igotz Mendi* stuck fast when so near to Germany. As to the German officers themselves, they were wild with anger at having to be interned, though the German ratings were only too delighted. For this long voyage begun in *Wolf* had not been wholly a picnic, and for some time past the men had lost all enthusiasm, become thoroughly disgruntled, and in bad mood. In fact, the cells on board were always full, and there was a long waiting list !

Wolf had a more successful ending than her prize. Nerger reached Germany safely on February 19, but had encountered heavy ice floes and fog likewise. He had long ago been given up for lost, yet after fifteen months of raiding in almost every sea of the globe, having cruised 451 days and steamed 64,000 miles, he

A MODERN SEA ROVER 279

had brought his ship back home. It was a fine achievement to have done what he endured on behalf of his country, and once more one sees how much can be accomplished by a disguised merchantman of very moderate speed which employs the right tactics and is able to preserve her mysteriousness. But Germany never sent any more raiders forth : the campaign came to a sudden end.

The question of raiders in the future does at once present itself. There will be ocean-going submarines of slow-diving ability, but great cruising range and serious formidability, to harass the trade-routes. But there will have to be borne in mind disguised steamers of the kind we have been considering. If a score of *Moewes* or the *Wolf* type were let loose at the beginning of hostilities to work along selected tracks, or in certain areas, the problem would be not easy of solution. Germany never went boldly into this surface raiding : she nibbled nervously at the task when she might have taken big mouthfuls.

On the other hand, the need for large numbers of light cruisers, and of merchant-vessels suitable for quick conversion into cruisers, suggests itself strongly. Seakeeping qualities, a long radius of cruising at economical speed with engines that can readily be quickened to high speed, an armament of guns and torpedo-tubes at least equal to that of any raider, are requisite. The least suitable commerce defender is the cruiser which is merely fast without staying power : it is necessary under modern conditions that she must have two entirely different sets of engines. One will be for slow patrolling along the busy sea-lanes such as between Brazil and West Africa, or wherever the rich trade flows : these engines will be of easy fuel consumption and capable of being overhauled whilst the other set is in use. The latter will be able to work up to maximum cruiser speeds so as to hurry towards any area where a raider is reported ; and, by superior speed, will be able to choose the range for shelling the raider when met with.

The cruiser in the late war has thus shown that a

combination of internal combustion engines with fast steam turbines is much to be desired. But the value of disguise has so well been established both by Q-ships and raiders that this ability to decoy cannot be neglected for a moment. The ideal commerce protector, whether engaged in convoying or patrolling, must so be designed that an arrangement of canvas screens, dummy funnels, masts, derricks, false upper works, and so on may serve to entice the raider into duel.

Great Britain is the one and only Power which has a chain of defended sea bases all round the world : she, at least, can start a naval war with a great initial superiority. The increasing use of oil fuel instead of coal, the much larger use of aircraft both by raiders and commerce protectors, the co-operation of the subtle submarine working with the raider or the cruiser, will, of course, modify the conditions to some extent ; yet nothing can upset the basic fact that the raider's deadliest enemy is a vessel that can conceal her superiority until the raider finds it is too late. The sinking of the would-be raider *Leopard* deserves to be studied with some of the best Q-ships' operations, and from this consideration there emerges a prophetic picture of the future.

BIBLIOGRAPHY

WHILST reliance has been placed chiefly on manuscripts and official confidential documents at the Admiralty, together with diaries and information obtained direct from personal sources, acknowledgment is due to the following printed references:

BLACKBURN, C. J. *How the Manx Fleet helped in the Great War.* Douglas, 1923.

"Carmania's" Historic Fight. (Printed privately.)

CORBETT, SIR JULIAN S. *Naval Operations*, Vols. I and III. 1920, etc.

FAYLE, C. ERNEST. *Seaborne Trade*, Vol. I. London, 1920.

HURD, ARCHIBALD. *A Merchant Fleet at War.* London, 1920. *The Merchant Navy*, Vol. I. London, 1921.

JELLICOE, ADMIRAL, VISCOUNT OF SCAPA. *The Grand Fleet, 1914–16.* London, 1919.

NERGER, FREGATTEN-KAPITAN K. A. *The Cruise of the "Wolf".* Berlin, 1918.

DOHNA-SCHLODIEN, KORVETTEN-KAPITAN BURGGRAF GRAF NIKOLAUS ZU. *The First Cruise of "Moewe".* Gotha, 1917.

The Second Cruise of "Moewe". Gotha, 1917.

SPINDLER, RESERVE-LIEUTENANT KARL. *Gun Running for Casement.* London, 1921.

THOMAS, LOWELL. *The Sea Devil.* London, 1928.
(Contains inaccuracies, but gives a lively account of Count Felix von Luckner's cruise in *Seeadler.*)

INDEX

Aalesund, Norway, 127
A. B. Johnson, 264
Abourkir, 41, 217
Abrolhos Rocks, 132, 139, 146, 161, 212
Achilles, 249-257
Africa, 197
Ajax, 48
Albemarle, 44, 46
Alcantara, 81, 221-229
Alda, 97
Algerine, 179
Allen, Captain (now Admiral) J. D., 84-88, 132, 133, 165
Almirante Condell, 67
Alsatian, 42, 219, 227
Amasis, collier, 70, 71
Amazon River, 53, 111
America, North, 15, 17, 18, 27, 78
America, South, 17, 23, 53, 55, 66, 98
America, U.S. of, 15, 18, 22, 26-28, 49, 56, 78, 98, 128, 129, 141, 149, 150, 168, 173, 179, 182, 205, 217, 230, 231, 236, 259
Amethyst, 207, 242
Amphion, 35, 36
Andes, 221-226, 229
Anne de Bretagne, 133, 134, 139
Antofagasta, 170
Antonin, 262
Appam, 201-205, 210, 211
Archangel, 38, 259
Arethusa, 190
Argentine, 66, 130, 139, 155
Argonaut, 129
Ariadne, 201
Arlanza, 31
Aquitania, 33, 152
Arucas, 31, 32, 129
Asnières, 242
Asquith, Mr., Prime Minister, 184, 185
Asuncion, 108, 112, 117, 121-123
Atkins, Acting Lieutenant P. S., 189, 190
Aud, 253-238, see *Libau*
Audacious, 48, 49, 185
Australia, 69
Australia, 16, 22, 167, 168, 267
Australian Squadron, 168
Austrian Consul, 129
Author, 200
Azores, The, 26, 53, 107, 128, 129, 241, 261

Baden, 55-57, 60, 62, 64, 181
Badewitz, Acting Officer, 208, 211, 240, 241
Bahamas, The, 25, 99, 100
Bahia Blanca, 56, 57, 65, 110, 113, 154, 155
Ballinas Bay, 179
Banff, 185
Bangor, 97
Bankfields, 180
Barbados, 53, 54, 106, 111, 122-124
Barbara Channel, 70, 71, 76, 83, 84
Barr, Captain J. C., 153, 154, 159, 160, 163
Barry, 27, 115, 117
Bavaria, 140
Bayo, 197
Beagle, 67
Beatty, Admiral, 248

Belfast, 196, 197
Belgica, 198
Bellevue, 134-136
Bellucia, 212
Berg, Sub-Lieutenant, 202, 204, 211
Bergen, 128
Bergensfjord, 219
Berlin, 15, 231, 236
Berlin, 14, 37-51, 157, 178, 185, 198, 218, 219
Bermuda, 99, 154, 210
Bernstorff, Ambassador, 231
Berwick, 98-105
Berwind, 110, 156
Bethania, 31, 32
Beluga, 272
Biermann, Captain, 35
Bilbao, 26
Biscay, Bay of, 19
Bjørgvin, 129
Blanche, 221
Bluebell, 234-236
Bonheur, 197
Bowes Castle, 111
Boy-Ed., Fregatten-Kapitan, 26, 27, 101, 181, 182, 191
Brandenburg, 42, 56, 128
Brazil, 17, 25, 58, 66, 81, 108, 109, 111, 117, 121, 132, 137, 139, 141, 198, 242, 243, 261
Brecknockshire, 243
Bremen, 14
Bremerhaven, 29
Bristol, 67, 73, 82, 83, 97, 99, 103-105, 114, 161, 181
British Yeoman, 262
Buenos Aires, 17, 25, 27, 31, 53, 57, 58, 70, 109, 114, 118, 136-139, 155, 163, 207, 261, 262
Burmah, 16

Cabot Strait, 99
Cadiz, 129
Caird of Grennock, 14
Calcutta, 14
Caligarian, 166
Callao, 64, 69, 97, 170, 180
Calliope, 221
Cambrian Grange, 239
Cambronne, 263
Campania, 14, 152
Canada, 18, 37
Canadian Convey, The, 37, 43, 44, 47, 51
Canadian Pacific Line, 166
Canary Islands, 17, 18, 23, 30, 31, 54, 66, 129, 200, 201
Canopus, 114, 143, 144, 162
Cap Trafalgar, 25, 110, 117, 155-163, 223, 243
Cape Corrientes, 180
Cape Finisterre, 200, 209
Cape Horn, 17, 26, 58, 59, 64, 71, 112, 131, 169, 170, 172, 173, 181, 263
Cape of Good Hope, 17, 243, 268, 277
Cape San Roque, 17, 18, 54, 55, 108, 109, 115, 119, 122, 134
Cape Santa Marta Grande, 57
Cape Town, 30
Cape Verdes, 23, 54, 113, 134, 202, 205, 206, 212, 244

283

INDEX

Cape Wrath, 196, 220, 259
Cardiff, 16, 27, 198, 232, 261
Carmania, 110, 121, 152–162, 165, 201, 223, 243
Carnarvon, 69, 73, 139
Caroline Islands, 78, 168
Caronia, 152
Casement, Sir Roger, 231, 233, 235
Castro, 231, 232
Celtic, 139
Centurion, 48
Cerrito Wireless Station, 80
Cervantes, 118
Chagos Archipelago, 19
Chair, Rear-Admiral Dudley de, 219, 227, 228
Chareus, 169
Charles Gounod, 261
Chasehill, 147, 148
Chile, 22, 61–63, 66, 71, 72, 78, 82, 90, 95–97, 117, 119, 141, 169, 172, 264
China Station, 166
Christmas Bay, 72
Clan Mactavish, 203, 204
Cleopatra, 189
Clyde, The, 37, 38, 45, 46
Cockburn Channel, 66, 71, 73, 83
Coco Island, 275
Coleby, 148
Columbella, 221
Colusa, 169
Competitor, 212
Comus, 221, 225
Conde, 99
Condor, 119
Conway Castle, 77, 96
Cook, Captain, 61
Cook Strait, 277
Corbridge, 198–200, 206
Cordelia, 220
Cormoran, 168
Cornish City, 115
Cornwall, 117, 118, 154, 161, 162
Coronel, 69, 76, 88, 172
Coronel, Battle of, 64, 73, 89, 93, 124, 149, 169, 180
Corrientes, 54–56
Corrientes Cape, 180
Coulson, Mr., 161
Cradock, Admiral Sir Christopher, 64, 98, 99, 103, 149, 154, 169
Crefeld, 112, 114, 115, 119, 120, 122
Cressy, 41, 217
Croats, 59
Cromarty Firth, 36, 42, 184, 185
Crooked Island, 100
"Cruiser Handbook", 25, 26
Cuba, 99, 101
Cumberland, 177, 272
Cumberland Bay, 90–93
Cunard Company, 152, 153, 156
Curaçao, 111

Dampier, 90
Day, Captain E. M., 30
Day, Captain Selwyn M., 218, 249–256
Dee, 269
Defence, 125
Demeterton, 245
Descartes, 99
Dickens, Mr., 161
Diego Garcia, 19
Djerissa, 212
Dohna-Schlodien, Count, 195–211, 237–248, 254
Dolphin, 176
Donaldson, 273
Dover Patrol, 215, 216
Drake, 210
Dramatist, 241
Dresden, 25, 52–97, 99, 109, 112, 127, 133, 141, 142, 155

Dromonby, 200
Drumcliffe, 53
Drummond, Mr., 154
Drummuir, 64, 65, 181
Duala, 129
Duchess of Cornwall, 239
Duke of Albany, 217
Duke of Cornwall, 217
Duke of Lancaster, see *Ramsey*
Dundee, 249–257
Dupleix, 262

EASTER ISLAND, 61, 62, 168–172, 175, 180, 264
Eber, 57, 110, 155, 157, 163
Ebernburg, 108, 110
Ecuador, 180
Eddie, 243
Edinburgh, 206
Edinburgh Castle, 125, 146, 176, 207, 243
Edmunds, Mr., 62, 63, 171
Edward VII, 196, 197
Elizabeth, 107
El Dorado, 62
Eleonare Woermann, 69, 70, 110
Elsinore, 180
Emden, 19, 52, 74, 124, 127, 166–168, 267
Empress, 33
Empress of Asia, 166
Empress of Japan, 166
Empress of Russia, 166, 167
Encore, 272
Encounter, 272
Engadine, 33
English Channel, 53
Esmeraldas, 244
Esplorador, 72, 75
Esquimalt, 179, 212
Essex, 32, 98, 99, 128, 201
Estrella, 208
Exmouth, 44

FALKLAND ISLANDS, 65, 66, 69, 82, 139, 168, 169, 172, 263
Falkland Islands, Battle of the, 66, 73, 81, 87, 127, 135, 168, 175
Falmouth, 28
Farn, 117–125, 140
Farringford, 198, 200
Fayle, Mr. T., 186
Felidu Atoll, 19
Fernando Noronha, 54, 109, 113, 117, 121, 136, 137, 175
Fernando Po, 135
Flamenco, 207
Florida, 99, 100
Floride, 175
Fox Bay, 70, 71
Frankenwald, 26
French Prince, 243
Friedrich der Grosse, 56, 98, 101
Fuller, Mr. F. C., 202
Fury, 49
Fylgia, 56

GABO ISLAND, 277
Galapagos Islands, 180
Galician, 30, 31
Galileo, 71, 81, 88
Geestemunde, 193
Geier, 78, see *St. Theodore*
Genoa, 232
George Washington, 56, 98
Georgic, 239
German-Australian Line, 14
German East Africa Line, 14
Germania, 259
German Levant Line, 14
Gibraltar, 162, 212
Gill Bay, 58

INDEX 285

Gillingham, 83, 84
Gladstone, 140
Gladys Royle, 261
Glanton, 122
Glasgow, 82, 83, 93–96, 109, 117, 121, 207
Gloucester, 145–148
Gneisenau, 62, 167, 170
Goeben, 145
Good Hope, 117, 121, 149
Gotha, 78, 80, 85, 88, 97
Governor, 245
Graecia, 128, 129
Grahn, Captain, 101, 102, 134
Grand Fleet, The, 36, 37, 40–45, 49, 80, 184, 185, 192, 197, 210, 212, 215, 248
Grant, Captain Noel, 153–165
Grasshof, Korvetten-Kapitän Carl, 78
Grief, see Rena, 225–229, 238, 248, 257
Grosse Kurfurst, 56, 98
Guam, Island of, 168
Guardicoupe, 147, 148
Guayaquil, 180
Guaymos, 58
Guben, see Grief
Gutenfels, 268

HADDOCK, COMMODORE, H. J., 49
Haiti, 52, 99
Halifax, Nova Scotia, 28, 262
Hall, Admiral Sir Reginald, 234
Hamburg, 185
Hamburg-Amerika Line, 14, 15, 25, 27, 28, 34, 53, 55, 78, 105, 109, 110, 128, 135, 140, 144, 266
Hamburg-Bremen-Africa Line, 14
Hamburg South American Line, 14, 108, 122, 155, 156
Hansa Line, 14, 108, 265
Harwich, 188, 190, 191
Havana, 25, 99, 105, 140
Hawke, 217
Heligoland Bight, 36, 37, 39–43, 188, 215, 259
Helle, Lieutenant zur, 70
Hemisphere, 136, 137, 175
Hendrick, 145
Highflyer, 30, 32, 202, 208
Highland Brae, 138, 143
Highland Hope, 114, 115
High Sea Fleet, 35, 36, 79, 80, 184, 210, 236
Hill, Leading Signalman, 86
Himalaya, 166
Hitachi Maru, 274, 275
Hogue, 41, 217
Holger, 121, 137–139, 143, 144
Holland, 15
Holmwood, 57, 58
Holsatia, 78, 79
Hong Kong, 166
Honolulu, 78
Honourable East India Company, 14
Horace, 208
Horngarth, 212, 262
Horn Reef, 188
Horta, 26
Hoste Island, 59, 60, 64
Hostilius, 53
Hotham, Captain Allen, 225
Hudson Maru, 242
Humber, River, 35, 214
Hurstdale, 122
Hyades, 56, 57, 109, 112

ICELAND, 30, 38
Igel, Wolf von, 231
Igotz Mendi, 275–278
Ile d'Oleron, 198
Ile d'Yeu, 198
Inconstant, 220
India, 18

Indian Prince, 108, 110, 112, 130
Indrani, 115, 122–125
Invercoe, 174
Irish Rebellion, The, 231
Irma, see Seeadler
Iron Duke, 40, 184, 185, 188
Isobel Browne, 173

Jacobsen, 173, 174
Jamaica, 32, 99, 103
James, Mr. Frederick Seton, 202
Japanese Fleet, 167
Java Sea, 267
Jean, 170–174, 242
Jellicoe, Admiral, 40, 41, 44, 45, 48, 126, 184, 185, 188, 190, 212, 220, 221, 227, 228, 237, 248
Jericoacoara, 54, 122
Jerram, Vice-Admiral Sir Thomas, 166, 167
John H. Kirby, 276
Josephine, 69
Juan Fernandez, 90–93, 180
Jumna, 269
Jutland, Battle of, 230, 237, 256, 258, 259

Kaipara, 31, 32
Kaiser, 40–42
Kaiser Wilhelm II, 56, 98
Kaiser Wilhelm der Grosse, 14, 28–34, 38, 50, 129, 178, 208
Kamaran Fort, 167
Karlsruhe, 52, 99–130, 134, 136, 139, 140, 148, 149, 154, 155, 160, 177, 178, 205, 206
Katherine, 244
Katherine Park, 58
Kattegat, The, 188, 233, 278
K.D.3, 140
Kelly, Captain W. A. Howard, 145
Kent, 81–89, 92, 132, 133, 165
Kildalton, 170–172
King Alfred, 201
King George V, 48, 239
King Orry, 218, 249, 250
Kingston, Jamaica, 32, 99
Kinneir, Captain D. R., 60
Kling, Lieutenant, 260
Knorr, Captain von, 187–191
Koesler, Grand Admiral von, 140
Köhler, Captain E., 52, 99–127, 131, 142, 148
Köhler, Sub-Lieutenant, 241
Kolberg, 43, 44
Konig, 259
Konigin Luise, 34, 35
Kosmos Line, 14
Kronprinzessin Cecilie, 25, 98
Kronprinz Wilhelm, 25, 27, 98, 101–103, 106–112, 127–151, 155, 163, 174–178, 205, 210, 221, 259

La Correntina, 130–132
La Plata, 130
La Rochefoucauld, 262
La Rochelle, 197
Ladrones Islands, 167, 168
Lancaster, 98, 99
Lansing, Mr., 182
Las Palmas, 25–27, 31, 32, 56, 66, 107, 112, 128, 129, 136, 137, 144, 155
Lavandeira Reef, 73, 80, 113–122, 125, 146
Lawson, Lieutenant F. H., 251, 255
Leake, Captain F. M., 249–253, 256
Leghorn, 232
Leipzig, 58, 62, 64, 170, 179–181
Leith, 185
Leonhardi, Korvetten-Kapitän, 26
Leopard, 249, 260, 280, see Rena
Libau, 232

INDEX

Lilac, 214, 215
Lisbon, 166, 200, 216
Liverpool, 48, 49
Lubinus, Lieut.-Commander, 117
Lucania, 14
Luce, Captain, 93–96
Luchs, 167
Luckner, Count Felix von, 258, 260–264
Lüdecke, Captain, 52, 54, 58, 66, 67, 70–97, 99, 109, 142
Lundy Island, 261
Lusitania, 18, 33, 179
Luxembourg, 207
Luxor, 69
Lockyer, Lieut.-Commander E., 153
Lody, Carl, 230
Lord Heneage, 235
Lough Swilly, 44, 45, 48, 49
Lynrowan, 118
Lynton Grange, 53
Lynx, 186

Macedonia (British), 148, 162, 163, 181, 207
Macedonia (German), 114, 144, 145, 148
Macquarie, 249
Madeira, 107, 136, 201–203
Madrid, 129
Magalana Bay, 179
Magdeburg, 31
Magellen Straits, 17, 25, 58, 64, 66, 67, 69, 71, 74, 81, 82, 83, 88, 89, 97, 131
Maldives Islands, 19, 274, 275
Maleta, 260
Mana, 62
Manchester Commerce, 47, 48
Manila, 264
Mantua, 42
Maple Branch, 113, 115
Maraca Island, 111, 206
Maranham, 54, 111
Maréchal Davout, 276
Maresfield, 212
Maria, 115
Mariana Quesada, 141
Marie, 180
Mariguana Island, 100
Marmora, 202
Maroni, 209
Marshall Islands, 167
Martin, Leading Signalman A. E., 256
Mary Ada Short, 175
Mas-a-Fuera, Island of, 61, 64, 76, 77, 80, 84, 90, 168, 169, 180, 181
Matunga, 273, 274
Mauretania, 152
Mazatlan, 179
Mediterranean, 19, 178
Merewether, Sir Edward, 202
Melbourne, 146
Memphis, 69
Mera, 69, 70
Merlet, Mr., 61
Meteor, 185–191, 195
Milward, Mr., 72, 81, 88, 97
Minelaying Raiders, 34–49
Minich, 242
Minikoi, 19, 269
Minnesotan, 67, 70, 71
Moewe, 194–216, 220, 225–227, 232, 237, 239–248, 254, 257, 262, 263, 266, 269, 279
Monmouth, 117, 121
Mont Agel, 134, 136
Monte Video, 17, 25, 31, 69, 70, 78, 80, 109–111, 113, 114, 117, 121, 130, 132, 134, 155, 169, 276
Moore, Rear-Admiral Sir Archibald, 201
Moray Firth, 36, 40, 42, 184, 185, 188, 214
Mount Temple, 238

Munster, 225
Mystery of Easter Island, 63, 171

Nantes, 241
Nantucket, 99, 103
Nauen Wireless Station, 127, 145
Nautilus, 43, 44
Navarra, 25
Nerger, Korvetten-Kapitän Karl August, 266, 268, 269, 273, 274, 278
Netherby Hall, 242
New Orleans, 144
Newport News, 22, 27, 141, 149, 176, 177, 179, 205, 210
New York, 22, 25, 26, 28, 31, 52, 53, 56, 58, 98, 100, 101, 107, 111, 119, 122, 123, 128, 136, 150, 166, 176, 177, 259, 276
New Zealand, 17, 22, 31, 264, 267, 270, 272
Niceto de Lorrinaga, 118
Niobe, 177
Nonesuch, 21
Norddiech Wireless Station, 25, 163
Norman Monarch, 212
North German Lloyd, 14, 15, 24, 28, 34, 56, 98, 101, 112, 128, 167, 232
North Wales, 64
Nurnberg, 62, 81, 88, 132, 165, 167
Nyanga, 31, 32

Odenwald, 105, 106, 146, 147
Odin, 268
Olaki, 244–246
Olinda Wireless Station, 55, 133
Olympic, 48, 49
Ophir, 202
Orama, 25, 82, 83, 93, 95, 207
Orange Bay, 59, 60, 64
Oregon, 62
Orfordness, 214
Orkneys, 197
Ortega, 60
Otavi, 135, 145
Otranto, 175

P. & O. Line, 166
Pagan Island, 167
Paley, Skipper Fred, 214, 215
Panama Canal, 22, 52, 69, 180, 241
Papen, Captain von, 182, 231
Para, 25, 53, 54, 123, 136
Paramount, 216
Pass of Balmaha, 259
Patagonia, 69, 70, 106, 111–113, 154, 206
Patey, Admiral, 70
Pathfinder, 217, 249
Patia, 221
Peel Castle, 216, 217
Pentland Firth, 196
Perce, 262
Pernambuco, 17, 27, 55, 56, 81, 108, 109, 112–114, 121, 133–137, 141, 145, 147, 148, 154, 162, 175, 205, 207, 242
Perseus, 268
Pertius d'Antioche, 198
Pfundheller, Captain, 37–49
Philadelphia, 128
Picton Island, 65, 66, 181
Pinmore, 262
Pisa, 177
Pittan, 108
Plana Cays, 100, 101
Plymouth, 29, 44
Pohl, Admiral von, 178, 190
Pontos, 109, 110
Port-au-Prince, 52, 99
Porto Rico, 53, 140, 146
Portsea, 212
Port Stanley, 69, 169

INDEX 287

Portugal, 26, 28, 98, 230, 237
Potaro, 138
President Grant, 98
Pretoria, 212
Priestfield, 132
Prinz Adalbert, 28
Prinz Eitel Friedrich, 63, 127, 149, 164–179, 210, 217
Prophet, 212
Prussia, 56, 57, 109, 110
Pruth, 118
Puerto Rico, 105, 125
Puerto Santa Elena, 70
Pugno, see Moewe
Punta Arenas, 25, 58, 66, 67, 70–76, 81, 113

"Q" Ships, 178, 182, 193, 195, 215, 228, 229, 246, 247, 258, 259, 280

Rabaul, 273, 274
Raby, Lieut.-Commander, 186
Radnorshire, 242
Rainbow, 179
Ramage, Commander G. N., 217
Ramsey, 183–191, 195, 214, 218, 224, 250
R. C. Slade, 264
Reina Victoria, 114
Rena, 223–225, 248–257, see Grief and Leopard
Reymann, Captain, 29, 30, 32
Rhakotis, 64
Rhodanthe, 242
Riasan, 168
Rio de Oro, 31, 32
Rio Iguassu, 115, 117
Rio Janeiro, 17, 25, 27, 57, 58, 109, 110, 112, 115, 139, 147, 174, 223, 263
Rio Negro, 122–127
River Plate, 58, 110, 112, 131, 132, 139, 147, 155
Riviera, 33
Robeck, Admiral de, 129
Rocas Reef, 18, 54–56, 109, 112, 113, 121, 207, 242
Roggeveen, Admiral, 61
Roland Line, 14, 67, 121, 137
Rosario, 175
Rose, Kapitän-Leutnant, 266
Rotterdam, 217
Routledge, Mr. and Mrs. Scoresby, 62, 171, 172
Royal Sceptre, 123
Rugg, Captain John, 269
Russia, 15, 186, 191

Sacramento, 64
Salif Fort, 167
Samland, 238
San Diego, 179
San Francisco, 22, 64, 78, 179, 181, 270
San Juan, 105, 106, 125, 140, 146
Santa Cruz, 144, 208, 240
Santa Ines Island, 76, 88
Santa Isabel, 57, 58, 64, 181
Santos, 25, 110, 221, 242
Saxon Prince, 209, 210, 238
Sayville Wireless Station, 99, 101
Scapa Flow, 37, 43, 49, 183, 184, 196, 197, 215, 221, 237
Scharnhorst, 62, 63, 167, 170
Scheer, Admiral, 237, 239
Schmehl, Kapitän-Leutnant, 266
Seeadler, 238, 258–264
Selkirk, Alexander, 90
Semanatha, 139, 147, 174
Setter II, 234, 235
Sevilla, 57
Seydlitz, 64, 65
Shearwater, 179
Short, Lance-Corporal G., 256
Siamese Prince, 56, 112

Sierra Cordoba, 70, 71, 73, 75–78, 88, 97, 131, 132
Sierra Leone, 212
Singapore, 78
Skagerrak, The, 188, 233, 278
Skerries, 172
So-a-Joao Islands, 111
Southport, 78
South Sea Islands, 180
Spain, 26, 98
Spee, Admiral Graf von, 60–66, 69, 70, 73, 77, 82, 114, 117, 127, 135, 142, 167–169, 172, 177, 180, 181
Spindler, Lieutenant Karl, 232–236
Squadron, 2nd Cruiser, 36, 42, 44,
   10th Cruiser, 215, 219–221, 227–229, 248
St. Paul Rocks, 113–118, 122, 134, 136–139, 145, 147, 175, 208, 242, 244, 262
St. Quentin Bay, 60, 64
St. Theodore, 78, 240–243
St. Thomas, West Indies, 25, 52–54, 105, 106, 241
St. Vincent, 81, 112, 128, 129, 136, 145, 175, 206, 208, 212, 230
Stadt Schleswig, 106, 111
Steiermark, 57, 155
Stephen, 26
Stetten, 266
Stoddart, Admiral, 69, 72, 73, 139, 146
Stokes Bay, 72, 81, 84
Storebror, 276
Strathroy, 112–117, 125
Studt, Lieut.-Commander, 125–127
Sturdee, Admiral, 65
Submarines:
   U Boats, 18, 178, 179, 187–189, 214, 217, 225, 228, 229, 230, 246, 257, 259
   "E 4", 41
   "U 9", 41
   "U 21", 249
   "U 22", 231–234
   "U 28", 188, 190
Suez Canal, 19
Suffolk, 98, 99, 103–106, 149
Supply Centres, Germany, 25–28, 53–58, 66, 70, 78, 124, 128, 137, 141, 144, 163, 182, 191
Sussex, 179, 230, 236
Sutley, 208
Sydney, 22
Sydney, 81, 146, 166

Talcahuano, 90
Tamar, 148
Tara, 44
Tenerife, 27, 30, 31, 66, 112, 120, 128, 129, 145, 205, 208
Thierfolder, Lieut.-Commander Paul, 102, 108, 110, 130–138, 142, 146–149, 175
Thierchsens, Captain, 169–177
Thistledhue, 132
Tierra del Fuego, 71
Tiger, 167
Tirpitz, Admiral, 100, 191
Titania, 167
Titanic, 135
Togoland, 57
Tory Island, 45, 46, 49, 214, 219
Trader, 201
Trinidad, 53, 111, 122
Trinidad, Island of, 25, 57, 108–110, 121, 129, 132, 138, 143, 154–157, 163, 243, 263, 276
Trondhjem, 51, 56, 223
Tsingtau, 167, 168, 175
Tubal Cain, 30
Turpin, 67
Turritella, 268–271
Tyne, River, 35, 214

INDEX

Tyrwhitt, Commander, 188, 190

Union, 131, 132
Uruguay, 25, 66, 173

Valentine, 180
Valparaiso, 58, 60–64, 77, 78, 90, 91, 95, 97, 168, 169, 171, 181
Vancouver, 22, 166
Vandyck, 122, 123
Vaterland, 56, 98
Venezuela, 111
Victorian, 129
Vienna, see Meteor
Vigo, 26
Viking, 262, see Viknor
Viking Orry, see King Orry
Viknor, 219
Vindictive, 30, 139, 166
Virgen del Socorro, 216
Voltaire, 238
Von der Tann, 135
Vulcan Company, 28

Wach'fels, 265–267
Wairuna, 270, 271
Walhalla, 107
Wardle, Captain T. E., 221–225, 229

Warrender, Admiral, 43
Washington, 26, 181, 182, 230, 236
Weddigen, Lieut.-Commander, 41
Wedel, Baron von, 219
Westburn, 208, 240
West Indies, 17
Wharton, Commander, 83
Whiten Head Bank Minefield, 197, 214
Wilfred, 138, 143, 144, 150
Willerby, 175
William Island, 76
William P. Frye, 173, 179
Willow Branch, 212
Windward Isles, 144
Windward Passage, 101, 103
Winslow, 271, 272
Wirth, Commander, 155, 156, 160
Woermann Line, 14, 110
Wolf, 130, 238, 267–279
Wolf, Lieut.-Commander, 241
Worcestershire, 268
Wordsworth, 269

YARMOUTH RAID, 259
Yarrowdale, 240–243, 248, 251
Young, Captain G. B. W., 221
Ypres, 49

ZEPPELIN RAID, 236

www.ingramcontent.com/pod-product-compliance
Lightning Source LLC
Chambersburg PA
CBHW061933220426
43662CB00012B/1891